AF734989

The Impact of Regulation on International Investment in Portugal

OECD
BETTER POLICIES FOR BETTER LIVES

Please cite this publication as:
OECD (2023), *The Impact of Regulation on International Investment in Portugal*, OECD Publishing, Paris, https://doi.org/10.1787/688b30c8-en.

ISBN 978-92-64-84374-5 (print)
ISBN 978-92-64-43643-5 (pdf)
ISBN 978-92-64-90694-5 (HTML)
ISBN 978-92-64-57093-1 (epub)

Photo credits: Cover © Yasonya/Getty Images.

Corrigenda to publications may be found on line at: www.oecd.org/about/publishing/corrigenda.htm.

Preface

Portugal has long recognised the importance of international investment for its economy and worked towards lowering barriers to foreign direct investment (FDI) over time. The accession to the European Community in 1986 marked an important historical milestone in this regard, helping to foster support for leveraging FDI to modernise Portugal's industrial and services sectors, integrate its economy into regional and international markets and promote convergence with the other European Union Member States.

Portugal has been committed to maintaining an open and enabling environment for foreign investment ever since, being today one of the most open economies to FDI among OECD member countries. Over the last decade, Portugal has also demonstrated a strong commitment towards creating a favourable business environment, as evidenced by its successful administrative and regulatory simplification programme *Simplex* and strides taken in the digitalisation of public services, among other initiatives.

Foreign investors continue to perceive Portugal's skilled workforce and the quality of its higher education institutes as highly attractive. They have also shown increasing interest in Portugal's renewable energy commitment in recent years, resonating with the country's leadership in green transition efforts, as one of the first countries in the world to set 2050 carbon neutrality goals, and its strong policy emphasis on the expansion of renewable electricity generation and increased energy efficiency.

These achievements, alongside the extensive reforms implemented after the economic crisis of 2011, have paved the ground for a recent increase in foreign investment projects. Portugal now enjoys one of the highest levels of inward FDI stocks among OECD countries after a decade of impressive growth, standing at 71% of GDP in 2021. As demonstrated in this report, foreign-owned firms in Portugal are bringing about many benefits to the Portuguese economy, contributing to sustainable development goals in areas such as productivity and innovation, job quality and skills, gender equality and low-carbon transition. By developing local sourcing and selling to international markets, foreign firms also help to deepen Portugal's integration into global value chains. They equally contribute to advance Portugal's digital transformation by investing in information and communication technologies (ICT) and infrastructure, promoting greater technology uptake by domestic firms, too.

Mobilising increasing levels of international investment remains, nonetheless, a strategic priority for Portugal for the next decade, as it can help address long-lasting structural challenges weighing on productivity growth. Particularly, more investment is needed in productivity-enhancing assets, such as machinery, equipment and intellectual property assets. Increased investment in ICT assets more broadly across industries and firms could also enable further productivity improvements and help to consolidate Portugal's reputation as an emerging technology and innovation hub. The timing for Portugal to further strengthen its appeal to foreign investment may be particularly important, as businesses reconfigure their supply chains in the light of the economic uncertainty surrounding the COVID-19 recovery and Russia's war of aggression against Ukraine. Amidst intensifying global competition for FDI, Portugal may also be able to leverage its recent track record in attracting increasing amounts of foreign investment.

This report supports these efforts by assessing the impact of regulation on foreign investment in Portugal. It proposes policy actions to further improve general aspects of the country's investment climate, affecting a wide range of firms economy-wide, as well as some targeted reforms to facilitate market entry and boost competitiveness in areas providing strategic support to Portugal's priority sectors for investment.

We believe that the assessment and policy considerations that this study puts forward will help key reform efforts in various domains, including some that are currently being scoped by the government. More broadly, it will support Portugal in the pursuit and implementation of its strategic priorities reflected in the *Acordo de Parceria Portugal 2030* and Portugal's Recovery and Resilience Plan. Ultimately, we hope that the suggested investment climate reforms will help Portugal advance on its path towards the twin green and digital transition.

The Government of Portugal and the OECD are very pleased to have joined forces in the preparation of this study. We thank the European Union for funding the work leading to this publication and for the support provided throughout the project development. We are also grateful to all Portuguese agencies, consulted companies and other stakeholders who contributed to this report.

Luís Filipe de Castro Henriques,

CEO, AICEP Portugal Global

Yoshiki Takeuchi,

Deputy Secretary-General, OECD

Foreword

A remarkable rebound and transformation have marked the development of the Portuguese economy in the last decade. Yet, overall investment levels in Portugal, from public and private sectors combined, are among the lowest in the European Union (EU). Further investment is necessary to support Portugal's long-term productivity growth and transition to a carbon-neutral society by 2050. Foreign direct investment (FDI) can play an important role in attaining these objectives, promoting growth and recovery from the economic repercussions of the COVID-19 pandemic and Russia's war of aggression against Ukraine.

Portugal has already taken steps to open its economy to foreign investment and has one of the lowest levels of statutory restrictions to FDI among OECD countries. However, a better understanding of how broader regulatory aspects and the overall business climate contribute to Portugal's FDI attractiveness is needed to keep improving the environment for foreign investment. Through targeted policy recommendations, this report suggests avenues for Portugal to strengthen its investment climate and ensure a continued positive impact of FDI on its economy.

Building on previous OECD Investment Regulatory Reviews, designed purposedly for assessing the impact of regulation on international investment and deriving policy recommendations to create more conducive business environments, this report assesses recent FDI trends and the broader economic and social benefits of foreign investment in Portugal. It benchmarks Portugal's investment regulatory environment against a group of peer economies to identify possible bottlenecks and explores, through an econometric analysis, the potential impact that some relatively stringent policies can have on foreign investment activity. Foreign investors' views, collected via a business consultation, complement the findings and help provide a comprehensive picture of Portugal's business environment.

The work leading to this publication was funded by the EU via the Technical Support Instrument, and implemented by the OECD, in co-operation with the Directorate-General for Structural Reform Support of the European Commission. An Advisory Group composed of representatives from DG REFORM, AICEP Portugal Global, Portugal's Ministry of Foreign Affairs and the Ministry of Economy and Maritime Affairs provided oversight and support in the project development. The extraordinarily active engagement of numerous Portuguese Government stakeholders throughout this project is testament to Portugal's recognition of the importance of FDI for its economy and its strong commitment to making of Portugal an increasingly attractive destination for foreign investors.

Acknowledgements

This report was prepared by a team comprised of Francesca Spinelli, Fernando Mistura, Polina Knutsson and Laura Kuusela from the Investment Division in the OECD Directorate for Financial and Enterprise Affairs, and Irene Oliván García from the Trade Policy Division in the Trade and Agriculture Directorate, under the general guidance of Ana Novik, Head of the Investment Division. Liv Gudmundson prepared the report for publication. Inés Gomez Palacio, Marie-Laure Garcia and Tuateba Ontoyin provided administrative assistance.

The authors are grateful to Maria João Veiga Gomes, Pedro Sousa Rodrigues and Luis Moura from AICEP Portugal Global (AICEP); Joana Almodovar from the Office for Strategy and Studies (GEE) in Portugal's Ministry of Economy and Maritime Affairs; and Milena Raykovska from the Directorate-General for Structural Reform Support (DG REFORM) in the European Commission for their support and engagement as part of the Advisory Group overseeing the project.

The authors would also like to thank Madalena Oliveira e Silva, Elisabete Velez, Alfonso Machado, Philomene Dias and Inês Silva from AICEP; Rita Bessone Basto, Gabriel Osório de Barros, Ana Martins, Guida Nogueira, Eva Pereira, Teresa Rebelo, Mariana Costa, Gonçalo Novo and Eugénia Pereira da Costa from GEE; José Salgado and Sara Santos from the Directorate for International Trade in the Ministry of Economy and Maritime Affairs; Inês Inverno and Carolina Arenga from the Ministry of Justice; Rui Velasco Martins from the Institute for Mobility and Transport; Manuel Cabugueira from the Competence Centre for Planning, Policy and Foresight in Public Administration; Claudia Barroso from the Administrative Modernization Agency; Antonio Santos from the Foundation for Science and Technology; and Joana Anjos from the Ministry of Labour, Solidarity and Social Security for their insightful feedback and inputs.

The report also benefitted from comments and inputs received from the following OECD colleagues: Ana Novik, Stephen Thomsen, Martin Wermelinger, Joachim Pohl, Stratos Kamenis, Sarah Dayan and Katharina Böhm from the Investment Division; John Drummond, Janos Ferencz, Frédéric Gonzales, Ana-Maria Muresan and Gustavo Ribeiro de Maceido from the Trade Policy Division; Jean-Christophe Dumont, Jonathan Chaloff and Ana Damas de Matos from the Directorate for Employment, Labour and Social Affairs; and Daniel Trnka, Paul Davidson and Supriya Trivedi from the Directorate for Public Governance.

Finally, the authors are grateful for the contributions of consulted senior executives of foreign-owned companies in Portugal, as well as those of several foreign and domestic chambers of commerce present in the country, whose experiences on Portugal's business environment further enriched the report. In particular, the authors would like to thank the following chambers of commerce for their support and/or participation: AmCham Portugal, British-Portuguese Chamber of Commerce, Câmara de Comércio e Indústria Luso-Francesa, Câmara de Comércio e Indústria Luso-Alema, Portugal-China Chamber of Commerce and Industry, Câmara de Comércio e Indústria Luso-Brasileira, Portuguese-Japanese Chamber of Commerce and Industry, Portuguese Chamber of Commerce and Industry, Confederação Empresarial de Portugal, Invest Lisboa and AED Cluster Portugal.

Table of contents

FIGURES

TABLES

Abbreviations and acronyms

ADR	Alternative Dispute Resolution
AI	Artificial Intelligence
AICEP	AICEP Portugal Global (Agência para o Investimento e Comércio Externo de Portugal)
AMNE	Activity of Multinational Enterprises
ANACOM	Portuguese National Telecommunications Authority (Autoridade Nacional de Comunicações)
BSC	Business Services Centre
CEPEJ	European Commission for the Efficiency of Justice
CEPII	Centre for Prospective Studies and International Information
CIT	Corporate Income Tax
COVID-19	Coronavirus Disease 2019
CPAI	Permanent Commission for Investor Support (Comissão Permanente de Apoio ao Investidor)
CRM	Customer Relationship Management
DGSTRI	Digital Services Trade Restrictiveness Index
EATR	Effective Average Tax Rate
EC	European Commission
EEA	European Economic Area
EIB	European Investment Bank
EPL	Employment Protection Legislation
ERP	Enterprise Resource Planning
EU	European Union
FDI	Foreign Direct Investment
FDI RRI	FDI Regulatory Restrictiveness Index
GDP	Gross Domestic Product
GEP-MTSSS	Strategy and Planning Office of the Ministry of Labour, Solidarity and Social Security (Gabinete de Estratégia e Planeamento do Ministério do Trabalho e Solidariedade Social)
GI	Greenfield Investment
GPA	Government Procurement Agreement
GVC	Global Value Chain
IAPMEI	Portuguese Agency for Competitiveness and Innovation (Agência para a Competitividade e Inovação)
ICE	Incentivo à Capitalização das Empresas
ICT	Information and Communication Technologies
IEA	International Energy Agency
IEFP	Portuguese Institute for Employment and Professional Training (Instituto do Emprego e Formação Profissional)
IMF	International Monetary Fund
INE	Statistics Portugal (Instituto Nacional de Estatística)
IoT	Internet of Things
IRENA	International Renewable Energy Agency
IT	Information Technology
IUTICE	Inquérito à Utilização Tecnologias Informação nas Empresas
LPI	Logistics Performance Index

M&A	Mergers & Acquisitions
MNE	Multinational Enterprise
OECD	Organisation for Economic Co-operation and Development
PII	Investment for the Interior (Projeto de Investimento para o Interior)
PIN	Potential National Interest (Potencial Interesse Nacional)
PMR	Product Market Regulation
PPP	Purchasing Power Parity
QP	Quadros de Pessoal
R&D	Research and Development
RFAI	Regime Fiscal de Apoio ao Investimento
RHS	Right Hand Side
RIA	Regulatory Impact Assessment
SCIE	Sistema de Contas Integradas das Empresas
SDG	Sustainable Development Goal
SEF	Portuguese Immigration and Borders Service (Serviço de Estrangeiros e Fronteiras)
SIFIDE II	Sistema de Incentivos Fiscais em Investigação e Desenvolvimento Empresarial
SIR	Responsible Industry System (Sistema da Indústria Responsável)
SME	Small and Medium-Sised Enterprise
STEM	Science, Technology, Engineering and Mathematics
STRI	Services Trade Restrictiveness Index
ULC	Unit Labour Cost
UN	United Nations
UNCITRAL	United Nations Commission on International Trade Law
VAT	Value Added Tax
WTO	World Trade Organisation
ZER	Responsible Business Area (Zona Empresarial Responsável)
ZLT	Technology Free Zone (Zona Livre Tecnológica)

Executive summary

Alongside an impressive economic rebound, foreign direct investment (FDI) in Portugal has grown rapidly over the last decade, resulting in one of the highest levels of inward FDI stocks among OECD countries. Yet, with overall investment levels remaining relatively low, Portugal would benefit from mobilising further FDI to help respond to long-term structural challenges weighing on productivity growth and to accelerate the country's digital and green transitions. FDI can also help modernise Portugal's industrial and services sectors, further integrate the economy into regional and international markets and promote convergence with more advanced European Union (EU) countries. It may also serve as a conduit to progress on several sustainable development goals, in relation to e.g. job quality and skills, gender parity, technology uptake and digitalisation. Strengthening appeal to FDI, including in manufacturing and other high value-added activities, is thus essential and features prominently in Portugal's priorities for the next decade (see the *Internacionalizar 2030* and the *Acordo de Parceria Portugal 2030* programmes).

Strict market entry conditions and other factors of the business environment may at times hold back FDI. While such regulation can serve important public policy objectives, it may unintendedly discourage investment, create barriers to entry or expansion, when excessively strict or burdensome. Alternative, less restrictive policies are sometimes possible and can positively affect FDI activity. The timing is apt to consider alternative policy approaches, as structural reforms envisaged in Portugal's Recovery and Resilience Plan are being scoped and as the uncertainty of the post-pandemic recovery and Russia's war of aggression against Ukraine weigh on investors' confidence and tighten competition for FDI worldwide.

This report assesses how regulatory reforms could help Portugal build a more conducive environment for investment. It evaluates Portugal's performance in attracting and retaining FDI in comparison to selected European peer economies and benchmarks the Portuguese regulatory framework for investment against those of peer economies. The report also quantifies the expected positive impact that further liberalising reforms could have on FDI flows. Foreign investors' views complement the assessment. Finally, the report provides policy considerations to further improve Portugal's investment climate and inform a whole-of-government approach to their planning and implementation.

Key findings

Investors benefit from Portugal's open regulatory framework, with fewer discriminatory statutory restrictions on FDI, more competition-friendly rules and fewer barriers to services trade and investment than OECD average. Regulatory harmonisation within the Single Market has lowered barriers for investors from the European Economic Area (EEA), and simplification efforts have reduced administrative and regulatory burden for firms. Funding opportunities, financial and regulatory incentives are in place to attract FDI and foreign talent. Investors praise Portugal's skilled labour force and the quality of higher education.

Nonetheless, a few remaining regulatory barriers and broader factors of the business climate may contribute to hold back FDI:

- Investors perceive business licenses and permits as particularly burdensome, despite recent simplification and consolidation of procedures, e.g. in industrial and environmental licensing.

- There is room to further advance regulatory impact assessment (RIA) and stakeholder engagement practices in the drafting of business regulation. For instance, RIA documents are not made available online and *ex post* evaluation of existing rules is not mandatory.
- Firms spend more time on tax compliance in Portugal than in most peer countries, despite simplification efforts by the tax authority. Foreign investors consider that tax regulation remains too complex, changes too frequently and clarification on new rules is difficult to obtain.
- Despite improvements in the efficiency of Portuguese courts in recent years, processing times remain long compared to peer countries, particularly in administrative courts.
- Skilled labour is the leading driver of FDI to Portugal, but skill shortages are increasingly a concern for investors in some sectors. Many investors do not use or are not aware of incentives for skill upgrading. Bottlenecks in the entry of non-EEA talent thwart efforts to recruit workers from abroad.
- Labour market duality continues to constitute an obstacle for productivity growth and social equity, despite recent measures limiting the excessive use of temporary contracts.
- Investors find the tax incentive for research and development effective, but certain other funding and incentives might be too complicated to apply for or insufficiently aligned with business needs. Many investors are not aware of existing support for firms' green and digital transitions.
- In professional services, ownership restrictions for non-licensed professionals, combined with rules restricting access to the profession for foreign practitioners, currently limit possibilities for FDI. Remaining obstacles in transport and logistics services, such as limitations on maritime cabotage by foreign-flagged vessels and non-competitive award of port service concessions can affect foreign and domestic firms in downstream industries economy-wide.

Key policy conclusions

Regulatory reforms and a more service-oriented approach in the implementation of business regulation could be considered to improve Portugal's ability to attract and retain FDI:

- Further streamline business licenses and equip authorities to issue licenses within statutory time limits and enforce tacit approval to increase predictability for investors.
- Make broader use of RIA and stakeholder engagement for the development of business regulation.
- Continue to streamline corporate taxation and strengthen assistance services and digitalisation to reduce tax compliance costs. Provide adequate means for taxpayers to adapt to new obligations.
- Reduce the length of court proceedings further by increasing digitalisation in courts, strengthening human resources in support functions and making more extensive use of out-of-court mechanisms.
- Raise investor awareness of government support for employee training and strengthen the alignment of such training with business needs and Portugal's strategic objectives.
- Step up efforts to improve the efficiency of the immigration authority and facilitate the hiring of non-EEA talent (e.g. leverage digital tools, allocate more resources to the processing of applications).
- Continue efforts to lessen labour market duality by further reducing the gap in protection between open ended and temporary contracts and to strike a better balance in labour market rigidity.
- Assess and streamline the investment incentives offering where possible to ensure that they reach their intended objectives while keeping added complexity to the tax system at a minimum. Promote awareness and take-up of existing incentives to support firms' green and digital transitions.
- Proceed with the implementation of the recently approved reform of regulated professions to open investment in these firms by non-licensed professionals. Consider lifting identified barriers in transport and logistics sectors to boost competitiveness.

1 Trends and impacts of foreign direct investment in Portugal

This chapter assesses Portugal's performance in attracting and retaining foreign direct investment (FDI) and explores the various economic, social and environmental benefits of foreign multinational activity in Portugal (e.g. green and digital transition, skills development, gender equality, technology uptake, integration into global value chains, regional development). Several data sources are used in the assessment, including official FDI statistics, cross-border mergers and acquisitions (M&A), and greenfield investment data, as well as firm-level data from Statistics Portugal (INE), among other economic indicators.

Key findings

- After a decade of impressive growth, Portugal has one of the highest levels of inward foreign direct investment (FDI) stocks across OECD member countries, at 71% of GDP in 2021. The uncertainty surrounding the COVID-19 pandemic and the economic consequences of Russia's war of aggression against Ukraine might, however, weigh on Portugal's near-term FDI activity prospects.
- Foreign investment is actively supporting Portugal's green and digital transitions, with significant amounts of investment flowing into renewable energy projects, digital technologies and infrastructure. There are also signs of rising investment activity in the manufacturing sector, which had typically been overlooked by foreign investors.
- More granular evidence shows that foreign affiliates in Portugal contribute to the development of Portugal's skills base and to job quality improvements, in terms of wage and gender parity. They are also supporting Portugal's integration into global value chains by purchasing inputs from local firms and selling to international markets.
- Despite being mostly concentrated in the Lisboa and Norte regions, foreign investors are present throughout the entire territory. Their characteristics and performance vary considerably across regions, reflecting differences in the industrial structure of the regions and in the specialisation profiles of the investors.
- Further FDI could help to expand and modernise the currently subdued capital base in many sectors, particularly with respect to productivity-enhancing assets, such as machinery, equipment and intellectual property assets. More investment in information and communication technology assets would also be beneficial more broadly across sectors and firms, including for Portugal to deliver on and sustain its reputation as a technology and innovation hub.
- Further diversification of the investor base, which remains largely concentrated in few traditional European partners, could also contribute to broadening economic opportunities by strengthening ties with other world leading investing economies and regions.

1.1. Introduction

The last decade marked the turnaround of the Portuguese economy. After going through a full-scale economic crisis in 2011, which led the government to request assistance from the European Union (EU) and International Monetary Fund (IMF) and implement a series of fiscal, financial and labour market reforms, Portugal underwent a remarkable economic rebound and transformation, restoring investor confidence, improving its economic competitiveness and resilience, and exiting the agreed economic adjustment programme earlier than expected in 2014 (IMF, 2018[1]; Gouveia et al., 2018[2]). Since then, Portugal has been sustaining an impressive economic record, drastically reducing unemployment and bringing previously large fiscal and current account deficits under control (OECD, 2021[3]). The COVID-19 pandemic, however, brought many of these positive developments to a sudden halt. Economic activity contracted by 8.4% in 2020, Portugal's deepest post-war recession. But the economy rebounded well in 2021 partly thanks to government support measures, which helped weather the economic shock. The outlook, however, remains uncertain as the pandemic and its economic effects may still linger in the near term (OECD, 2021[3]). Russia's invasion of Ukraine might also weigh on Portugal's economic prospects due to possible disruptions in global supply chains and increased volatility of commodity prices.

While the pressing attention of authorities remains in navigating the economy through these uncertain times, in the longer term Portugal will need to address some of its long-lasting structural challenges.

Particularly, Portugal could mobilise further investment to support long-term productivity growth in view of adverse demographic trends and support its transition to a carbon-neutral economy by 2050 (IMF, 2018[1]; EC, 2020[4]). Overall investment levels in Portugal remain among the lowest in the EU (20.3% of GDP against 22% of GDP in the EU in 2021) despite steady improvement over recent years.

Foreign investment can play an important role in addressing these challenges. Beyond capital and jobs, foreign investors can contribute to develop and transfer knowledge and technology, introduce innovative management methods and help upstream and downstream sectors upgrade their products, through close links that could further support productivity growth, particularly for domestic small and medium-sized enterprises (SMEs) (OECD, 2022[5]). They can also bring other social benefits related to job quality, gender equality, digital transition and carbon neutrality (OECD, 2019[6]). As shown throughout this chapter, existing foreign investors are already contributing to advancements in many of these areas in Portugal and, hence, to setting the country on a more sustainable development path. Efforts to further attract foreign investors and retain existing ones could thus prove to be strategic for addressing Portugal's productivity challenge and for accelerating its green and digital transition.

Foreign investors may also provide crucial support for the economic recovery following the COVID-19 pandemic.[1] Like Portugal, many countries will grapple with recurring outbreaks, but those who manage to remain attractive destinations post-COVID-19 will have an edge in retaining and mobilising new foreign investment. Increasing the level of international investment is already part of Portugal's strategic priorities for the next decade (the *Internacionalizar 2030* programme approved by the Council of Ministers in July 2020 and the *Acordo de Parceria Portugal 2030* programme approved by the Council of Ministers in March 2022 in the context of the Multiannual Financial Framework 2021-27 and the European Structural and Investment Funds). This is a critical time to pursue this strategy.

Moreover, foreign investment may help to weather some of the economic challenges posed by Russia's war against Ukraine. Aside from the regretful human losses and humanitarian damages, the war has steepened pressures on the supply of energy, agriculture and minerals, causing significant moves in commodity prices and prompting many countries to revise their strategic priorities. In March 2022, EU countries adopted the Versailles Declaration reaffirming the EU's intentions to enhance energy security, strengthen defence capabilities and reduce dependencies on critical resources, such as digital technologies, agricultural products and raw materials.[2] As showed in this chapter, Portugal has been advancing in many of these fronts already, including with the support of international investors, and may look towards accelerating the pursuit of such strategies and exploring associated opportunities with their support.

This report examines how regulatory reforms could help Portugal build a more enabling and competitive environment for investment, particularly foreign direct investment (FDI), contributing ultimately towards achieving Portugal's strategic priorities enshrined in the *Acordo de Parceria Portugal 2030* and in its Recovery and Resilience Plan. This chapter assesses trends and patterns of FDI as well as its contribution to sustainable development in Portugal. Section 1.2 reviews Portugal's overall investment situation in comparison to a group of benchmark European economies to better understand how it could best support long-term productivity growth. Section 1.3 examines trends and patterns of FDI, cross-border mergers and acquisitions (M&A) and greenfield investment in Portugal and in the benchmark countries. It looks at their evolution, capital composition and sectoral distribution and at the origin of investors. It also explores the more detailed sectoral information of M&A and greenfield investment data to examine to what extent foreign investors are contributing to advance Portugal's low-carbon and digital transition. Lastly, Section 1.4 exploits the richness of Portuguese micro-data to describe the broader effects of FDI on skill development and gender equality, on technology uptake and digitalisation, and on the linkages with domestic firms as well as their integration into global value chains (GVCs). The regional impact of FDI is also considered in this section.

1.2. Investment is needed to support long-term productivity growth

1.2.1. Portugal's productivity has plateaued during the last decade

Like many other developed countries, Portugal has a rapidly ageing and decreasing population.[3] In the longer term, the resulting declining share of workers to the total population will weigh on labour's contribution to economic growth. This demographic evolution will also intensify demand for health care, pension and social services and increase the pressure on the public sector (IMF, 2018[1]).

Raising productivity is thus necessary to cope with Portugal's adverse demographic trends and to continue improving people's living standards. Productivity has plateaued over the last decade and is no longer converging with the average top 15 most productive European economies (TOP15).[4] The productivity gap with the TOP15 stood at about 60% over the period 2011-21 (Figure 1.1 A). While Portugal's productivity level is still higher than in some countries in the benchmark group, the latter are seeing their productivity levels converge faster to TOP15 levels (Figure 1.1 B).[5] Similar trends hold across the manufacturing and business services sectors excluding real estate.

Figure 1.1. Real labour productivity (hours-based)

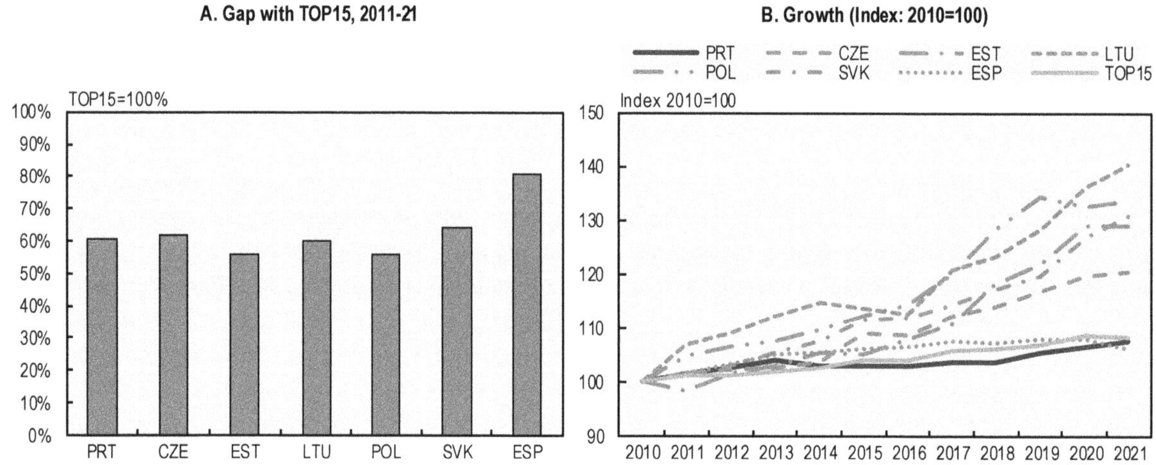

Note: Real labour productivity based on GDP per total hours worked; a similar trend holds for labour productivity measured on a per employee basis. Panel A reflects the median labour productivity gap with the average top 15 most productive European economies (TOP15) in USD million, constant prices, 2015 Purchasing Power Parity over the period 2011-21. Panel B reflects real labour productivity growth in national currency, constant prices. TOP15 refers to the average of the 15 most productive European economies indicated in endnote [4]. Information on the benchmark group selection is available in endnote [5].
Source: OECD (2021[7]), *Productivity Statistics Database*, https://www.oecd.org/sdd/productivity-stats/.

1.2.2. Investment has been relatively weak and unable to raise capital stock levels

Along with improvements in labour skills and in labour market efficiency and broader efforts to enhance domestic firms' absorptive capacity, particularly of SMEs (IMF, 2018[1]; Alves, 2017[8]; OECD, 2022[5]), productivity improvements could be achieved with further capital deepening. Total public and private investment – i.e. gross fixed capital formation – has been weak and unable to raise capital stock to levels similar to those of the average TOP15 economy. The ratio of investment to GDP has declined for most of the last decade before starting to recover in 2017. Yet it remains somewhat lower than in most peer economies: 20.3% of GDP in 2021 compared to 22% on average in the benchmark group and 21.7% in the TOP15. When looking at investment by the corporate sector, the gap with TOP15 economies has recently narrowed; however, compared with some peers, corporate investment in Portugal has been considerably lower during the last decade. While the median level of investment to GDP by the corporate sector was 10.7% in Portugal over the period 2011-21, it was 13.7% on average in the benchmark group and 12.4% in the TOP15, about 30% and 15% greater than in Portugal respectively (OECD, 2021[9]).

Portuguese workers would particularly benefit from having at hand better machinery, tools and technology that would enable them to work more efficiently and increase productivity. The level of capital stock per worker remains relatively low and the wedge with the average TOP15 economy has been growing more recently (Figure 1.2 A). This is particularly the case in the manufacturing sector, for which Portugal's level of capital stock per worker stood at 70% of the TOP15 level in 2017. In turn, many services sectors (e.g. construction, distribution, transportation, among others) present relatively high levels of capital stock per worker, but this may partly reflect the misallocation of capital over the years before the Portuguese crisis when large amounts of credit-fuelled resources were drawn into non-tradable activities (Alves, 2017[8]; OECD, 2014[10]). Also, across sectors, capital invested has been mostly allocated to construction assets as opposed to potentially more productivity-enhancing assets, such as machinery, equipment and intellectual property assets (Figure 1.2 B). This divergence is much more pronounced than in the average TOP15 economy and across the benchmark group, and has strongly accentuated in the manufacturing sector over the last decade.

Figure 1.2. Net capital stock per worker is on a declining trend

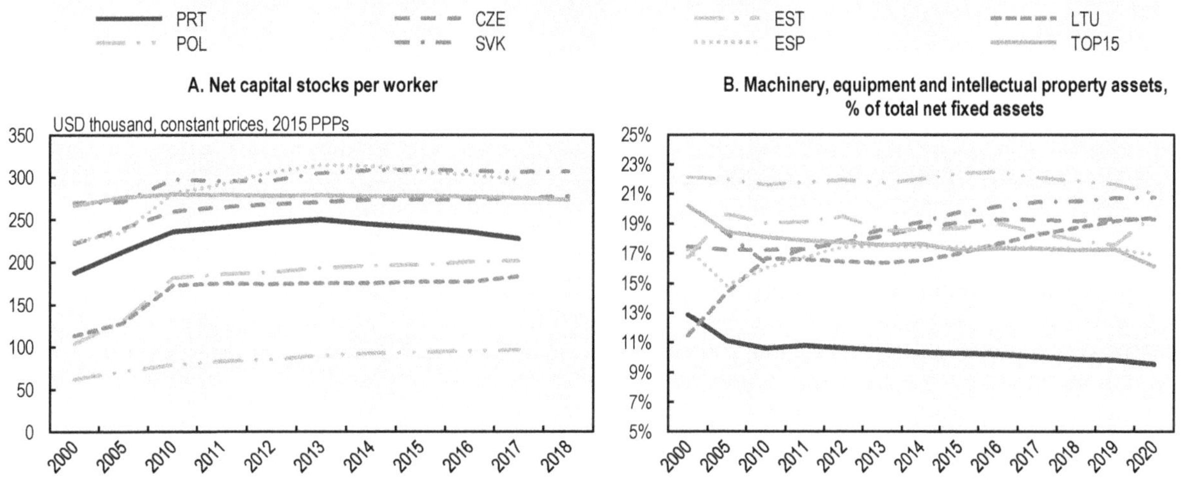

Note: Panel B data correspond to the share of machinery and equipment and weapon system (transport equipment, ICT equipment and other machinery, equipment and weapons) and intellectual property products (computer software and databases, research and development assets, etc.) in total net fixed assets. Total net fixed assets include construction assets (dwellings and other buildings and structures) and cultivated biological resources in addition to the aforementioned assets. The average top 15 most productive European economies (TOP15) in Panel B excludes Switzerland and Iceland due to the lack of data.

Source: OECD (2020[11]), *Structural Analysis database*, https://www.oecd.org/sti/ind/stanstructuralanalysisdatabase.htm; OECD (2021[12]), *Annual National Accounts database*, https://stats.oecd.org/Index.aspx?DataSetCode=SNA_TABLE9A.

1.2.3. Investment in ICT assets remain relatively subdued

Portugal's reputation as an attractive technology and innovation hub is increasing.[6] Yet, investment in information and communication technology (ICT) assets in Portugal has still to pick up across industries. Net ICT capital stock per worker is still much lower in Portugal than in the average TOP15 and is also much lower than in most of the benchmark group (Figure 1.3). Moreover, it has been relatively stable over the past decade in Portugal while it has been growing in most benchmarked economies and in the TOP15. The relatively slow uptake in ICT investment thus far can increasingly become a drag for Portugal's digital transition and a significant barrier to productivity improvements in the long term (Andrews, Criscuolo and Gal, 2016[13]). A shortfall in ICT assets can also hamper the green transition, as digital technologies play a prominent role in improving energy efficiency (IEA, 2019[14]). Low ICT investment can further amplify the existing digital divides between companies reaping the benefits of technological developments and those struggling to update their business models due to limited digital assets (EIB, 2019[15]) (see Section 1.4.3 for detailed information on technology uptake by Portuguese firms). Foreign investment can be an important complement to the measures envisaged in the Portuguese Recovery and Resilience Plan to boost the country's ICT stock.

Figure 1.3. Net ICT capital stock per worker

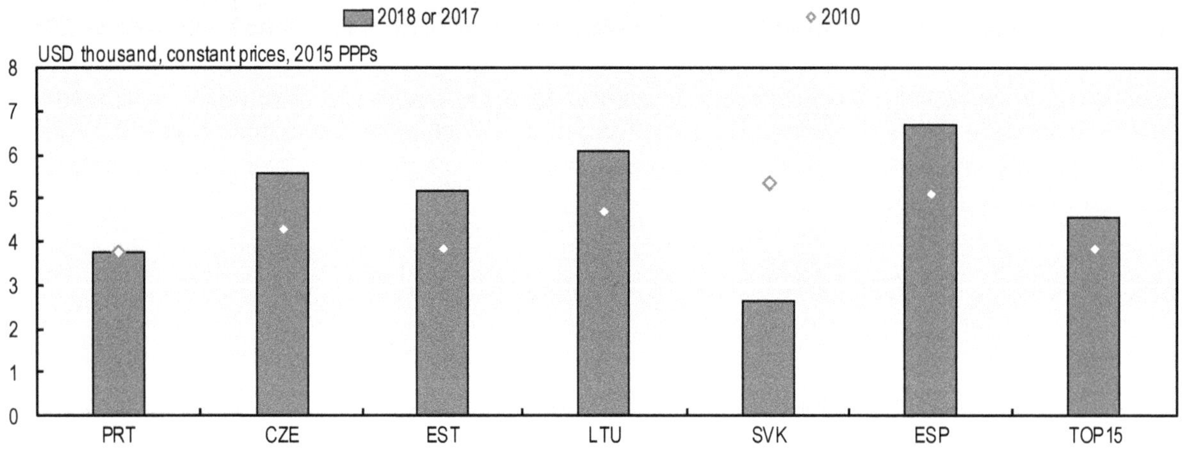

Note: ICT capital refers to computer hardware, telecommunications equipment, software and databases. The average top 15 most productive European economies (TOP15) excludes Iceland, Germany and Switzerland due to the lack of data. Poland is also omitted for this reason.
Source: OECD (2020[11]), *Structural Analysis database*, https://www.oecd.org/sti/ind/stanstructuralanalysisdatabase.htm.

1.2.4. Portugal preserved labour cost competitiveness in recent years

Currently, unit labour costs (ULCs) in Portugal remain lower than in the average TOP15 economy and in some of the economies in the benchmark group, which helps to keep Portugal as an attractive location to investors, although many of its peers prove to be quite competitive too (Figure 1.4).[7] Portugal has been able to keep unit labour costs relatively under control over the last decade, having one of the slowest growing rates across the benchmark countries.

Figure 1.4. Unit labour costs

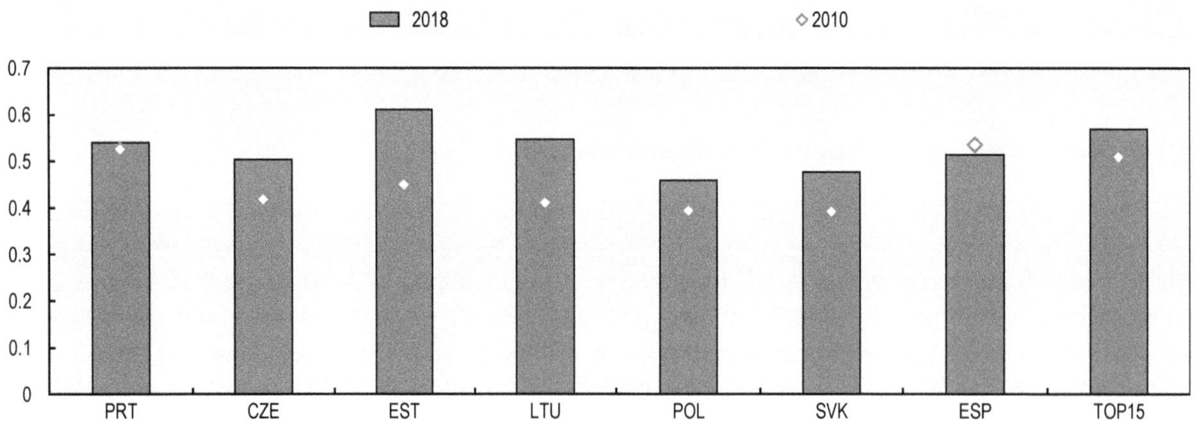

Note: Unit labour costs measure the average cost of labour per unit of output and are calculated as the ratio of total labour costs to real output.
Source: OECD (2020[11]), *Structural Analysis database*, https://www.oecd.org/sti/ind/stanstructuralanalysisdatabase.htm.

Maintaining relative cost advantages over time can prove challenging, however, without productivity gains. Total unemployment was 6.6% in 2021, one of the lowest levels since 2004 (World Bank, 2021[16]). Investors are already struggling to find qualified workers for certain positions, particularly those requiring information technology (IT) and digital skills, as demand for talent has been outgrowing supply in some areas. Investors consider supporting high-tech industries and innovation and developing talent as key areas of focus to maintain Portugal's competitive position in the global economy (Ernst & Young, 2020[17]; Ernst & Young, 2021[18]; INE, 2018[19]).

1.3. Foreign investment trends

Foreign investors can and in many ways are already contributing to addressing many of Portugal's long-term sustainable development challenges (see Section 1.4). International investment can also play a critical role in accelerating the green and digital transition, including to partly address the consequences of the COVID-19 pandemic and the war in Ukraine. Stepping up efforts to attract foreign investors and retain existing ones could thus prove to be strategic for making further progress on these priorities.

1.3.1. FDI in Portugal has grown rapidly over the last decade

Portugal has one of the highest levels of inward FDI stocks across OECD countries and compares favourably against most of the benchmark group (Figure 1.5 A). At end-2021, inward FDI stocks as a share of GDP stood at 71%, having risen slightly below the average of the benchmark group since 2015. However, over the last decade (2011-21), they have grown at an impressive 6% compound annual growth rate. Such growth has not been nearly matched by any of the benchmarked countries during the period. Most of this growth has been driven by equity capital injections. In the shorter period between 2015 and 2021, for which comparable data are available for most benchmark countries, equity capital injections accounted for over 60% of FDI inflows on average. In turn, FDI into most peer economies has been largely associated with reinvested earnings (Figure 1.5 B).

Figure 1.5. Portugal has relatively strong inward FDI stocks and has seen a significant increase in new equity capital injections in recent years

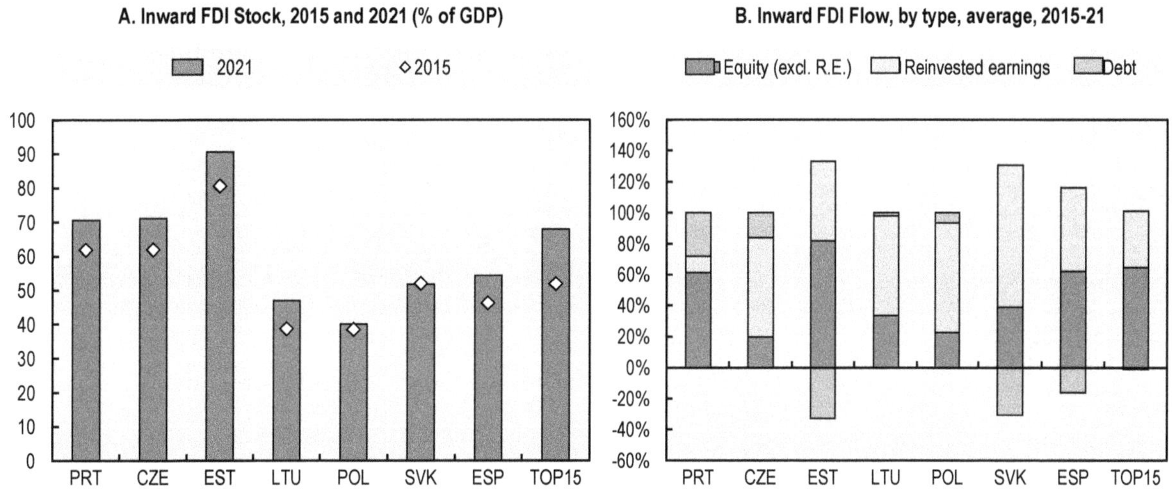

Note: Inward FDI stock and flow data on a directional basis, excluding resident special purpose entities.
Source: OECD (2022[20]), *International Direct Investment Statistics*, https://www.oecd.org/corporate/mne/statistics.htm.

1.3.2. Foreign investment activity may be tapering off as uncertain economic outlook continues to weigh on recovery prospects

Although higher frequency data on foreign investment, such as cross-border mergers and acquisitions (M&A) deals and greenfield investment projects, are in some ways conceptually different from FDI statistics, they are a great complement to official FDI statistics as they can help to identify broader investment dynamics taking place in recent periods with greater sectoral detail and, thus, contribute to explaining underlying trends in FDI. They also help to inform about investors' mode of entry. As in other developed economies, cross-border M&As represent an important entry mode for foreign investors in Portugal, correlating highly with FDI equity flows. In turn, the contribution of announced greenfield investment projects tends to be much smaller overall.[8]

Cross-border M&A activity has been relatively more important in Portugal than in selected economies in recent years (Figure 1.6 A).[9] However, the sum of all deal values as a share of Portugal's GDP has been on a declining trend since 2015, despite some strong upward M&A activity occurring in 2020 and 2021, thanks to several large-scale M&A deals. In contrast, the number of deals completed in Portugal, which had declined sharply during the pandemic, has recovered to a level slightly below the pre-pandemic level. The economic disruptions from the COVID-19 pandemic and possible long-term consequences of Russia's war against Ukraine might, however, continue to weigh on cross-border M&A activity in Portugal. In 2022, the number of completed cross-border M&A transactions was still about 10% lower than back in 2018 before the pandemic, and in value terms it stood at roughly 50% of the level observed in 2018.

Figure 1.6. Uncertain outlook might curb the upward trends in M&A and greenfield activity

Cross-border M&A deal values and greenfield investment as shares of GDP, 2-year moving average

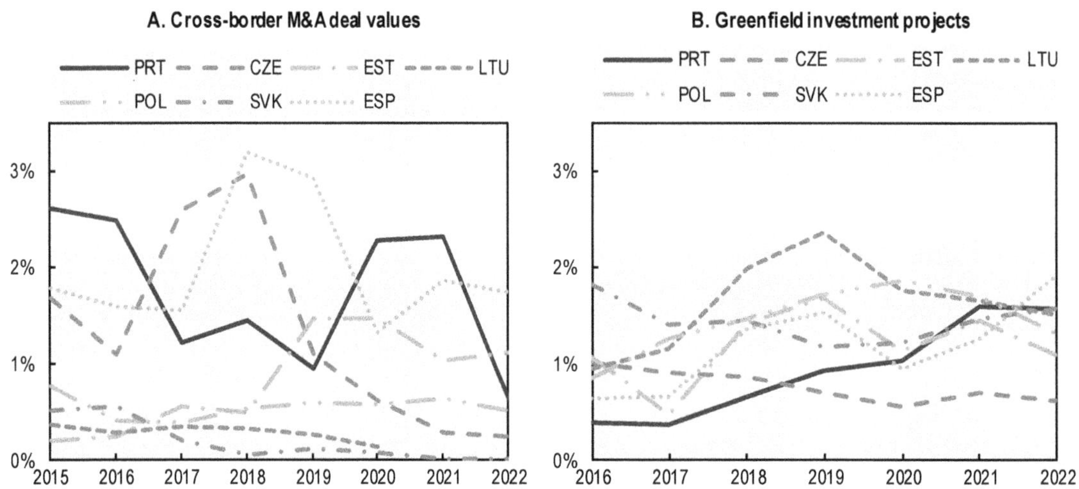

Note: M&A deals refers to the aggregated value of completed cross-border M&A deals that give the investor 10% or more of the voting shares of the acquired company. Greenfield investment refers to the total value of announced capital expenditure. All values are deflated by producer price indices (2020=100).
Source: Refinitiv M&A database, Financial Times fDi Markets database and OECD (2021[12]), *Annual National Accounts database*, https://stats.oecd.org/Index.aspx?DataSetCode=SNA_TABLE1.

The COVID-19 outbreak also hit greenfield investment projects hard (OECD, 2020[21]; 2021[22]). In 2020, the number of greenfield projects in Portugal fell by 36% compared to 2019, but already in 2021 greenfield investment activity had recovered.[10] In 2022, it continued to grow reaching its peak at year-end. Similarly to M&A, however, the uncertainty surrounding the global economic outlook might still pose challenges for investment projects. While greenfield investment has been on the rise over the past few years, with the share of announced and undertaken greenfield investment projects to GDP increasing steadily over the years, the trend has slowed down in 2022 (Figure 1.6 B).[11]

1.3.3. Further diversification of the investor base could be beneficial

With the increasing role played by new outward investors in international markets, it could be strategic for Portugal to intensify efforts to diversify further its investor base, which remains predominantly based on traditional European investors, although there are signs of further investor diversification taking place in recent years.

Most cross-border M&As in Portugal come from the intra-EU market (Figure 1.7 A). Although less numerous, M&A transactions by investors located outside the Single Market are often larger: total deal value of extra-EU M&A was nearly 20% higher than that of intra-EU deals over the reported period.

Figure 1.7. Portugal attracts both EEA and non-EEA M&A investors

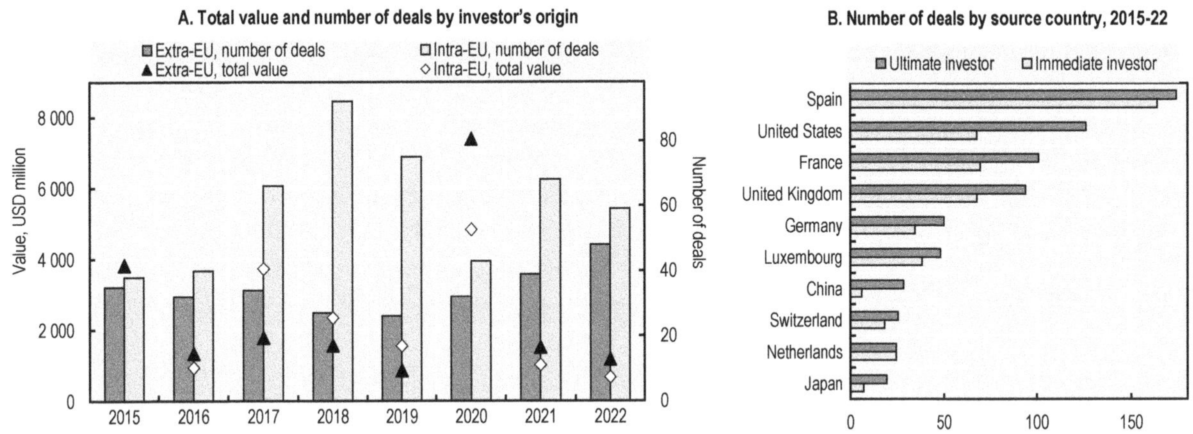

Note: Intra-EU refers to the investment originating in the EU's Single Market (the EU, Iceland, Liechtenstein, Norway and Switzerland); Extra-EU comprises all the countries outside the EU's Single Market. Panel A reports investor origin on the ultimate basis, Panel B on the ultimate and immediate basis as recorded in Refinitiv.
Source: Refinitiv M&A database.

Figure 1.8. Most greenfield projects come from the EEA

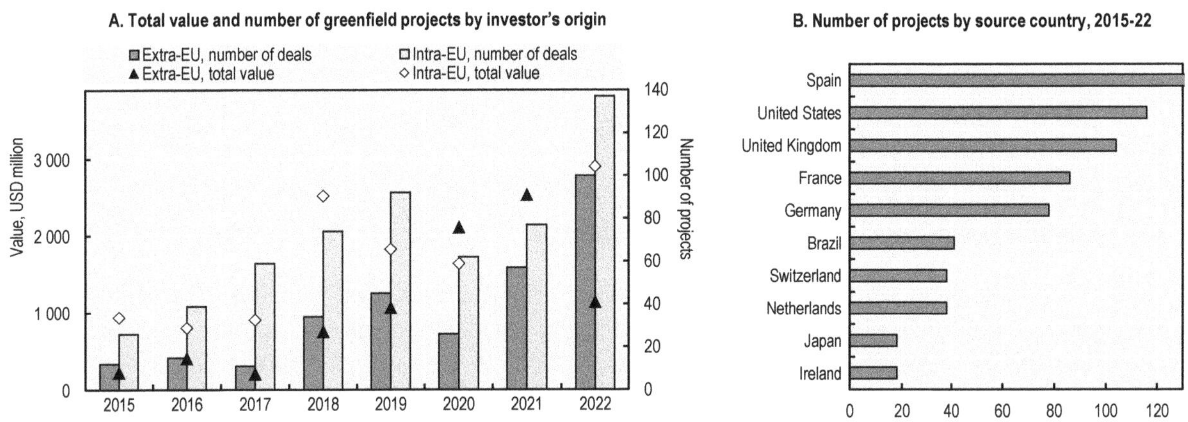

Note: Intra-EU refers to the investment originating in the EU's Single Market (the EU, Iceland, Liechtenstein, Norway and Switzerland); Extra-EU comprises all the countries outside the EU's Single Market. The data provider reports only a single source country per greenfield project (the immediate investor).
Source: Financial Times fDi Markets database.

The largest number of M&A deals in Portugal originated in Spain, both on an immediate and ultimate investor basis (Figure 1.7 B). Many cross-border transactions in the last decade were also undertaken by investors from the United States, the United Kingdom and France, all of which were home to more ultimate than immediate investors. In value terms, the People's Republic of China (hereafter 'China') and Brazil are also among the top sources of M&As in Portugal from an ultimate owner point of view.

Intra-EU investors have equally been the main proponents of greenfield projects in Portugal, both in terms of the number and value of announced projects, but extra-EU investors have been catching up in recent years (Figure 1.8 A), as measured on an immediate investor basis.[12] From 2015 to 2022, the number of greenfield projects announced both by intra and extra-EU investors gradually increased, reaching its peak in 2022 when several larger projects took place.

Like for M&As, most greenfield investment projects in Portugal originate in Spain, France and the United Kingdom, even on an immediate investor basis – the only one available for these data (Figure 1.8 B). The United States, Germany and Brazil are also home to a great number of greenfield investors in Portugal. These countries are also among the leading investors when looking at the value of announced investment, along with Korea.

The geographical distribution of leading foreign investors in Portugal observed in recent years is broadly in line with the more historical perspective portrayed by the Bank of Portugal's new statistical series on FDI positions by the ultimate investing country (Figure 1.9), with Spain, France and the United Kingdom also accounting for a substantial share of FDI stocks. The presence of Portugal among the major ultimate investors denotes the existence of "round-tripping" investment, i.e. funds transferred abroad by investors resident in Portugal that are then channelled back to the country in the form of direct investment through intermediary entities abroad, for instance in the Netherlands and Luxembourg (59% and 17% respectively) (Banco de Portugal, 2021[23]).[13]

Figure 1.9. Foreign direct investment position by ultimate investor, 2021

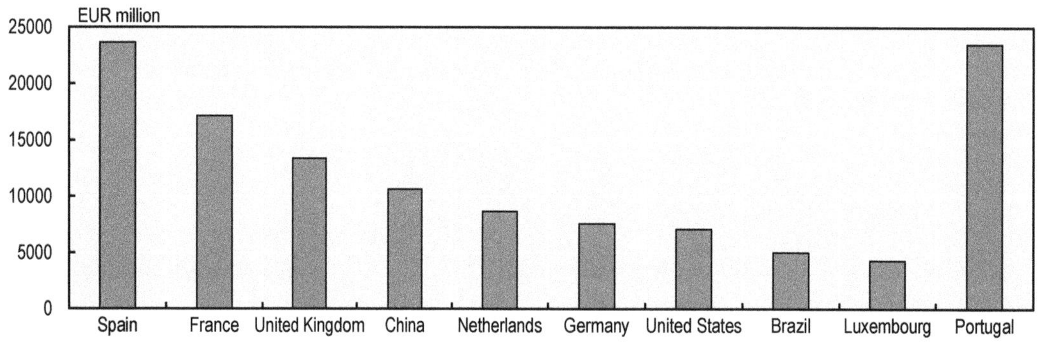

Source: Banco de Portugal (2021[23]), *New statistics on foreign direct investment by ultimate investor: statistical press release*, https://bpstat.bportugal.pt/conteudos/noticias/1579/.

1.3.4. Manufacturing and ICT sectors have proved attractive to foreign investors

Portugal's manufacturing sector has been historically overlooked by foreign investors. The manufacturing share in total inward FDI stocks is the lowest across the benchmark group. Across the benchmarked economies, only in Portugal and Estonia the manufacturing sector is underrepresented in the stock of inward FDI and the extent of such divergence is greater in Portugal. Recent trends, however, point to rising investment activity in export-oriented manufacturing industries (e.g., mineral and metal products, chemicals, machinery, agro-food, transport material) (OECD, 2022[5]).

Manufacturing accounted for most cross-border M&As in Portugal in the last decade (Figure 1.10 A). The sector's share in all foreign M&As in Portugal is, however, just 18%, among the smallest in benchmarked economies with only Estonia's share being lower (16%). The relative number of deals in the manufacturing sector has been steadily declining since 2014, to the point that the share of the sector in the total number of M&A transactions has fallen from 27% in 2014 to 17% in 2022 on a 3-year moving average basis. Likewise, the share of manufacturing in total deal values contracted from 28% in 2014 to 2% in 2022.[14]

Figure 1.10. Portugal's manufacturing attracts many M&As and greenfield projects

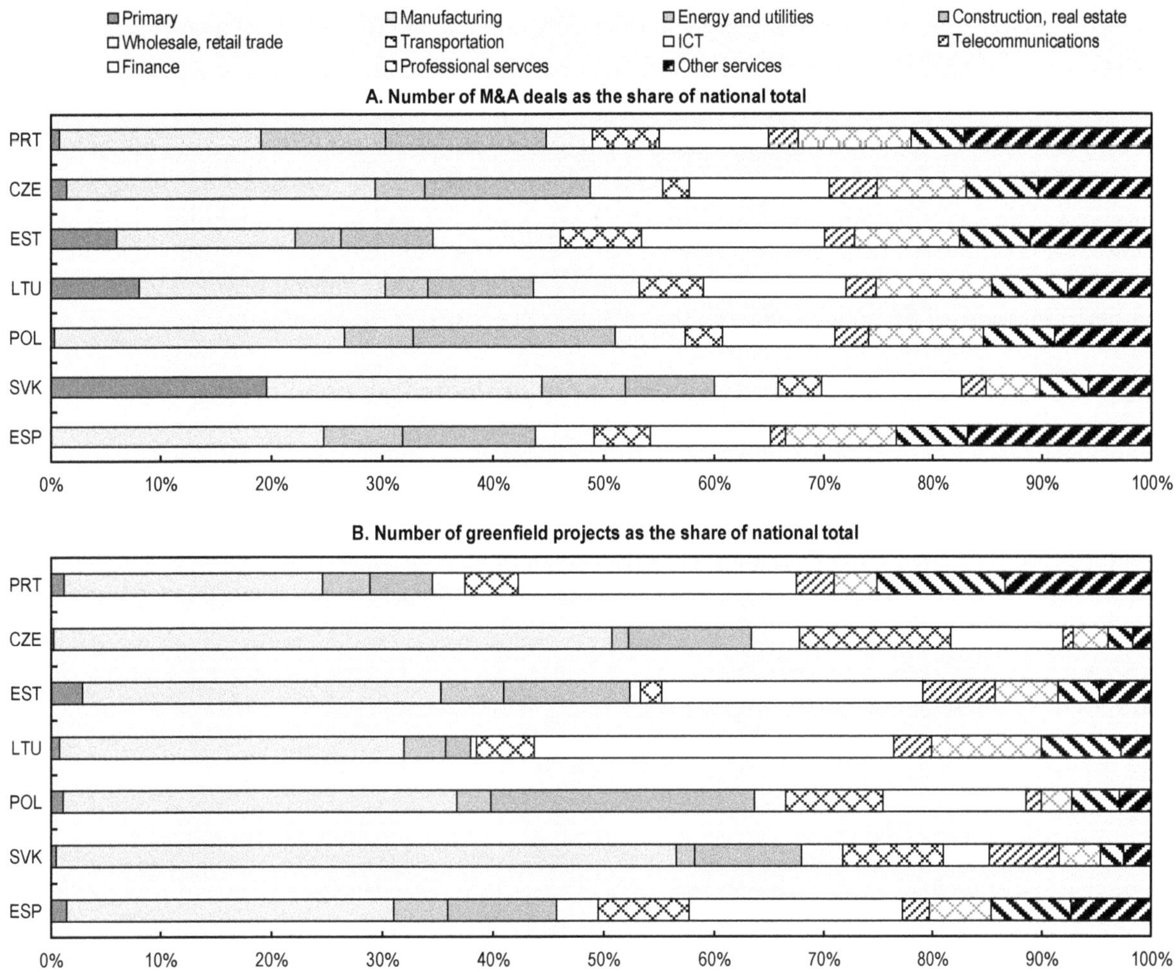

Note: Other services include accommodation, food services, health, social work, arts and administrative activities. Data are from 2012 to 2022.
Source: Refinitiv M&A database; Financial Times fDi Markets database.

A sizeable portion of greenfield projects into Portugal also went to the manufacturing sector (20%), albeit lower than in the benchmarked countries (Figure 1.10B). Over the years, the share of manufacturing in Portugal's greenfield activity has been quite stable, accounting for nearly a quarter of all projects and a fifth of total greenfield investment, while the sector is steadily losing its relevance in peer countries.

Manufacturing plays a prominent role in foreign investment supported by AICEP Portugal Global, the country's investment promotion agency (AICEP, 2022[24]). Over recent years, the sector's share accounted for 78% of total value of investment contracts, with most projects targeting the automotive industry (26%) and chemicals (17%).

Despite these developments, overall FDI activity continues to be largely concentrated in services sectors, notably in financial and professional services which accounted for the largest shares of total inward FDI stocks as of end-2021, although both sectors have seen their shares decline considerably over the last decade.[15] The sectors that have been driving FDI growth in Portugal more recently are energy and utilities, information and communication, accommodation and food services, transportation and storage, and real estate activities.

Energy and utilities, for instance, accounted for 11% of all cross-border M&A deals in Portugal and was the largest sector in terms of investment value (25%) over the period analysed, driven largely by rising activity in the renewable energy sector (see Section 1.3.5). While relatively less pronounced in terms of numbers of projects (5%), energy and utilities activities absorbed the largest share of greenfield investment in value terms (22%) too over the period assessed.

In turn, FDI activity in the ICT sector has been mostly associated with greenfield investment projects. A third of greenfield projects in Portugal target ICT, the second largest share in the benchmark group after Lithuania (34%). While in value terms the sector's share is smaller (15%), it is still the third largest in the group. This contrasts somewhat with the M&A trend, where the share of cross-border M&A deals in ICT is the lowest among peers (12%) and has changed little over time. In comparison, in Estonia, for instance, the sector's share went up from 9% in 2014 to 26% in 2022 on a 3-year moving average basis, making it the leading recipient of ICT deals in the group (18% over the period of observation).

1.3.5. Foreign investment into renewable energy projects has been on the rise

Renewable energy has dominated both cross-border M&A and greenfield investment in the energy sector in Portugal in recent years (Figure 1.11A-B). Renewables accounted for 96% of all cross-border M&As in the energy sector (and 5% of all cross-border M&As in Portugal). This is in stark contrast with most peer economies, where transactions in fossil energy dominated, the share of renewables averaging only 37% of all energy sector cross-border M&As. Greenfield projects in fossil energy have been generally less prevalent across countries.

Figure 1.11. Renewable energy dominates M&A and greenfield investment in energy

Share of total number of deals (Panel A) and projects (Panel B)

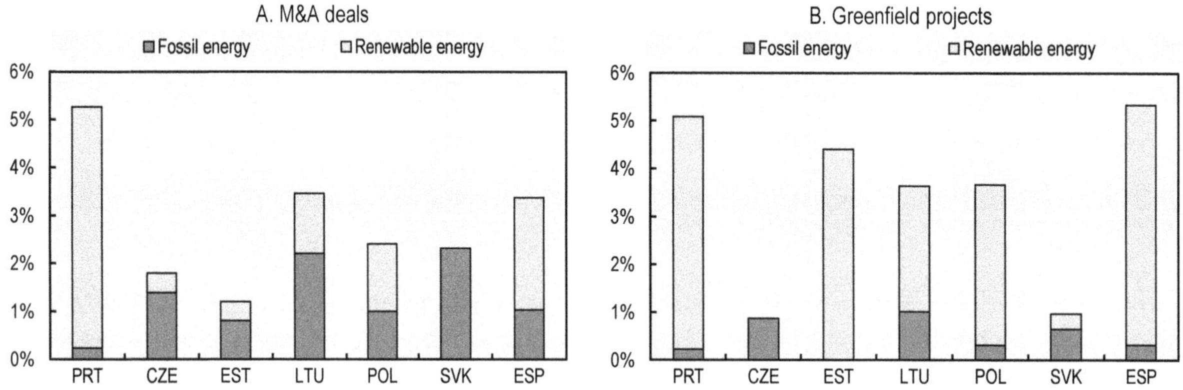

Note: Renewable energy includes the production of energy from naturally replenishing sources, i.e. solar, wind, geothermal, marine, biomass and hydroelectric energy. Fossil energy includes the generation of fuels, such as coal, oil and natural gas, and related extraction activities. Nuclear energy is not considered. M&A deals refer to completed ones, greenfield projects refer to announced investment plans. M&A data cover the period from 2012 to 2022. Greenfield data are from 2015 to 2022.
Source: OECD elaborations on Refinitiv M&A and Financial Times fDi Markets databases.

Most foreign investment in the Portuguese renewables sector were in solar energy (Figure 1.12). For instance, in 2020, new projects in solar photovoltaic and storage capacity were announced by Korean investors and Chinese investors. In 2018, a German investor also acquired a solar plant in the Algarve region. Hydropower and marine energy also attract foreign investors. In 2020, for instance, Swedish investors established a subsidiary in Porto to develop wave energy projects. In the same year, a group of French investors acquired six hydropower plants from EDP Energias de Portugal for USD 2.4 billion.

Figure 1.12. Solar power attracts most foreign investment

Distribution of deals and projects in renewables by energy source

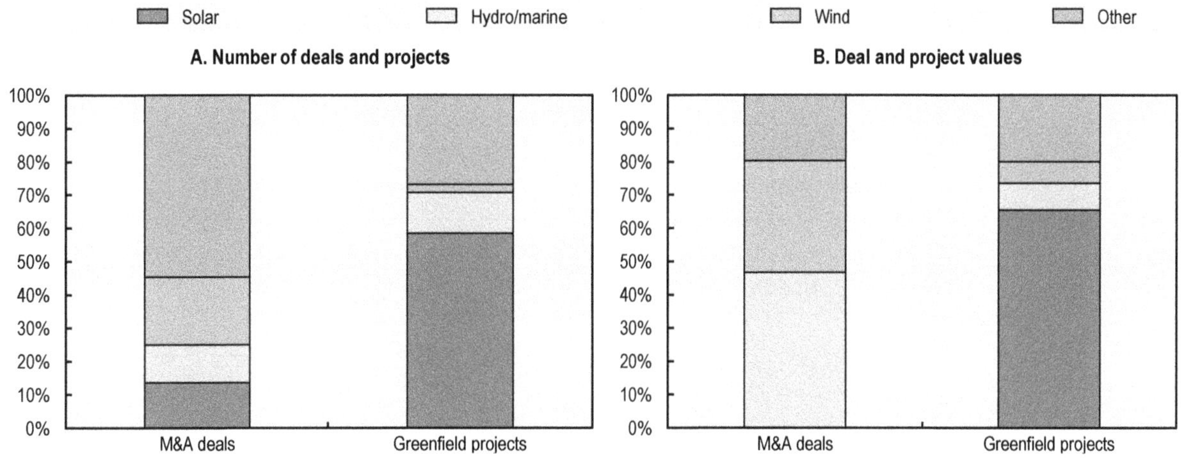

Note: Deal values of all M&As in solar energy were undisclosed. Other renewable energy refers to transactions where the source of the alternative energy is unknown. M&A data cover the period from 2012 to 2022. Greenfield data are from 2015 to 2022.
Source: OECD elaborations on Refinitiv M&A and Financial Times fDi Markets databases.

The increasing appetite of foreign investors for renewable energy projects in Portugal resonates with Portugal's leadership and policy orientation in this matter, being among the first countries in the world to set 2050 carbon neutrality goals and placing great emphasis on the expansion of renewable electricity generation as a means to achieve carbon neutrality, together with increased energy efficiency and broad electrification of energy demand. In its long-term strategy for carbon neutrality (Portugal's Roadmap for Carbon Neutrality 2050), Portugal has set the goal for renewables to cover 46-47% of final energy consumption by 2030, 71-72% by 2040 and 86-88% of final energy consumption by 2050. In 2020, renewables already covered a significant portion (30%) of the total energy consumption – one of the highest rates among the International Energy Agency (IEA)'s members (IEA, 2021[25]). However, after rising by almost 10 percentage points from 2005 to 2010, the growth in the share of renewables in total energy consumption has been relatively modest in comparison to the benchmarked group (Figure 1.13 A).

Portugal's energy demand is still largely supplied by imported fossil fuels, which accounted for roughly 73% of Portugal's total energy supply in 2019 (43% oil, 24% natural gas and 6% coal), driven particularly by demand from transport and industrial sectors (IEA, 2021[25]). All these are imported as Portugal has no domestic oil, natural gas or coal. The remaining part is sourced domestically from Portugal's domestic energy production sources, which are almost entirely renewable sources, notably bioenergy, wind and hydro. Impressive strides were made in expanding domestic renewable energy production over 2005-12, when it passed from covering 18% of total energy supply to 27%, largely due to growth in wind generation supported by a feed-in tariff scheme. Solar energy has also been trending up slightly more recently (IEA, 2021[25]). But such increments in domestic energy production have slowed down and, together with seasonal variations in the output of Portugal's hydropower plants, impeded a more pronounced reduction in Portugal's energy import dependency. As of end-2019, Portugal remained one of the most external energy dependent economies among IEA countries.

Boosting investment in renewable energy generation and energy efficiency is thus critical both to ensure carbon neutrality targets are achieved and to decrease energy import dependency. Adding renewable energy capacity to the grid might also contribute to further curtail electricity prices, which remains an area of concern for investors despite recent improvements (EIB, 2020[26]) (Figure 1.13 B). Over the last decade, the cost of electricity from utility-scale solar plants and onshore wind farms has dropped drastically to levels below those of various fossil fuel-fired options, increasingly undercutting even the cheapest and least sustainable forms of existing coal-fired power plants (IRENA, 2021[27]).[16] The war in Ukraine has further underlined the potential benefits of expanding Portugal's renewable energy production capacity.

Figure 1.13. Renewable energy intensity and industrial electricity prices

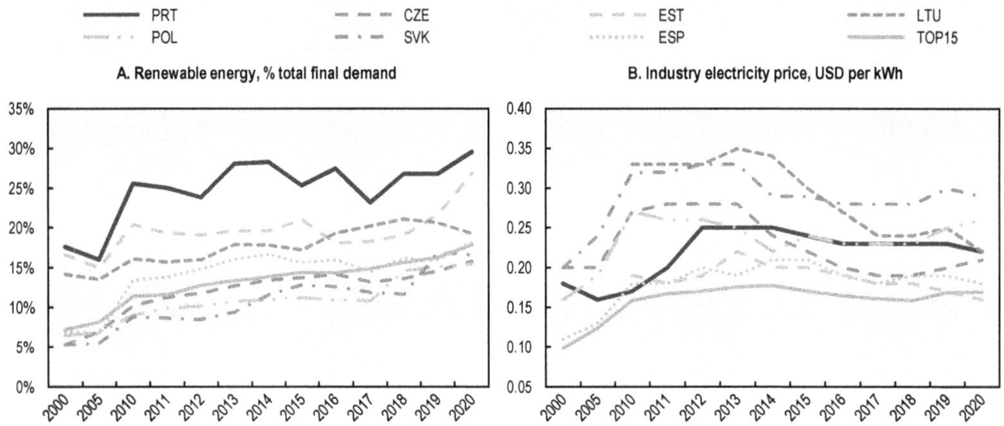

Note: Industry electricity prices are expressed at constant 2015 USD using PPP per kilowatt-hour. They represent the annual average end-user price for industrial users. To ensure better comparability with data on residential prices (not-showed here, but available in the database), the price is deflated by the GDP deflator and includes value added tax.
Source: IEA (2022[28]), *World Energy Balances Highlights*, https://www.iea.org/data-and-statistics/data-product/world-energy-balances-highlights; OECD (2021[29]), *Green Growth Indicators*, https://stats.oecd.org/Index.aspx?DataSetCode=GREEN_GROWTH#.

1.3.6. Foreign investment is also flowing into digital technologies and infrastructure

The digital economy has attracted a significant share of inward FDI across Portugal and the benchmarked economies, with software and IT services accounting for most investment (Figure 1.14).[17] Although Portugal hosts many cross-border M&As in digital sectors, their share in the total number of foreign deals was the second lowest in the benchmark group (16%). Greenfield projects into the digital economy were relatively more numerous, amounting to 37% of all greenfield investment announced in Portugal, surpassed only by Estonia (39%) and Lithuania (37%). Portugal is also attracting foreign investment in business services centres (BSC), particularly IT-related services. According to a recent survey, IT stands for over 40% of functions performed by BSCs in Portugal (AICEP and IDC Portugal, 2019[30]).

Most foreign investment into the Portuguese digital economy targets software and IT services (Figure 1.15 A). However, in value terms, software and IT services account for only half of all announced greenfield investment, whereas a substantial share of capital comes from projects in telecommunications (44%). The telecommunications sector clearly dominates in the value of foreign M&A activity (97%) (Figure 1.15 B).

Beyond the direct investment into digital technologies and infrastructure, foreign investors can also play an important role in Portugal's digital transition by providing funding for the start-up ecosystem. In 2020, the top 25 Portuguese technological start-ups raised 60% of their funding from foreign sources, with the United States (32%) and Singapore (17%) being the leading contributors, followed by other EU economies (EIT Digital, 2020[31]). The vibrant development of Portugal's start-up ecosystem, fuelled by the growing number of business incubators and accelerator programmes, strengthens the country's image as an attractive destination for foreign capital (Portugal Ventures, 2022[32]).[18]

Figure 1.14. The digital economy attracts foreign investment, but there is room for more

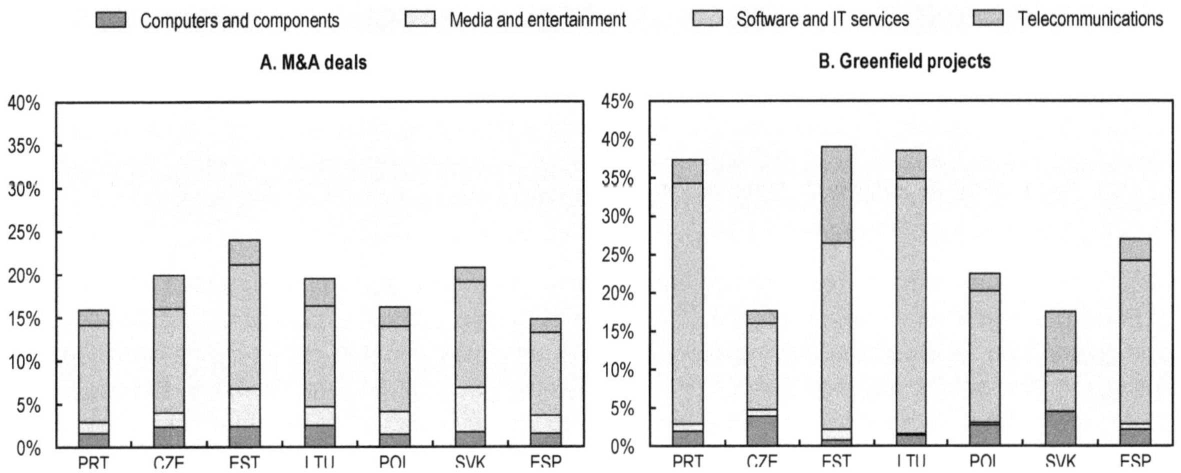

Note: The classification of M&A deals and greenfield projects into the subsectors of the digital economy is based on the activity classification in the source data. M&A deals refer to completed ones, greenfield projects refer to announced investment plans. M&A data cover the period from 2012 to 2022. Greenfield data are from 2015 to 2022.
Source: OECD elaborations on Refinitiv M&A and Financial Times fDi Markets databases.

Figure 1.15. Most transactions are in software and IT services, most value is in telecommunications

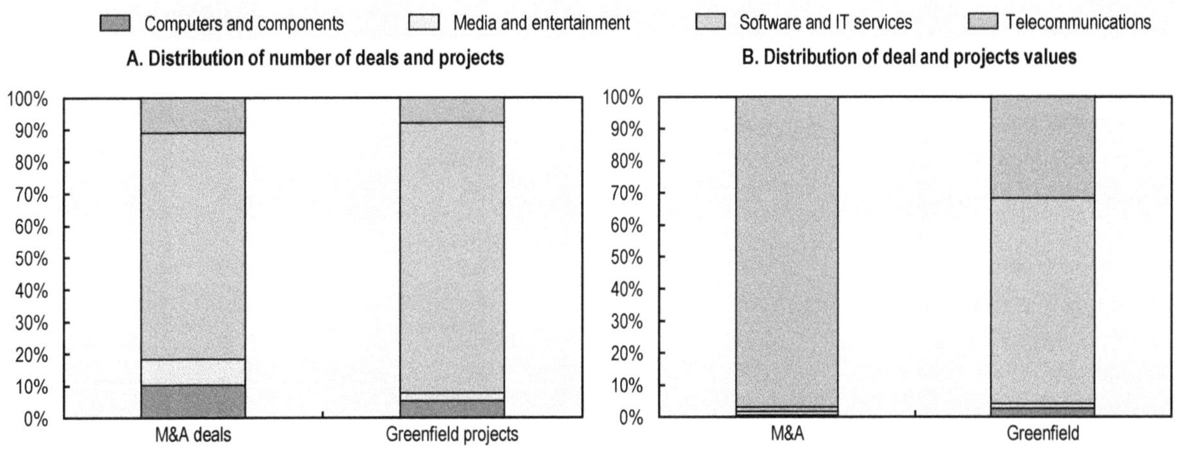

Note: The classification of M&A deals and greenfield projects into the subsectors of the digital economy is based on the activity classification in the source data. M&A deals refer to completed ones, greenfield projects refer to announced investment plans. M&A data cover the period from 2012 to 2022. Greenfield data are from 2015 to 2022.
Source: OECD elaborations on Refinitiv M&A and Financial Times fDi Markets databases.

1.4. FDI contribution to sustainability and inclusiveness in Portugal

Investment is central to growth and sustainable development. It can support the expansion of an economy's productive capacity in a sustainable manner and drive job creation and income growth. Most investment is undertaken by domestic firms, but FDI can provide additional advantages beyond its contribution to the capital stock and as an additional source of tax revenues. It can directly contribute to progressing on several areas of the Sustainable Development Goals (SDGs) (e.g. productivity and innovation, job quality and skills, gender equality and carbon emissions) by stimulating allocative efficiencies across and within sectors (e.g. when concentrated in more sustainable activities and when outperforming the average firm in its sector in respect to sustainable outcomes). It can also indirectly serve as a conduit for the local diffusion of technology and expertise and improved access to foreign markets, and potentially for other sustainable development outcomes, if its competitive pressure and linkages to the domestic economy pushes customers and firms throughout the value chain to improve their sustainable performance (OECD, 2021[33]). Several of these potential FDI contributions to sustainable development are assessed below, exploiting the richness of Portugal's micro-level statistics on firms and employees.

In 2020, foreign-owned firms[19] represented only 2% of all firms in Portugal but contributed substantially to the Portuguese economy: they employed 18% of the domestic workforce, accounted for 28.4% of total value added and 24.6% of business-funded research and development (R&D). Aside from the direct contribution to economic activity, foreign multinational enterprises (MNEs) are also found to bring broader benefits to Portugal. As shown below, they contribute to the development of Portugal's skills base and to job quality improvements, in terms of wage and gender parity. They are equally contributing to speed up the country's rate of digitalisation and, by purchasing inputs from local businesses and selling to international markets, are also supporting Portugal's integration into GVCs.

Table 1.1. Foreign firms perform better than Portuguese ones

Characteristics of foreign and domestic firms by size group (average values)

	Foreign firms			Domestic firms		
	Micro	SMEs	Large	Micro	SMEs	Large
Distribution of firms						
Total number of firms	5 048	4 718	439	376 115	59 932	771
Share of firms in manufacturing	8%	21%	41%	11%	29%	26%
Share of firms in services	83%	71%	52%	71%	53%	59%
Firm characteristics						
Number of employees	4.3	52.2	939.3	3.5	27.9	787.0
Labour productivity, in thousands (EUR)	47.4	46.2	41.1	19.2	23.3	32.1
Sales, in thousands (EUR)	2 328	16 177	148500	273	3 025	104 068
Export intensity	27%	25%	38%	4%	11%	22%
Domestic purchases, in thousands (EUR)	619	4 579	36585	22	330	14 580
R&D expenditure, EUR	437	4 600	58543	121	2 138	121 989
Share of high-skilled employees	48%	37%	30%	24%	22%	24%
Monthly wage, EUR	1 474	1 326	1 193	778	943	1 091
Share of female employees	44%	44%	44%	45%	40%	44%

Note: Micro-firms are enterprises with less than ten employees, SMEs employ 10-249 workers, and large firms have 250 or more employees. Labour productivity is value added per employee. Export intensity is the ratio of exports to firm sales.
Source: Own calculations based on Statistics Portugal (INE), QP and SCIE, 2009-20.

Micro-level evidence shows that most foreign-owned businesses in Portugal are micro-enterprises (49%) or SMEs (46%), with only 4% being large-sized (Table 1.1). Most foreign firms are in the services sector, although many large foreign enterprises operate in manufacturing. For every size group, foreign companies are larger, more productive and generate more sales than their Portuguese peers. They are also more integrated in GVCs, as shown by their higher export intensities and larger volumes of domestic purchases. They hire more skilled workers and pay higher wages. On average, foreign micro-enterprises and SMEs invest more in R&D than their domestic counterparts. Foreign-owned SMEs employ slightly more women than their domestic peers, while shares of female employment are very similar in foreign and domestic companies of the other size groups.

1.4.1. FDI supports skill development in Portugal

Foreign enterprises tend to hire more high-skilled workers than domestic firms, possibly because their business operations might involve more advanced technologies or more complex tasks, which increases the demand for skilled labour and can raise the host country's skill intensity (OECD, 2019[6]). Moreover, foreign MNEs tend to pay higher wages to their employees, especially to highly qualified ones (Hijzen et al., 2013[34]; Setzler and Tintelnot, 2021[35]). Foreign businesses can increase the supply of skills by training their own employees and employees of partner firms, but also by inducing domestic firms to invest in skill development to stay competitive. Upskilling of the domestic workforce can also take place through mobility of labour from foreign to local firms.

Foreign firms employ more high-skilled workers

In Portugal, foreign affiliates employ more high-skilled workers than domestic businesses in most sectors of the economy (Figure 1.16). Discrepancies in skill intensity in some sectors, such as construction and manufacturing, reflect the differences in the industrial specialisation with foreign enterprises operating in more technology-intensive activities. In other sectors, such as ICT and electricity, foreign-owned businesses employ more high-skilled workers than their domestic counterparts even within narrowly defined economic activities, likely because they perform more technologically advanced tasks. Skill intensity in foreign firms is higher even when looking only at workers in managerial positions.[20] Additional estimates show that foreign enterprises are more skill-intensive even when compared to domestic firms with the same characteristics.[21]

Figure 1.16. Foreign businesses employ more high-skilled workers

Share of employees in high-skilled occupations

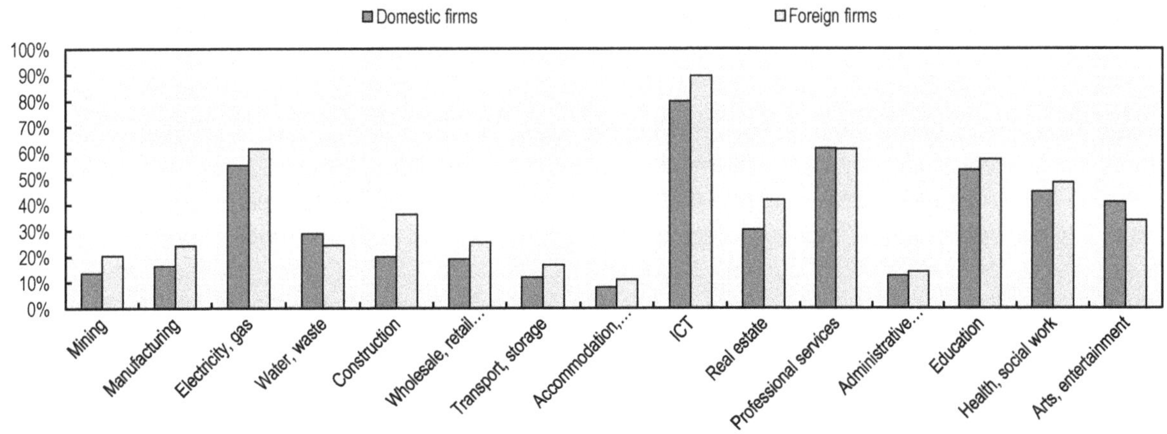

Note: High-skilled occupations include managerial, professional, technical and associated professional occupations.
Source: Own calculations based on Statistics Portugal (INE), QP and SCIE, 2009-20.

Foreign firms pay higher wages

Foreign-owned firms pay higher wages than domestic firms. The wage premium holds even when comparing employees and firms with similar characteristics.[22] Furthermore, the premium exists for all skill groups (Figure 1.17). It is estimated that wages paid by foreign firms to employees in high-skilled occupations are 7.3% higher than in domestic firms, whereas the estimated wage premiums for medium and low-skilled occupations are 4% and 4.5%, respectively.[23]

The foreign wage premium exists even after accounting for the differences in observable firm and worker characteristics, suggesting that other factors might explain why foreign firms reward their workers more generously. For instance, foreign wage premium might reflect greater complexity of tasks that employees of foreign firms perform (Nilsson Hakkala, Heyman and Sjöholm, 2014[36]) or better management practices, possibly adopted from headquarters (Bloom et al., 2021[37]; Hjort, Li and Sarsons, 2020[38]). It is also plausible that employees of foreign companies systematically differ from workers of domestic firms in ways that cannot be captured by the data but are important for wage setting (e.g. fluency in foreign languages).

Figure 1.17. Foreign firms reward skills better

Estimated wage premium in foreign firms by skill group

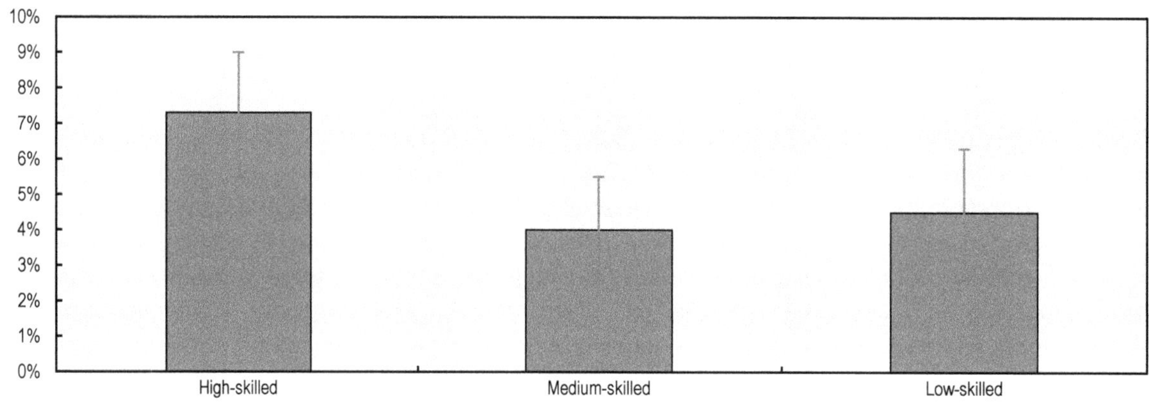

Note: The figure shows the estimated effects of foreign ownership on hourly wages and their respective 95% confidence intervals. The regressions control for individual (education and experience) and firm characteristics (size, productivity and export intensity), as well as industry-year and regional effects. High-skilled occupations include managerial, professional, technical and associated professional occupations. Medium-skilled occupations refer to clerks, craft and related trades workers, plant and machine operators, and assemblers. Low-skilled occupations include service workers, shop and sales workers and elementary occupations.
Source: Own calculations based on Statistics Portugal (INE), QP and SCIE, 2009-20.

FDI contributes to the diffusion of skills

Foreign businesses can contribute to upskilling workers through training. One indication that foreign companies actively invest in employee training comes from the Portuguese ICT use survey (IUTICE): nearly two-thirds of surveyed foreign firms (62%) reported providing training to their employees to develop their ICT skills, whereas only around a third of domestic firms (36%) did so. Among foreign companies, training was offered extensively by both large firms (76%) and SMEs (53%), whereas employees of domestic companies were substantially more likely to access training if they worked in large firms (63% offered ICT training), than those working for domestic SMEs (30%).

FDI can also support skill upgrading in the host economy through labour mobility. Micro-level evidence shows that from 2009 to 2020, nearly 979 000 workers in Portugal had experience working in a foreign-owned firm, that is 24% of all the working population in Portugal. Over time, around 259 000 of these employees, representing nearly 6.5% of all workers, left foreign MNEs and started working in domestic companies.[24] This labour mobility translates into a growing share of domestic businesses employing workers with experience from foreign MNEs. In 2020, 18% of domestic firms employed one or more workers with recent experience from foreign-owned enterprises, against 5% in 2012. On average, workers moving from foreign to domestic enterprises experienced a 2% increase in real hourly wages.[25]

Experience acquired in foreign MNEs might be seen as especially valuable to their domestic competitors if, for instance, employees of foreign multinationals gain insights about international markets, embrace superior management practices or learn to use advanced technologies (Balsvik, 2011[39]). A recent study finds that Portuguese employers value experience accumulated in firms with international operations, as seen from the wage premium that workers coming from these firms get (Mion, Opromolla and Ottaviano, 2020[40]). This result is consistent with the notion that employees of foreign affiliates are bringing new knowledge and skills when changing their jobs to start working in domestic companies.

1.4.2. Foreign MNEs contribute to gender equality

Through their demand for female workers, foreign affiliates can affect employment and wage gaps. Their corporate practices, such as hiring and promotion, can influence women's opportunities for career progression, including their ability to reach leadership positions. More demanding international and national standards, including responsible business conduct principles, may prompt foreign firms to include gender equality considerations in their corporate strategy. Foreign-owned businesses can also enhance women's labour market prospects in local enterprises, if domestic companies adopt more gender-inclusive employment policies to imitate successful foreign firms (OECD, 2019[6]).

Foreign firms offer women better opportunities in some sectors

As in other OECD countries, female employment in Portugal is concentrated in low value-added services sectors, such as education, health and social work activities, which typically offer lower pay (OECD, 2019[6]). Domestic firms employ relatively more women in these sectors than foreign affiliates (Figure 1.18 A). Female participation is very similar between foreign and domestic companies in other economic activities, although foreign firms have noticeably higher shares of women working in wholesale and retail trade and in transport and storage.[26]

Figure 1.18. Better female employment opportunities in retail and storage

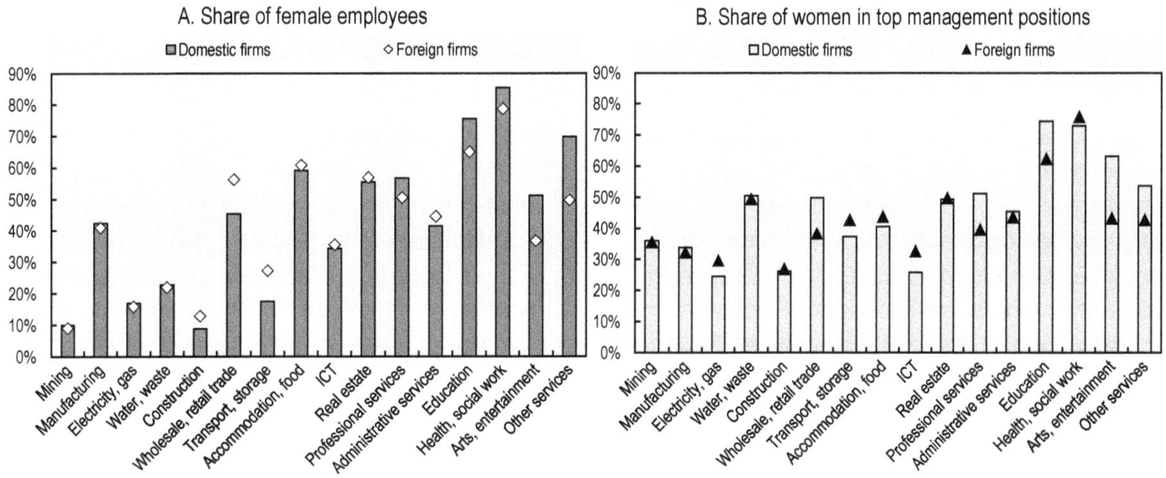

Note: Top management positions include "Senior Executives" as defined by the classification of employees into hierarchical levels reported in the micro-data (the levels are defined according to Portuguese Decree-Law No. 121/78 of 2 July 1978). These positions include occupations responsible for the main strategic decisions of the firm: the organisation of firm's resources, strategic planning, etc.
Source: Own calculations based on Statistics Portugal (INE), QP and SCIE, 2009-20.

In many sectors, women are less likely to reach the top levels of management. The share of female executives is over one half only in sectors traditionally dominated by women (education, arts, health and social work). However, foreign firms employ more women in senior positions than their domestic counterparts in many sectors, including ICT, transport and storage, accommodation and food services (Figure 1.18 B).

Women earn more in foreign firms, but they face slightly larger pay gaps

Foreign-owned companies pay higher wages to female employees than domestic firms. In 2020, the median monthly wage of women working in foreign firms was EUR 972 and EUR 796 in domestic firms (for comparison, men's median wages were EUR 1 144 in foreign and 856 in domestic enterprises).

A slightly higher gender pay gap is observed in foreign firms than in domestic ones, when accounting for employees' education, experience and occupation, as well as the differences in firm characteristics (size, productivity and export intensity; see Annex Table 1.A.3).[27] However, the estimated wage penalty in foreign firms disappears completely for women in high-skilled occupations and in top management positions.[28]

The absence of foreign wage penalty for women in highly skilled and top management positions is in line with the finding that wage discrepancies tend to be smaller for highly skilled workers. The gender wage gaps may also vary considerably across industries due to the differences in investors' sectoral specialisation and technological profiles.[29]

1.4.3. Foreign firms support Portugal's digitalisation

Foreign MNEs can support the host country's digital transition by investing in digital technologies and infrastructure (see Section 1.3.6), and by transferring ICT solutions across borders. Some studies find that the development of key digital technologies is highly concentrated in a few source countries, hence, foreign investors can play an important role in technology diffusion by sharing new tools and practices with their affiliates, but also with partners and customers in the host economy (OECD, 2019[41]).

FDI supports ICT diffusion in Portugal

Although Portugal enjoys high levels of Internet penetration, with 60% of businesses connected to high-speed broadband, technology uptake by Portuguese firms remains well below best performing OECD and EU countries, especially among SMEs (OECD, 2021[3]; EC, 2021[42]). For instance, Portuguese SMEs lag substantially behind in the adoption of cloud computing, which can help firms scale up without incurring costly investment into IT infrastructure.

Foreign firms in Portugal extensively use digital technologies,[30] thus actively exploiting opportunities to strengthen innovation capacity and optimise costs. Overall, foreign affiliates' uptake of key digital technologies is 1.1 to 2 times higher than of domestic enterprises, and compared to domestic SMEs, foreign-owned ones are more likely to use most of the selected technologies (Figure 1.19). Domestic large companies use cloud technologies more extensively than their foreign counterparts do, although higher shares of foreign businesses adopt industrial robots, 3D printing and artificial intelligence technologies.[31] For many firms in Portugal, online sales are an important source of revenue, as reflected in the country's relatively high e-commerce uptake compared to other EU economies (EC, 2021[42]). Among SMEs selling online, both domestic and foreign-owned ones generated over a fifth of their turnover online (Figure 1.20). The share of web sales in large firms is generally lower, partly reflecting the fact that larger enterprises tend to depend on a mix of electronic and more traditional sales channels (OECD, 2019[43]). In general, for a given firm size, firms with higher labour productivity and export intensity tend to generate a larger share of their revenue from online sales (Annex Table 1.A.4).[32]

Figure 1.19. Foreign firms extensively use digital technologies, while domestic SMEs lag behind

Share of firms using a given technology, 2021 or latest available year

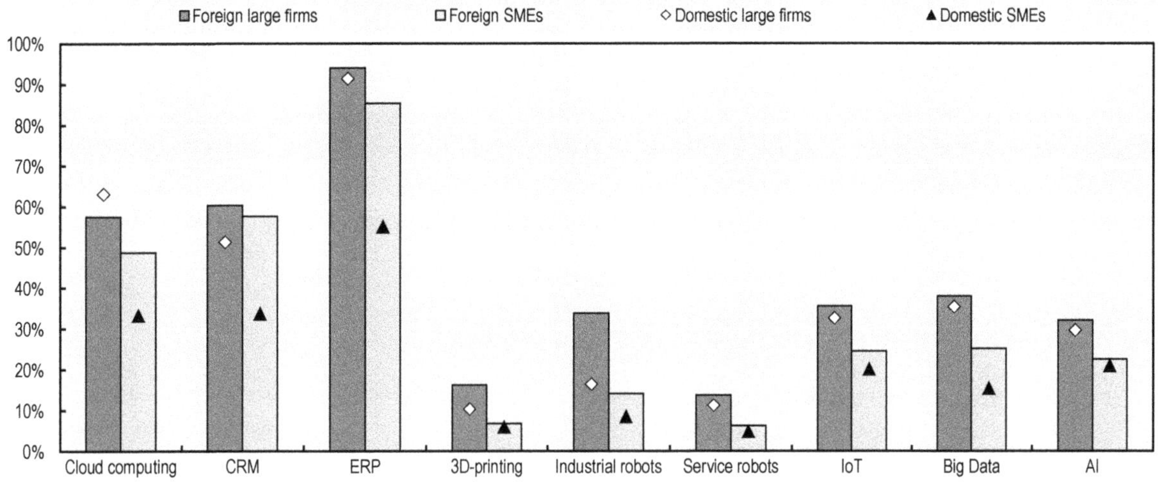

Note: Cloud computing is the delivery of information technology services over the Internet. Customer relationship management (CRM) software organises data about customers, employees and suppliers. Enterprise resource planning (ERP) systems integrate information on business processes. 3D-printing includes use of 3D printers to create three-dimensional physical objects. Industrial robots are automatically controlled machines used in industrial automation. Service robots are machines that can perform tasks involving interaction with people or other devices with some autonomy. The Internet of Things (IoT) is the use of interconnected devices that collect/process data and can be controlled over the Internet. Big data uses tools to analyse data in complex formats. Artificial Intelligence (AI) refers to the use of selected technologies to make decisions with some autonomy. Data on robots refer to 2018, Big Data and 3D printing to 2020. SMEs are firms with 10-249 employees, large firms with 250 or more.
Source: Own calculations based on Statistics Portugal (INE), QP, SCIE and IUTICE, 2018-21.

Figure 1.20. Participation in online sales

Share of firms selling online and share of e-sales in total sales, 2021

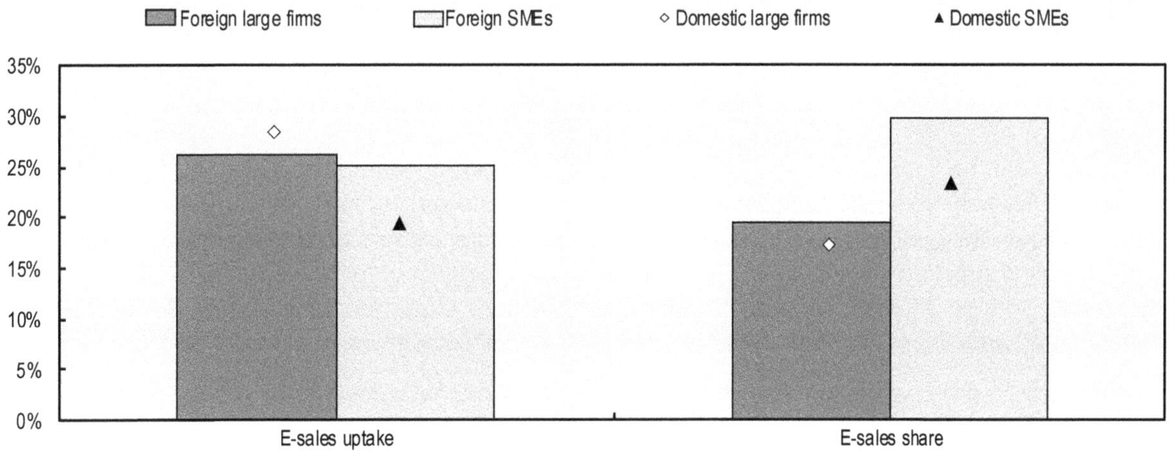

Note: E-sales uptake refers to the share of firms selling their goods or services online. E-sales share is the average share of online sales in the revenue of firms that are selling online. SMEs are firms with 10-249 employees, large firms have 250 or more employees.
Source: Own calculations based on Statistics Portugal (INE), QP, SCIE and IUTICE, 2020-21.

Various firm characteristics influence the decision to sell online, but other factors can be important too.[33] Micro-data evidence from the Portuguese ICT use survey suggests that many firms in Portugal abstain from online sales because their goods or services are not fit for electronic transactions (43% domestic firms, 44% foreign; Figure 1.21 A).[34] Costs of introducing sales on the web, logistics related to the transport of goods and services and difficulties with the legal framework are also cited among the key obstacles, with the latter being reported slightly more often by foreign firms, particularly those from outside the European Economic Area (EEA).[35] When asked about the difficulties for web sales within the EU, 18% of domestic and 15% foreign e-sellers indicated high costs of delivery and return as the main challenge (Figure 1.21 B).

In terms of destination markets, most online sales by firms in Portugal target domestic consumers. In 2020, web sales within Portugal accounted for 88% of all electronic orders received by foreign MNEs and 86% by domestic enterprises. Foreign markets make up a slightly higher share of online sales of domestic businesses than for foreign firms, possibly because many foreign firms enter Portugal with the intention to serve the Portuguese consumer.

Figure 1.21. Various factors hinder the uptake of e-commerce

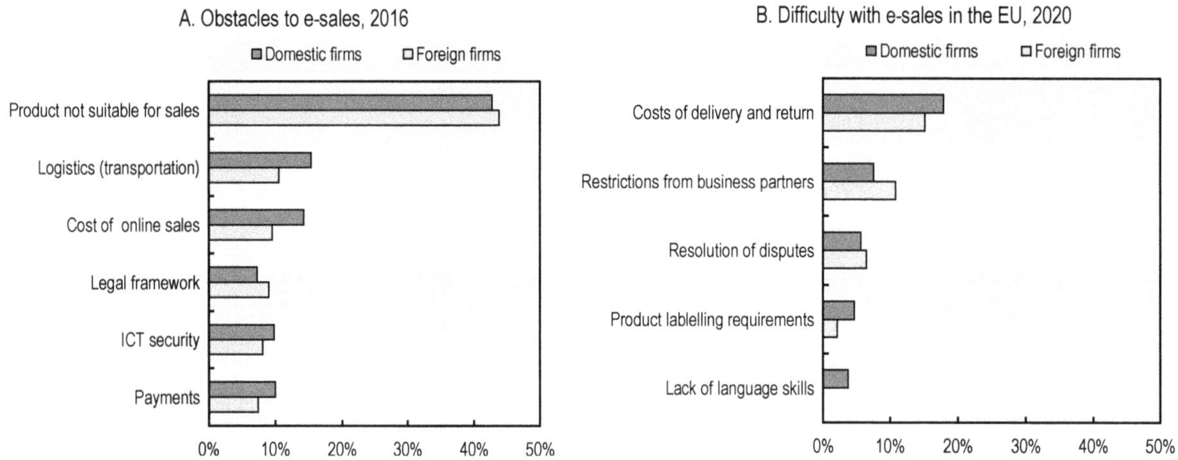

Note: Panel A presents shares of firms reporting a given obstacle to online sales (of all firms that participated in the survey). Panel B presents shares of firms selling online reporting a given difficulty with online sales within the EU. The latest data available are for 2020 as the above questions were only included in the more recent survey.
Source: Own calculations based on Statistics Portugal (INE), QP, SCIE and IUTICE, 2016-20.

1.4.4. FDI facilitates the integration of domestic firms into global value chains

Foreign firms can be important buyers of domestically produced goods and services. Backward linkages of foreign MNEs help domestic businesses access new markets and improve the competitiveness of their products. These linkages can also stimulate knowledge transfers if foreign firms demand higher-quality inputs from local suppliers and are willing to share their technology or corporate practices (OECD, 2019[6]). Furthermore, foreign affiliates can enhance the host country's export performance by selling their own outputs abroad and also by incorporating inputs from domestic companies in products destined for export.

These features can be particularly critical for a country like Portugal whose level of trade is relatively low for a small open economy. Despite impressive strides over the past decade, with exports of goods and services rising rapidly as a share of GDP, partly supported by structural reforms that followed from the economic adjustment programme, Portugal's level of trade to GDP ratio still stood at 86% of GDP in 2021, while it averaged 137% across the benchmarked countries. This low level is particularly marked with respect to merchandise trade, but also holds true for services trade, albeit to a much lower extent. In comparison to the benchmarked countries, and despite improvements in the last decade, Portugal's export basket is also still dominated by relatively lower complexity goods and services (i.e. involving less sophisticated productive know-how), which can be a constraint for long-term income growth (Hausmann, Hwang and Rodrik, 2006[44]).[36]

Foreign affiliates based in Portugal source extensively from local firms

In 2020, foreign-owned enterprises located in Portugal purchased most of their inputs from Portuguese businesses (77% of services, 53% of goods).[37] Intermediate inputs sourced domestically accounted for nearly half of foreign firms' output (47%), indicating that foreign-owned investors incorporate a substantial amount of domestic value added in their production. Industries where foreign firms rely heavily on domestic goods include wholesale and retail trade (43% of turnover) and manufacturing (25%). Domestically sourced services accounted for more than half of foreign firms' turnover in professional services (50%) and transport and warehousing (46%).

Foreign MNEs boost Portugal's export performance

Apart from its capital contribution, FDI plays an important role in Portugal's export performance. While representing only a small fraction of the entire business population, foreign firms were responsible for 46% of total exports by Portugal (39% of services exports and 53% of merchandise exports) in 2020, a share that has been growing over time (38% in 2010). Their contribution is especially important in key exporting industries: in 2020, foreign MNEs accounted for nearly 55% of Portugal's overall international sales in ICT, 52% in manufacturing and 32% in wholesale and retail trade (Figure 1.22).

Figure 1.22. Foreign firms contribute significantly to Portuguese exports

Share of foreign affiliates in total export value and in the number of firms, 2020

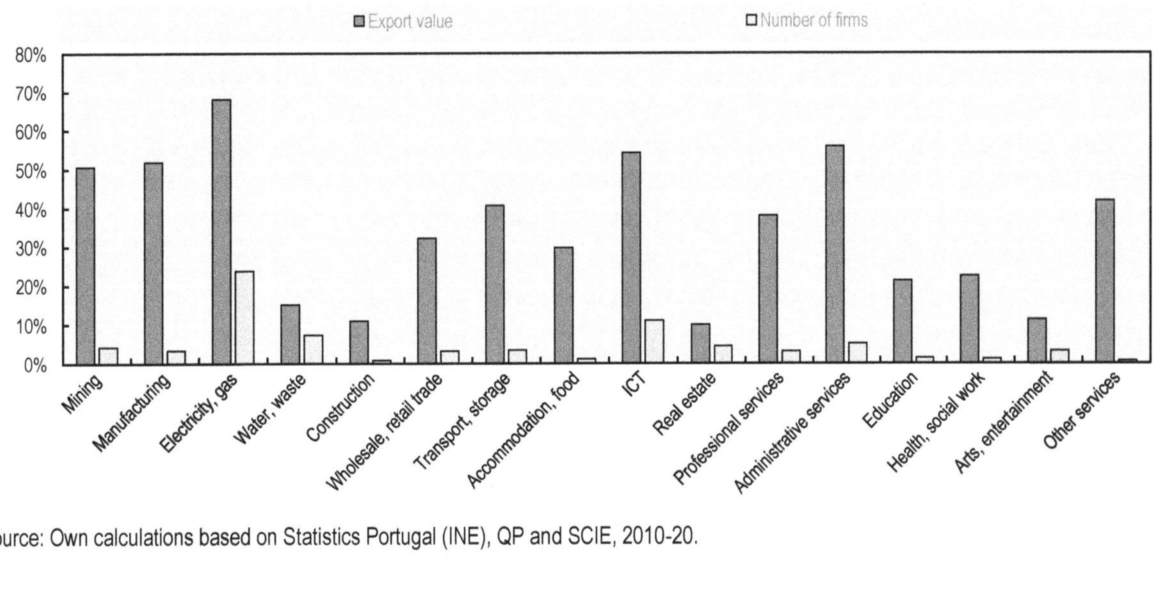

Source: Own calculations based on Statistics Portugal (INE), QP and SCIE, 2010-20.

Foreign firms are more likely to export than domestic companies. In 2020, more than half of all foreign-owned firms sold their goods or services in international markets, whereas only 17% of domestic enterprises did so. Among the businesses that exported, foreign-owned enterprises sold a larger share (48% of total sales of a median firm) of their turnover on international markets than their domestic counterparts (14% of total sales of a median domestic company).

Over the past decade, export intensity of foreign firms has been steadily increasing, mostly driven by accommodation and food services, professional services, wholesale and retail trade (Figure 1.23).[38]

Figure 1.23. Export intensity of foreign services exporters has been on the rise

Median export intensity of firms selling abroad

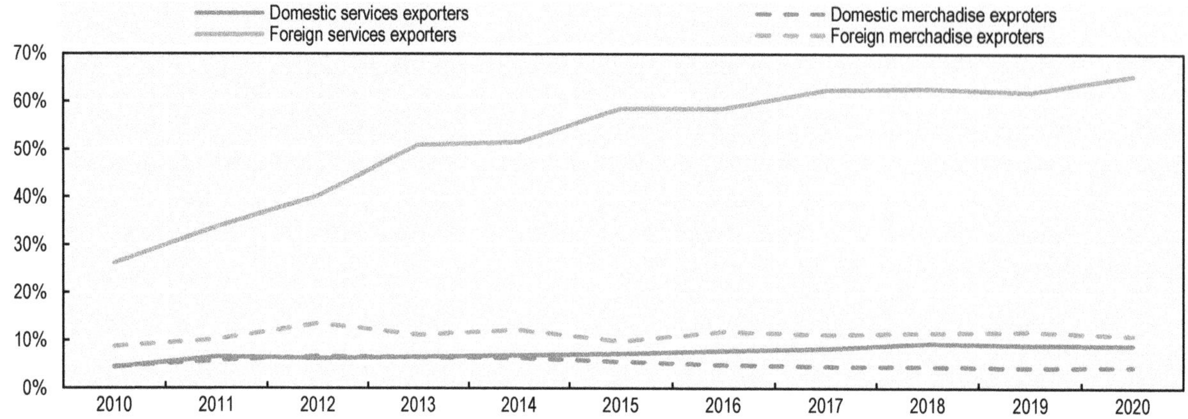

Note: Export intensity is measured as the share of exports in firms' turnover.
Source: Own calculations based on Statistics Portugal (INE), QP and SCIE, 2010-20.

Foreign MNEs provide additional channels for GVC integration

In 2020, domestic purchases by foreign-owned firms in Portugal accounted for slightly over a quarter of all domestic purchases in Portugal (25% of services and 26% of goods). By incorporating local goods and services into production, part of which is exported abroad, foreign companies promote greater integration of Portuguese firms in global value chains.

Similarly, a greater use of imported inputs by both domestic and foreign exporters is an indication of increasing integration into GVCs. Figure 1.24 shows that around a third of Portuguese gross exports reflects value added from imported inputs and the share climbed up from 28% in 2010 to 31% in 2018. The share of foreign content is substantially larger in the Czech Republic (42%) and the Slovak Republic (48%), reflecting greater reliance of these economies on inputs sourced from abroad. This suggests that there is room for enhancing Portugal's level of GVC integration and export performance.

Figure 1.24. A large share of domestic inputs is embedded in gross exports

Share of foreign and domestic value added in gross exports, 2018

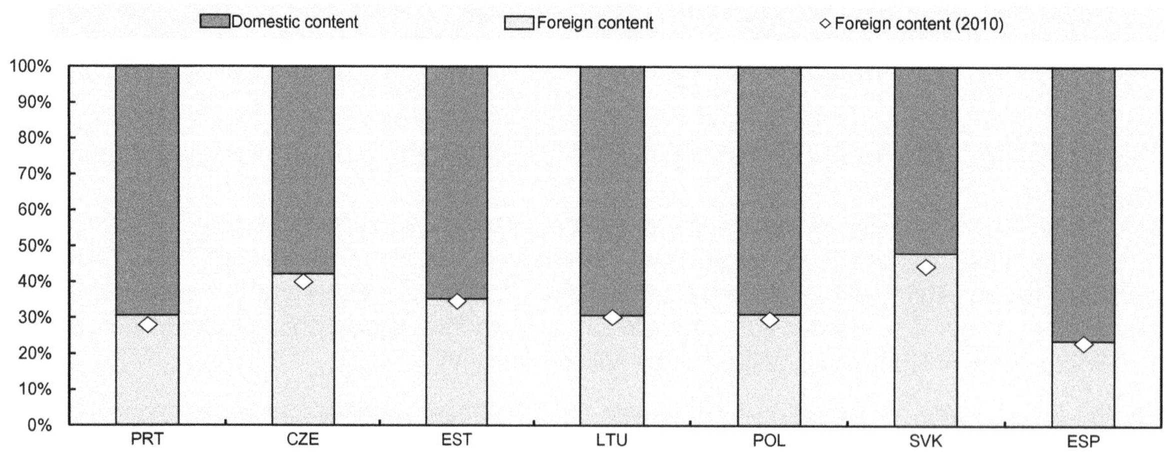

Source: OECD (2021[45]), *Trade in Value Added database*, https://www.oecd.org/sti/ind/measuring-trade-in-value-added.htm.

Exported products embody a substantial share of services inputs. When all those intermediate services that went into producing goods (and services) are accounted for, their contribution amounts to more than half (57%) of the value added exported by Portugal (Figure 1.25). The largest share of the service content embedded in gross exports in Portugal is produced domestically (43% in 2018). In contrast, the Czech Republic and the Slovak Republic rely on foreign services inputs more extensively (19% and 20% respectively). Thus, although foreign services contribute substantially to Portugal's exports, there is even further potential for Portugal to strengthen its integration into global production networks, including through more foreign investment into services.

Figure 1.25. Services contribute extensively to gross exports, 2018

Services embodied in gross exports, 2018

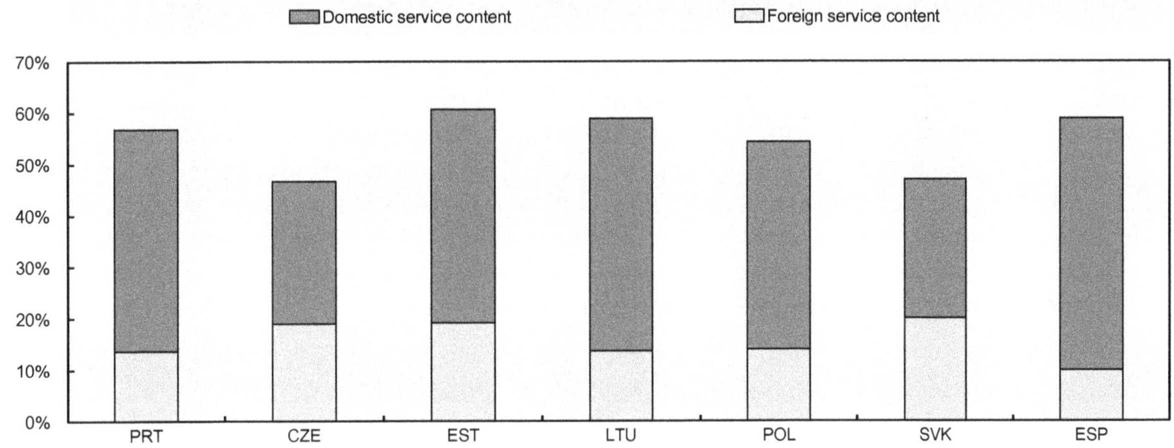

Source: OECD (2021[45]), *Trade in Value Added database*, https://www.oecd.org/sti/ind/measuring-trade-in-value-added.htm.

1.4.5. Benefits of FDI may not materialise automatically

Strong linkages can facilitate FDI spillovers…

The strength of supplier linkages between foreign and domestic firms tends to be critical for the ability of host economies to benefit from activities of foreign MNEs (Görg and Greenaway, 2004[46]). For instance, a recent study argues that knowledge spillovers from FDI into the Portuguese textiles sector in the 1970s were limited, as foreign investors generated few linkages with local producers (Lopes and Simões, 2017[47]). In contrast, in the 1980s, local producers of automotive parts managed to substantially upgrade their capabilities thanks to their extensive interactions with Renault's manufacturing facility, which allowed many of these firms to become suppliers of Renault plants outside Portugal. In the 2000s, Siemens set up a number of new training centres in Portugal, strengthening linkages with local universities, which in turn attracted highly skilled individuals and spurred business creation (Lopes and Simões, 2017[47]).

… but other factors can be important for the benefits of FDI to materialise

A recent OECD report assesses the extent to which different FDI diffusion channels are at play in Portugal, focusing on the linkages between FDI and domestic SMEs (OECD, 2022[5]). The report concludes that although foreign MNEs appear better integrated into Portugal's economy than in comparable countries, strengthening capabilities of firms in high-tech sectors and advancing the innovation potential of domestic SMEs would facilitate linkages with foreign investors in Portugal. The study also proposes several policy options that could enhance the impact of FDI for SMEs. Several other studies have also pinpointed key factors that influence the strength of positive effects of FDI on the Portuguese economy. For instance, Teixeira and Tavares-Lehmann (2014[48]) find that knowledge sharing between foreign MNEs and Portuguese businesses is stronger for more R&D-intensive local firms. Crespo, Fontoura and Proença (2009[49]) show that geographical proximity between foreign and domestic enterprises in Portugal also facilitates the occurrence of FDI spillovers. Benefits of FDI may also fail to materialise when the host economy lacks absorptive capacity or experiences low labour mobility (OECD, 2019[6]).

Beyond factors that might hinder the accrual of potential positive FDI spillovers, there is also the need to have appropriate policies and institutions to address any potential adverse impact that may directly or indirectly result from the presence of foreign firms (e.g. potential crowding out of local firms, wider wage inequality and regional disparity, greater pressures on existing infrastructures and natural resources, etc.) (OECD, 2021[33]).

1.4.6. Foreign firms are unevenly distributed across Portugal

Foreign-owned businesses are largely concentrated around Lisbon (Figure 1.26). Compared to domestic companies, the concentration of foreign micro-firms and SMEs is twice as high. Large foreign enterprises are also significantly overrepresented in the capital region, which might partially reflect that the Lisboa region hosts many head offices of foreign companies, even if they operate in other regions as well.[39] Many foreign-owned companies locate in the Norte region, although to a lesser extent than domestic ones. The Centro region also hosts a substantial share of foreign-owned businesses, but disproportionately fewer micro-enterprises and SMEs compared to domestic peers. Foreign presence in other regions is much lower, but similar to the distribution of domestic firms.

Figure 1.26. Lisboa and Norte regions host the majority of foreign firms

Number of firms as percentage of total

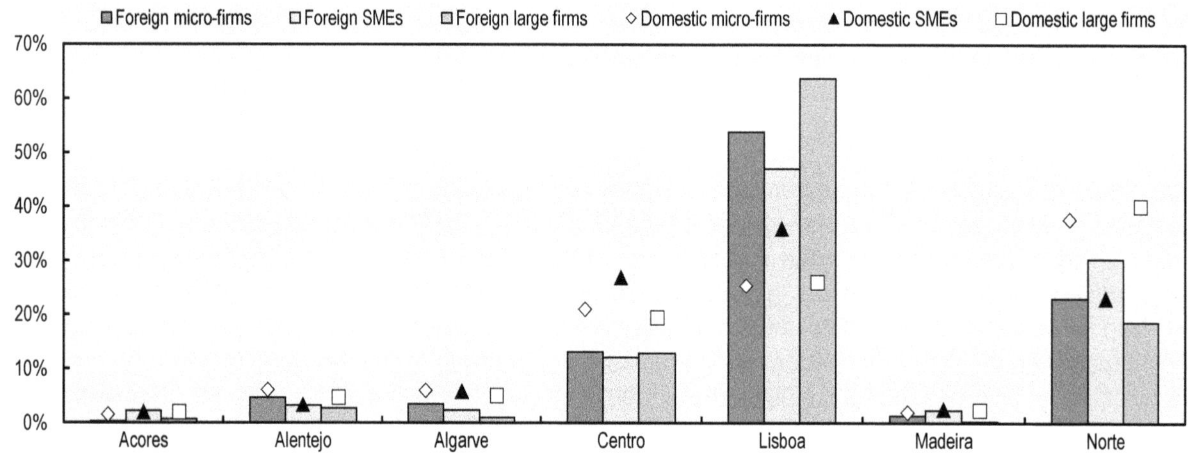

Note: The bars represent the number of foreign firms of a given size group as percentage of the total number of foreign firms in that size group. The symbols show the number of domestic firms of a given size group as percentage of the total number of domestic firms in that size group.
Source: Own calculations based on Statistics Portugal (INE), QP and SCIE 2010-20.

Characteristics and performance of foreign affiliates vary considerably across regions, reflecting differences both in the industrial structure of the regions themselves and in the specialisation profiles of foreign investors (Table 1.2). Most productive and skill-intensive firms are located in the Lisboa region. Although only a relatively small number of companies operate in Madeira, the region hosts foreign firms that are among the most productive and skill-intensive, driven largely by businesses performing data hosting and processing. Most export-intensive foreign firms are located in the Norte and Centro regions. Both regions host many manufacturing exporters, whereas Norte also enjoys a large presence of ICT firms that extensively sell their services abroad. Foreign companies in Algarve employ on average more women, particularly in accommodation and food services. The share of women is also among the largest in foreign companies operating in Norte, mostly reflecting the high female participation in manufacturing of food, clothing and leather products.

Table 1.2. Characteristics of foreign firms vary across regions

Characteristics of foreign firms by region (average values)

	Acores	Alentejo	Algarve	Centro	Lisboa	Madeira	Norte
Labour productivity, in thousands (EUR)	38.4	39.0	27.2	37.6	53.7	43.4	39.5
Share of high-skilled employees	34%	29%	26%	30%	49%	40%	33%
Share of female employees	32%	43%	55%	44%	47%	49%	45%
Export intensity	9%	27%	10%	32%	22%	31%	36%
Domestic purchases, in thousands (EUR)	1 584.6	3 447.9	171.7	4 389.8	6 223.3	347.9	3 789.3

Note: Labour productivity is value added per employee. Export intensity is the ratio of exports to firm sales.
Source: Own calculations based on Statistics Portugal (INE), QP and SCIE, 2009-20.

1.5. Conclusion

Portugal needs to mobilise further investment to support long-term productivity growth in view of adverse demographic trends and to accelerate the transition to a carbon-neutral economy by 2050, the latter becoming increasingly strategic in view of Portugal's external energy dependency and current rampant energy prices. Despite recent improvements, overall investment levels remain relatively low, particularly with respect to productivity-enhancing assets, such as machinery, equipment and intellectual property assets. Increased investment in ICT assets more broadly across industries and firms could also enable further productivity improvements and help to strengthen Portugal's reputation as a technology and innovation hub.

Foreign investors can be important partners to address these challenges. Indeed, as shown in this chapter, FDI can play a valuable role in addressing Portugal's productivity challenge as well as serve as a conduit to progress on many other SDGs. Evidence from the micro-data analysis shows that foreign affiliates in Portugal support skill development, contribute to more gender-inclusive corporate practices, speed up the host country's digital transformation and provide new channels to integrate domestic businesses into global production networks. Foreign investment is also actively contributing to accelerate Portugal's green and digital transition, with significant amounts of investment flowing into renewable energy projects, digital technologies and infrastructure in recent years.

Portugal has long turned to FDI as a vehicle for capital renewal and innovation, taking several steps to promote and further open the economy to foreign investors over time. Currently, Portugal holds one of the highest levels of inward FDI stocks to GDP ratio across OECD member countries. Yet, there are still several areas where FDI could be further leveraged. Portugal's investor base, for instance, remains largely concentrated in traditional European partners. In addition to greater resilience, further diversification could broaden Portugal's economic opportunities by strengthening its ties with other world leading outward investing economies and more dynamic regions. Relatively little FDI has also gone into the manufacturing sector, although there are signs of foreign investment activity picking up in the sector more recently. Further FDI could help to modernise the capital base of tradable activities more broadly and ensure that Portugal's recent trade expansion and gains in competitiveness are sustained over the long run.

Economic uncertainty brought up by the COVID-19 pandemic and Russia's war against Ukraine will also likely have near and long-term consequences for global FDI flows, and for Portugal as a recipient country. Besides the economic shock and other disruptions associated with such events, recent shifts in economic and political priorities at the EU level towards reducing economic dependencies, strengthening defence capabilities and bolstering the green and digital transition might also bring new investment opportunities and give a boost to existing ones. Portugal may benefit from its recent track record in attracting increasing amounts of FDI, notably in the renewable energy and digital sectors, including to facilitate foreign investment more broadly and take advantage of any arising opportunity.

The next chapter assesses Portugal's investment and trade regulatory environment to identify possible inefficiencies that may be holding back foreign investment from reaching its full potential. It provides a comparative overview of regulation and laws affecting the entry and operation of foreign businesses in Portugal and in the benchmark countries, as well as of other behind-the-border rules impacting business operations more widely (e.g. labour market regulation, non-competitive practices and red-tape).

References

AICEP (2022), *Investimento Direto Estrangeiro contratualizado com a AICEP, no âmbito do PT2020, 2015-2021.* [24]

AICEP and IDC Portugal (2019), "Business Service Centres in Portugal". [30]

Alfaro, L. and M. Chen (2012), "Surviving the Global Financial Crisis: Foreign Ownership and Establishment Performance", *American Economic Journal: Economic Policy*, Vol. 4/3, pp. 30-55. [60]

Alves, R. (2017), "Portugal: A Paradox in Productivity", *International Productivity Monitor*, Vol. 32, pp. 137–160. [8]

Andrews, D., C. Criscuolo and P. Gal (2016), "The Best versus the Rest: The Global Productivity Slowdown, Divergence across Firms and the Role of Public Policy", *OECD Productivity Working Papers*, No. 5, OECD Publishing, Paris, https://doi.org/10.1787/63629cc9-en. [13]

Andrews, D., G. Nicoletti and C. Timiliotis (2018), "Digital technology diffusion: A matter of capabilities, incentives or both?", *OECD Economics Department Working Papers*, No. 1476, OECD Publishing, Paris, https://doi.org/10.1787/7c542c16-en. [62]

Balsvik, R. (2011), "Is labor mobility a channel for spillovers from multinationals? evidence from norwegian manufacturing", *Review of Economics and Statistics*, Vol. 93/1, pp. 285-297, https://doi.org/10.1162/REST_a_00061. [39]

Banco de Portugal (2021), "New statistics on foreign direct investment by ultimate investor: statistical press release", https://bpstat.bportugal.pt/conteudos/noticias/1579/. [23]

Bloom, N. et al. (2021), "Pay, Productivity and Management", *NBER Working Papers*, https://doi.org/10.3386/W29377. [37]

Bøler, E., B. Javorcik and K. Ulltveit-Moe (2018), "Working across time zones: Exporters and the gender wage gap", *Journal of International Economics*, Vol. 111, pp. 122-133, https://doi.org/10.1016/J.JINTECO.2017.12.008. [51]

Crespo, N., M. Fontoura and I. Proença (2009), "FDI spillovers at regional level: Evidence from Portugal", *Papers in Regional Science*, Vol. 88/3, pp. 591-607, https://doi.org/10.1111/J.1435-5957.2009.00225.X. [49]

Desai, M., C. Foley and K. Forbes (2008), "Financial Constraints and Growth: Multinational and Local Firm Responses to Currency Depreciation", *Review of Financial Studies*, Vol. 21/6, pp. 2857-88. [61]

EC (2021), "Digital Economy and Society Index 2021: Integration of digital technology". [42]

EC (2021), *European innovation scoreboard 2021*, European Commission, Directorate-General for Internal Market, Industry, Entrepreneurship and SMEs, Publications Office of the European Union, https://doi.org/10.2873/725879. [67]

EC (2021), *New European Alliance to accelerate startups growth*, https://digital-strategy.ec.europa.eu/en/news/new-european-alliance-accelerate-startups-growth#:~:text=The%20European%20Startup%20Nations%20Alliance%20(ESNA)%20is%20a%20new%20entity,stage%20of%20their%20life%20cycle. [56]

EC (2020), "Country Report Portugal 2020", *Commission Staff Working Document SWD(2020) 521 final*, European Commission Brussels, February 26. [4]

EC (2020), *European innovation scoreboard 2020*, European Commission, Directorate-General for Internal Market, Industry, Entrepreneurship and SMEs, Publications Office, https://doi.org/10.2873/6063. [66]

EIB (2020), *EIB Investment Survey 2020 – Country Overview: Portugal*, European Investment Bank. [26]

EIB (2019), "The digitalisation of small and medium-sized enterprises in Portugal", https://www.eib.org/attachments/thematic/digitalisation_of_smes_in_portugal_summary_en.pdf. [15]

EIT Digital (2020), *Scale Up Portugal*. [31]

Ernst & Young (2021), *As the winds change, is Portugal just flying or soaring?*, EY Attractiveness Survey: Portugal, June. [18]

Ernst & Young (2020), *How can a resilient Portugal become a platform for sustainable investment in the future?*, EY Attractiveness Survey: Portugal, July. [17]

Falck, S. (2016), "Foreign-to-domestic labour mobility in Sweden", *Regional Science Policy & Practice*, Vol. 8/3, pp. 111-125, https://doi.org/10.1111/RSP3.12077. [54]

Görg, H. and D. Greenaway (2004), "Much Ado about Nothing? Do Domestic Firms Really Benefit from Foreign Direct Investment?", *The World Bank Research Observer*, Vol. 19/2, https://doi.org/10.1093/wbro/lkh019. [46]

Gouveia, A. et al. (2018), "The Portuguese economy: Short essays on structural changes", *Gabinete de Planeamento, Estratégia, Avaliação e Relações Internacionais Ministério das Finanças, Lisbon, Portugal.* [2]

Hausmann, R., J. Hwang and D. Rodrik (2006), "What you export matters", *Journal of Economic Growth*, Vol. 12, March, pp. 1-25. [44]

Heyman, F., F. Sjöholm and P. Tingvall (2007), "Is there really a foreign ownership wage premium? Evidence from matched employer–employee data", *Journal of International Economics*, Vol. 73/2, pp. 355-376, https://doi.org/10.1016/J.JINTECO.2007.04.003. [52]

Hidalgo, C. and R. Hausmann (2009), "The building blocks of economic complexity", *Proceedings of the National Academy of Sciences*, June 30, pp. 10570-10575. [55]

Hijzen, A. et al. (2013), "Foreign-owned firms around the world: A comparative analysis of wages and employment at the micro-level", *European Economic Review*, Vol. 60, pp. 170-188, https://doi.org/10.1016/J.EUROECOREV.2013.02.001. [34]

Hjort, J., X. Li and H. Sarsons (2020), "Across-Country Wage Compression in Multinationals", *NBER Wokring Paper*, https://doi.org/10.3386/W26788. [38]

IDC Portugal (2021), "Startup & Entrepreneurial Ecosystem Report: Portugal 2021", https://idcportugal.com/wp-content/uploads/2021/Startup_Final.pdf (accessed on 15 March 2022). [57]

IEA (2022), *World Energy Balances Highlights*, https://www.iea.org/data-and-statistics/data-product/world-energy-balances-highlights. [28]

IEA (2021), *Portugal 2021: Energy Policy Review*, International Energy Agency, France. [25]

IEA (2019), *Energy efficiency and digitalisation*, https://www.iea.org/articles/energy-efficiency-and-digitalisation. [14]

IMF (2018), "Portugal: Selected Issues", *IMF Country Report No. 18/274*, International Monetary Fund, Washington, D.C., September. [1]

INE (2018), "Inquérito aos Custos de Contexto 2017", Instituto Nacional de Estatística, July 27. [19]

IRENA (2021), *Renewable Power Generation Costs in 2020*, International Renewable Energy Agency, Abu Dhabi. [27]

Lanz, R. and S. Miroudot (2011), "Intra-Firm Trade: Patterns, Determinants and Policy Implications", *OECD Trade Policy Papers*, No. 114, OECD Publishing, Paris, https://doi.org/10.1787/5kg9p39lrwnn-en. [64]

Lopes, T. and V. Simões (2017), "Foreign investment in Portugal and knowledge spillovers: From the Methuen Treaty to the 21st century", *https://doi.org/10.1080/00076791.2017.1386177*, Vol. 62/7, pp. 1079-1106, https://doi.org/10.1080/00076791.2017.1386177. [47]

Martins, P. (2005), "Inter-firm employee mobility, displacement, and foreign direct investment spillovers", *Univesity of London Quenne Mary*, Vol. manuscript, https://kooperationen.zew.de/fileadmin/user_upload/Redaktion/DFGFLEX/ws2Martins.pdf (accessed on 25 January 2022). [53]

Mincer, J. (1974), *Schooling, Experience, and Earnings. Human Behavior & Social Institutions No. 2.*, Columbia University Press, https://eric.ed.gov/?id=ED103621 (accessed on 7 December 2021). [50]

Mion, G., D. Opromolla and G. Ottaviano (2020), "Dream Jobs: A comparison of career prospects in Portuguese firms", *CESifo Working Paper no. 8430*, http://www.RePEc.org (accessed on 21 December 2021). [40]

Nilsson Hakkala, K., F. Heyman and F. Sjöholm (2014), "Multinational firms, acquisitions and job tasks", *European Economic Review*, Vol. 66, pp. 248-265, https://doi.org/10.1016/J.EUROECOREV.2013.12.003. [36]

OECD (2022), *International Direct Investment Statistics*, https://www.oecd.org/corporate/mne/statistics.htm. [20]

OECD (2022), *Strengthening FDI and SME Linkages in Portugal*, OECD Publishing, Paris, https://doi.org/10.1787/d718823d-en. [5]

OECD (2021), *Annual National Accounts database*, https://stats.oecd.org/Index.aspx?DataSetCode=SNA_TABLE9A. [12]

OECD (2021), *FDI in Figures: Global FDI flows rebound to exceed pre-pandemic levels*, https://www.oecd.org/investment/investment-policy/FDI-in-Figures-October-2021.pdf (accessed on 11 January 2022). [22]

OECD (2021), "FDI Qualities Policy Toolkit: Policies for Improving the Sustainable Development Impacts of Investment", https://www.oecd.org/investment/investment-policy/FDI-Qualities-Policy-Toolkit-Consultation-Paper-2021.pdf. [33]

OECD (2021), *Green Growth Indicators*, https://stats.oecd.org/Index.aspx?DataSetCode=GREEN_GROWTH#. [29]

OECD (2021), *OECD Economic Surveys: Portugal 2021*, OECD Publishing, Paris, https://doi.org/10.1787/13b842d6-en. [3]

OECD (2021), *OECD National Accounts at a Glance database*, OECD Publishing, https://stats.oecd.org/Index.aspx?DataSetCode=NAAG (accessed on 10 January 2022). [9]

OECD (2021), *Productivity Statistics database*, https://www.oecd.org/sdd/productivity-stats/. [7]

OECD (2021), *The Role of Firms in Wage Inequality: Policy Lessons from a Large Scale Cross-Country Study*, OECD Publishing, Paris, https://doi.org/10.1787/7d9b2208-en. [63]

OECD (2021), *Trade in Value Added database*, https://www.oecd.org/sti/ind/measuring-trade-in-value-added.htm. [45]

OECD (2020), *COVID-19 disruptions send global FDI plunging 50%*, https://www.oecd.org/investment/investment-policy/FDI-in-Figures-October-2020.pdf (accessed on 11 January 2022). [21]

OECD (2020), *Structural Analysis database*, https://www.oecd.org/sti/ind/stanstructuralanalysisdatabase.htm. [11]

OECD (2019), *FDI Qualities Indicators: Measuring the sustainable development impacts of investment*, http://www.oecd.org/fr/investissement/fdi-qualities-indicators.htm. [6]

OECD (2019), *Measuring the Digital Transformation: A Roadmap for the Future*, OECD Publishing, Paris, https://doi.org/10.1787/9789264311992-en. [41]

OECD (2019), *Unpacking E-commerce: Business Models, Trends and Policies*, OECD Publishing, Paris, https://doi.org/10.1787/23561431-en. [43]

OECD (2017), *AMNE Database – Activity of Multinational Enterprises*, https://www.oecd.org/sti/ind/amne.htm. [58]

OECD (2014), *OECD Economic Surveys: Portugal 2014*, OECD Publishing, Paris, https://doi.org/10.1787/eco_surveys-prt-2014-en. [10]

OECD (2009), *OECD Benchmark Definition of Foreign Direct Investment 2008: Fourth Edition*, OECD Publishing, Paris, https://doi.org/10.1787/9789264045743-en. [65]

Portugal Ventures (2022), *Portugal Ventures celebrates 10 Years Growing Entrepreneurship*, https://www.portugalventures.pt/en/news/portugal-ventures-comemora-10-anos-a-fazer-crescer-o-empreendedorismo/. [32]

Setzler, B. and F. Tintelnot (2021), "The Effects of Foreign Multinationals on Workers and Firms in the United States", *The Quarterly Journal of Economics*, Vol. 136/3, pp. 1943-1991, https://doi.org/10.1093/QJE/QJAB015. [35]

Teixeira, A. and A. Tavares-Lehmann (2014), "Human capital intensity in technology-based firms located in Portugal: Does foreign ownership matter?", *Research Policy*, Vol. 43/4, pp. 737-748, https://doi.org/10.1016/J.RESPOL.2014.01.001. [48]

World Bank (2021), "Population ages 65 and above (% of total population) - Portugal", *World Development Indicators*, The World Bank Group, https://data.worldbank.org/indicator/SP.POP.65UP.TO.ZS?locations=PT (accessed on 10 January 2023). [59]

World Bank (2021), "Unemployment, total (% of total labor force) (national estimate) - Portugal", *World Development Indicators*, The World Bank Group, https://data.worldbank.org/indicator/SL.UEM.TOTL.NE.ZS?locations=PT (accessed on 10 January 2023). [16]

Annex 1.A. Methodology

The analysis draws on data from *Quadros de Pessoal* (QP), from which an employer-employee dataset covering all firms in Portugal with at least one employee can be obtained.[40] The sample is restricted to wage earners between 18 and 65 years of age and working full time. Additional firm-level data come from the *Sistema de Contas Integradas das Empresas* (SCIE), which covers all economic activities excluding agriculture, fisheries and the financial sector. Firms are defined as foreign if the ultimate controlling investor as reported in SCIE is outside Portugal. In addition, a given firm is considered foreign if foreign capital is at least 50% as reported in QP. Survey data from *Inquérito à Utilização Tecnologias Informação nas Empresas* (IUTICE) provides information on the use of digital technologies by firms. All monetary values are in 2020 prices.

The effects of foreign ownership are estimated by augmenting the worker-level Mincer equation with an indicator variable for the firm's ownership (Mincer, 1974[50]). The wage regression takes the following form:

$$\ln w_{ijst} = \beta_1 Forown_{jt} + X_{it}'\gamma + Z_{jt}'\delta + \alpha_{st} + \theta_r + \varepsilon_{ijst}$$

where w_{ijst} is the hourly base wage of individual *i* employed by firm *j* operating in industry *s* in year *t*. $Forown_{jt}$ is a binary variable taking value 1 for foreign firms and 0 for domestic. X_{it}' is a vector of observable individual characteristics (education, working experience and experience squared). Z_{jt}' is a vector of observable firm characteristics. In the preferred specification, it includes firm headcount, labour productivity and export intensity. Some specifications also include intangible assets intensity and the share of R&D employees, but since these variables are missing for many firms, the results from these models are seen as complementary to the main analysis based on the preferred specification. Industry-year fixed effects α_{st} and regional effects θ_r capture systematic variation in wages across industries over time and regions.

The effects of foreign ownership on gender wage gap are estimated by adding a female dummy and its interaction with an indicator variable for the firm's ownership, building on Bøler, Javorcik and Ulltveit-Moe (2018[51]). Occupational fixed effects (ϑ_o) are added to control for systematic variation across occupations:

$$\ln w_{ijst} = \beta_1 fem_i + \beta_2\, Forown_{jt} + \beta_3 fem_i * Forown_{jt} + X_{it}'\gamma + Z_{jt}'\delta + \alpha_{st} + \theta_r + \vartheta_o + \varepsilon_{ijst}$$

In this specification, β_1 represents the gender pay gap, assuming that the other variables adequately account for differences in employee qualifications; β_2 is the difference between wages in foreign and domestic firms; β_3 shows how the gender pay gap differs between foreign and domestic firms (a negative statistically significant coefficient would suggest that the gender pay gap is larger in foreign companies).

Annex Table 1.A.1. Estimation results: Share of highly skilled employees and foreign ownership

	(1)	(2)	(3)
Foreign-owned	0.092***	0.090***	0.077***
	(0.004)	(0.004)	(0.004)
Ln(Employment)		-0.034***	-0.031***
		(0.001)	(0.001)
Ln(Labour productivity)		0.034***	0.036***
		(0.001)	(0.001)
Export intensity		0.055***	0.053***
		(0.003)	(0.003)
Intangible assets intensity			0.103***
			(0.004)

	(1)	(2)	(3)
Share of R&D employees			0.107***
			(0.013)
Observations	2 587 660	1 835 344	1 522 493
Adjusted R-squared	0.178	0.181	0.184

Note: Dependent variable is the firm-level share of employees with highly skilled occupations. All specifications include a constant, industry-year and region fixed effects. Standard errors in parentheses clustered at firm level. ***, ** and * denote statistical significance at 1%, 5% and 10% levels respectively.
Source: Own calculations based on Statistics Portugal (INE), QP and SCIE, 2009-20.

Annex Table 1.A.2. Estimation results: Wage premium and foreign ownership

	All employees	All employees	All employees	Low-skilled	Medium-skilled	High-skilled
Foreign-owned	0.143***	0.060***	0.062***	0.045***	0.040***	0.072***
	(0.009)	(0.007)	(0.007)	(0.009)	(0.007)	(0.009)
Experience		0.015***	0.015***	0.009***	0.013***	0.025***
		(0.000)	(0.000)	(0.001)	(0.000)	(0.000)
(Experience^2)/100		-0.011***	-0.011***	-0.010***	-0.012***	-0.024***
		(0.001)	(0.001)	(0.001)	(0.001)	(0.001)
Education		0.055***	0.055***	0.021***	0.027***	0.060***
		(0.001)	(0.001)	(0.001)	(0.001)	(0.001)
Ln(Employment)		0.008***	0.007***	0.003**	0.006***	0.050***
		(0.001)	(0.001)	(0.002)	(0.002)	(0.002)
Ln(Labour productivity)		0.141***	0.141***	0.083***	0.133***	0.160***
		(0.003)	(0.003)	(0.003)	(0.003)	(0.004)
Export intensity		0.030***	0.029***	0.039***	0.008	0.072***
		(0.006)	(0.006)	(0.009)	(0.006)	(0.009)
Intangible assets intensity			0.052***			
			(0.010)			
Share of R&D employees			0.201***			
			(0.033)			
Observations	23 079 726	20 441 267	18 072 166	6 151 393	9 495 705	4 685 783
Adjusted R-squared	0.262	0.443	0.444	0.303	0.386	0.431

Note: Dependent variable is hourly base wage in logarithms. Columns 4-6 show the results for the subsamples defined with respect to the skill level. All models include a constant, industry-year and region fixed effects. Standard errors in parentheses clustered at firm level. ***, ** and * denote statistical significance at 1%, 5% and 10% levels respectively.
Source: Own calculations based on Statistics Portugal (INE), QP and SCIE, 2009-20.

Annex Table 1.A.3. Estimation results: Gender wage gap and foreign ownership

	All employees	All employees	All employees	All employees	High-skilled	Top managers
Female * Foreign-owned	-0.077***	-0.027***	-0.024***	-0.017**	-0.007	-0.009
	(0.014)	(0.007)	(0.007)	(0.007)	(0.009)	(0.01)
Female	-0.084***	-0.088***	-0.088***	-0.077***	-0.065***	-0.047***
	(0.003)	(0.002)	(0.002)	(0.002)	(0.002)	(0.003)
Foreign-owned	0.251***	0.076***	0.075***	0.066***	0.076***	0.054***
	(0.027)	(0.008)	(0.008)	(0.007)	(0.010)	(0.015)
Ln(Employment)		0.009***	0.008***	0.014***	0.049***	0.088***
		(0.001)	(0.001)	(0.001)	(0.002)	(0.004)
Ln(Labour productivity)		0.137***	0.136***	0.123***	0.156***	0.165***
		(0.004)	(0.003)	(0.001)	(0.004)	(0.006)
Export intensity		0.031***	0.031***	0.030***	0.070***	0.093***

	All employees	All employees	All employees	All employees	High-skilled	Top managers
		(0.006)	(0.006)	(0.006)	(0.009)	(0.013)
Intangible assets intensity			0.054***			
			(0.010)			
Share of R&D employees			0.188***			
			(0.031)			
Observations	23 079 726	20 441 267	18 072 166	20 431 651	4 685 783	1 318 045
Adjusted R-squared	0.057	0.454	0.454	0.548	0.434	0.48
Occupation FE				YES	YES	YES

Note: Dependent variable is hourly base wage in logarithms. The next to last column reports the results for individuals with high-skilled occupations. The last column presents the results run for the individuals in top management positions. Education, experience and its square are included, but omitted from the table for brevity. All specifications include a constant, industry-year and region fixed effects. Standard errors in parentheses clustered at firm level. ***, ** and * denote statistical significance at 1%, 5% and 10% levels respectively.
Source: Own calculations based on Statistics Portugal (INE), QP and SCIE, 2009-20.

Annex Table 1.A.4. Estimation results: E-sales and foreign ownership

	E-sales uptake	E-sales uptake	E-sales share	E-sales share
Foreign-owned	0.01	0.012	2.809	3.077*
	(0.024)	(0.025)	(1.783)	(1.804)
Ln(Employment)	0.184***	0.185***	-2.265***	-2.262***
	(0.005)	(0.005)	(0.344)	(0.355)
Ln(Labour productivity)	0.016*	0.014	2.403***	2.288***
	(0.010)	(0.010)	(0.826)	(0.870)
Export intensity	-0.218***	-0.240***	6.643**	5.635**
	(0.036)	(0.037)	(2.855)	(2.923)
Intangible assets intensity		-0.044		-1.539
		(0.042)		(2.512)
Share of R&D employees		0.244		8.07
		(0.151)		(11.816)
Observations	41 237	39 400	6 593	6 428
Adjusted R-squared			0.097	0.094
Pseudo R-squared	0.167	0.167		

Note: The first two columns report estimation results from the probit regressions, where the dependent variable is a binary indicator for the firm's e-sales uptake. The last two show results from the OLS regression with the share of e-sales in firm sales as the dependent variable. All columns include a constant, industry-year and region fixed effects. Standard errors in parentheses clustered at firm level. ***, ** and * denote statistical significance at 1%, 5% and 10% levels respectively.
Source: Own calculations based on Statistics Portugal (INE), QP, SCIE and IUTICE, 2009-20.

Notes

[1] Foreign affiliates tend to be more resilient in times of crises due to their linkages and access to their parent companies financial resources (Alfaro and Chen, 2012[60]) (Desai, Foley and Forbes, 2008[61]).

[2] On 10 and 11 March 2022, EU leaders adopted the Versailles declaration on the Russian aggression against Ukraine, as well as on bolstering defence capabilities, reducing energy dependencies and building a more robust economic base.

[3] For the most part of the last decade, population growth has been negative; before, from 2000 to 2010, it grew at below unit and declining rates. The share of the population above 65 years old now represents roughly 23% of the total population, versus 16% back in 2000 (World Bank, 2021[59])).

[4] The top 15 most productive European economies (TOP15) includes Austria, Belgium, Denmark, Finland, France, Germany, Iceland, Ireland, Italy, Luxembourg, the Netherlands, Norway, Sweden, Switzerland and the United Kingdom.

[5] The selected benchmark group is formed of the following countries: the Czech Republic, Estonia, Lithuania, Poland, the Slovak Republic and Spain. These countries either share some economic similarities with Portugal (in terms of the structure of manufacturing exports and services sectors value added), or are found to frequently compete with Portugal as destinations for foreign investment projects in priority sectors (according to Portugal's Investment Promotion Agency, AICEP Portugal Global).

[6] Portugal hosts Europe's largest technological event since 2016, the Web Summit, and is home to a buoyant start-up ecosystem with 13% more start-ups per capita than the average in Europe and largely driven by technology-based start-ups, fintechs and health-based ventures (IDC Portugal, 2021[57]). Portugal also featured among the group of Strong Innovators in the annual European Innovation Scoreboard 2020, an indicator which compares research and innovation performance in Europe (EC, 2020[66]). In 2021, however, it was downgraded to the group of Moderate Innovators (EC, 2021[67]).

[7] The sectoral perspective reveals where Portugal's competitive edge is more at stake. In manufacturing, ULCs in Portugal were already at par with the average top EUR15 economy at end-2018. In services, ULCs still remain below the average top EUR15 economy but the wedge has been shrinking since 2014.

[8] FDI equity capital flows encompass four types of transactions: purchase or sale of equity in the form of M&As (typically the largest component in developed economies), greenfield investment, extension of capital and financial restructuring. The gaps between FDI equity flows and value of M&A transactions might be driven by any of the other components. In addition, deal values that are not reported in Refinitiv might contribute to the difference between the two data series.

[9] The evidence reported in this sub-section is based on completed M&A deals over the period from 2012 to 2022. Although a bit less than three-quarters of the sample have undisclosed deal values, the total deal value is a meaningful measure, as values of larger deals tend to be reported.

[10] This is partly the result of a number of large projects announced, such as investment projects in the solar energy sector by Hanwha Q Cells (Korea) and Shanghai Electric (China).

[11] Caution is needed in the interpretation of greenfield investment data. In addition to undertaken greenfield investment projects, the data include projects that are *announced* in a given year, as reported by the Financial Times fDi Markets database. Announced projects might be realised at a later stage or, in some cases, withdrawn. Moreover, capital investment as reported in the data source should be interpreted with caution, as many values are estimates based on information available from other greenfield projects in the same country, sector and business function (e.g. sales office, R&D facility, etc.). Another possible limitation of the database is that it might be missing projects not covered in the sources used to collect the underlying data. Although, due to these shortcomings, there might be some discrepancy between the reported data and the realised investment, the trends observed in the data are still informative about the countries' ability to attract greenfield investment.

[12] The geographic distribution of the ultimate investors is likely to be different, notably because some greenfield projects seem to originate in countries that are often used as conduit for FDI. According to the

fDi market data, 7% of greenfield investment in Portugal came from Luxembourg, 3% from the Netherlands, whereas Bermuda, Panama and Macau together accounted for about 2% of the invested capital. These are all economies used by ultimate investors to transit funds elsewhere.

[13] A variety of reasons can be associated with round-tripping, including the method used to allocate FDI to the ultimate investing economy, tax optimization, property rights protection, risk diversification and access to better financial services (OECD, 2009[65]).

[14] The decline of M&A activity in Portugal's manufacturing can be observed also before the COVID-19 outbreak: by 2019, the share of deal numbers went down to 16.9% and the share of deal values to 4.4% on a three-year moving average basis.

[15] Professional services, however, continue to attract a relatively significant number of investors, particularly greenfield ones. From 2015 to 2022, 12% of all greenfield projects occurred in the sector. This is much more than in the benchmark group.

[16] The global weighted-average levelised costs of electricity from new capacity additions of utility-scale solar photovoltaics and onshore wind, for instance, are estimated to have declined by 85% and 56%, respectively, between 2010 and 2020, bringing them to a level roughly 27% and 22% lower than that of the cheapest fossil-fuel competitor, namely coal-fired plants (IRENA, 2021[27]). The levelised cost of electricity represents the net present cost of electricity generation for a generating plant over its lifetime.

[17] The classification of M&A deals and greenfield projects into the subsectors of the digital economy builds on the activity classification in the source data. The activities are identified as belonging to the digital economy based on the classification in OECD (2019[41]), where sectors are defined as digital if they produce digitally ordered and/or digitally delivered goods and services or if they enable this production.

[18] Strengthening its reputation as a country committed to promote start-up growth, in 2021, the Portuguese Government established the European Startup Nations Alliance in partnership with 26 EU countries, Iceland, and the European Commission (EC, 2021[56]).

[19] Firms are defined as foreign (or foreign-owned) if the ultimate controlling investor is outside Portugal as reported in the SCIE dataset. In addition, a given firm is considered foreign if reported foreign capital is at least 50% as reported in the QP data. The data sources are described in Annex A.

[20] Skill intensity of managers was measured in terms of the years in education. Managerial positions are defined as "Senior Executives" based on the classification of employees into hierarchical levels available in the micro-level data (the levels are defined according to Portuguese Decree-Law No. 121/78 of 2 July 1978). Managerial positions include occupations responsible for the main strategic decisions of the firm, such as the organisation of the firm's resources and strategic planning.

[21] Foreign enterprises are more skill-intensive than domestic firms even after correcting for differences in firm size, labour productivity, export intensity, industry-year and regional specificities; estimation results are reported in Annex Table 1.A.1.

[22] In the main specification, employee-level control variables include education and experience. Firm-level characteristics are firm size, labour productivity, export intensity, and industry-year and regional effects. The wage premium holds even when additional control variables are included, i.e. intangible assets intensity and the share of R&D workers. The estimation results are reported in Annex Table 1.A.2, while Annex 1.A details the estimation approach.

[23] These estimates (please see Annex Table 1.A.2) are in line with the existing literature. The average wage premium in foreign-owned firms in advanced economies tends to range from about 2% to 12% (Heyman, Sjöholm and Tingvall, 2007[52]; Hijzen et al., 2013[34]; Setzler and Tintelnot, 2021[35]). Foreign wage premium for low and medium-skilled occupations and the small difference in the premium between these two groups are consistent with the notion that foreign firms pay higher wages because they engage in more complex tasks (Nilsson Hakkala, Heyman and Sjöholm, 2014[36]).

[24] This labour mobility is substantially larger than the one observed in Portugal in the 1990s (Martins, 2005[53]). Yet, it appears lower than in some countries where comparable data are available, for instance Norway (Balsvik, 2011[39]) and Sweden (Falck, 2016[54]).

[25] The change in wages after the move from foreign to domestic firms varies substantially across workers. It can depend on a multitude of factors, including workers' qualifications, as well as the characteristics of new and former employers (e.g. industry, region, etc.).

[26] The higher share of female employees in transportation and storage in foreign-owned businesses is mostly driven by the presence of foreign firms in warehousing and support activities for transportation (employing nearly a half of total employment), where foreign firms have a higher share of female employees (36%) than domestic businesses (30%). In this sub-sector, nearly two-thirds of women work as clerks (68% in foreign and 60% in domestic firms). In wholesale and retail trade, foreign firms employ more women as service and sales workers, but fewer in clerical occupations than domestic businesses.

[27] The gender wage gap is measured as the difference between median earnings of men and women relative to median earnings of men. The preferred specification controls for individual and firm characteristics to ensure that the comparison of wages paid by foreign and domestic firms is based on individuals of similar qualifications (see results in Annex Table 1.A.3). This approach does not address sorting of women and men across these qualifications, which would be more relevant in the analysis of the drivers of gender wage gaps (e.g. the extent to which social norms influence women's ability to get into certain occupations or industries).

[28] This result might also be related to the finding that the relationship between firms' productivity and wages in Portugal is much stronger for high skilled than low skilled workers and it is stronger for women than men (OECD, 2021[63]). Given that foreign firms tend to be more productive (see Table 1.1), this suggests that foreign employers might translate a greater share of their productivity gains with their female employees than domestic companies do.

[29] For instance, lower wage discrepancy in foreign ICT firms than in domestic ones seems to be associated with the higher skill intensity of foreign employers. Higher pay gaps in foreign companies operating in accommodation and food services might come from their specialisation in low-cost segments of the sector.

[30] These digital technologies were selected for their potential to increase firm productivity (Andrews, Nicoletti and Timiliotis, 2018[62]). Accelerated adoption of most of these technologies features explicitly in the objectives formulated under Portugal's Industry 4.0 Strategy, which aims at promoting a fast and inclusive uptake of digital technologies by Portuguese businesses.

[31] In the IUTICE survey, Artificial Intelligence refers to systems that rely on computer vision, speech recognition, natural language processing, machine or deep learning to collect and/or use data to make predictions, recommendations or decisions with certain level of autonomy.

[32] In addition, the estimates show that foreign ownership is positively and significantly correlated with the share of online sales once firm characteristics are controlled for, likely reflecting the greater exposure of foreign MNEs to international markets.

[33] For instance, businesses with greater headcount are more likely to sell on the web (see estimation results in Annex Table 1.A.4), whereas firm ownership, labour productivity, intangible assets intensity or the share of R&D employees have no effect on the probability of selling online, suggesting that other factors might affect e-commerce participation.

[34] The survey does not provide any details about why some firms report that their goods and services are not fit for online sales. Possible reasons might include perishability of goods (fruits and vegetables), legal constraints (e.g. tobacco) and the need in physical proximity for the transaction (dental care).

[35] Given that the latest available data for this survey question refer to 2016, it is possible that the relative significance of various obstacles to e-commerce has changed in the recent years. Other factors, not covered by the survey, might also be important (e.g. digital security, privacy and consumer protection).

[36] This is reflected in Portugal's performance in the Economic Complexity Index published in the Atlas of Economic Complexity by Harvard's Growth Lab, which measures how diversified and complex a country's export basket is in terms of the level of sophistication of productive know-how embedded in its exports (Hidalgo and Hausmann, 2009[55]). The complexity of a country's exports is found to strongly predict income levels and where complexity exceeds expectations for a country's income level, the country is predicted to experience faster growth in the future (Hidalgo and Hausmann, 2009[55]).

[37] Although these statistics are not available for peer economies, the OECD Activity of Multinational Enterprises (AMNE) database provides a comparison. According to AMNE statistics, in 2016, foreign affiliates in Portugal sourced 62.2% of their inputs locally, less than in Spain (73%) and Poland (65%), suggesting that there is a room for more extensive integration of foreign firms into domestic value chains. Yet, the share of local sourcing by foreign affiliates in Portugal is well above the share observed in other small open economies (57% in Lithuania, 55% in the Czech Republic, 53% in Estonia and 52% in the Slovak Republic), where affiliates rely on imported inputs more extensively (OECD, 2017[58]).

[38] The increasing services exports intensity of foreign firms might be partly attributed by intra-firms trade in service, i.e. flows of services between parent companies and their affiliates or among the affiliates, which typically include management and consulting services, R&D services, etc. (Lanz and Miroudot, 2011[64]).

[39] The micro-level data only report one location for every firm.

[40] The QP survey is conducted by the Strategy and Planning Office of the Ministry of Labour, Solidarity and Social Security (GEP-MTSSS). Further information can be obtained at their website or via the National Statistics Institute (INE) website.

2 Portugal's domestic policy and regulatory setting for foreign investment

This chapter provides an overview of the policy and regulatory setting for foreign direct investment in Portugal, benchmarking the domestic regulatory framework against those of a selected group of peer countries. It examines at-the border and behind-the border regulation applied horizontally across all sectors of the economy, with potential impacts on foreign investment decisions and Portugal's general business environment. The chapter also assesses regulatory aspects that might affect investment in selected sectors providing strategic support to the economy: professional services, transport services, logistics services, and digital trade. In addition, it evaluates the degree of similarity of Portugal's regulation to other OECD and EEA countries, analysing to what extent regulatory barriers are lower for intra-EEA investors due to Single Market harmonisation.

Key findings

- Portugal has a relatively open regulatory environment for foreign direct investment and services trade with more competition-friendly regulation than the OECD average. Nonetheless, there is room to improve Portugal's investment climate by narrowing the gap with peer economies that have more open regulatory settings, according to OECD metrics.
- Foreign investors in Portugal, including non-EEA investors, benefit from relatively open market entry. Only certain non-EEA acquisitions of strategic assets are potentially subject to investment screening. Yet, transparency and flexibility in the implementation of the screening mechanism could be improved.
- Portugal could further strengthen regulatory impact assessment and stakeholder engagement practices to ensure that the effects of new regulation on businesses are better understood and unnecessary administrative burden is minimised. Measures to further reduce the length of judicial proceedings could also improve confidence in the business environment.
- In certain supporting services sectors, regulatory barriers to competition and investment are higher than in some benchmark countries. In particular, among professional services, engineering and accounting and auditing services continue to be relatively strictly regulated. Domestic regulatory barriers in transport and logistics services sectors could also be eased, and improving the efficiency of customs procedures would benefit firms in transport, logistics, courier and distribution services sectors.
- Portugal has made the digital transition a strategic goal for business development. However, economy-wide restrictions to movement of people can hinder access to digital knowledge and information and communication technology professionals.
- Regulatory harmonisation in the EU's Single Market has reduced barriers for intra-EEA investors in Portugal in all sectors. However, intra-EEA investors in benchmark countries benefit, in most sectors, from more open regulatory environments.

2.1. Introduction

Foreign investment may be held back by domestic regulation affecting market entry and operation of foreign businesses. In addition to explicit restrictions to foreign direct investment (FDI), such as rules limiting equity participation of foreign investors in locally incorporated companies, a range of behind-the-border factors shaping the general business environment may add costs and challenges for foreign companies in a host country. Where such regulatory barriers are overly strict, they may entail unnecessary economic costs, both in terms of foregone investment and associated benefits, such as additional tax revenues and potential business opportunities for domestic suppliers and business partners, as well as in terms of potential efficiency gains, which could derive from greater competition and market contestability associated with foreign investment.

The literature shows that addressing such regulatory barriers can have a positive impact on investment. Introducing liberalising reforms that even partially reduce FDI restrictions, such as investment screening or equity limits, could significantly increase a country's stock of FDI.[1] Moreover, countries with a more restrictive regulatory environment for services trade are significantly less likely to attract foreign investment in services than countries with a more liberal regulatory set-up.[2] Additionally, divergence between the regulatory settings of the investor's country of origin and the host country reduce cross-border investment.[3] Striking the right balance in the regulatory framework is therefore key for an effective and enabling investment environment.

This chapter reviews several regulatory aspects that foreign investors face at the border and behind the border in Portugal, benchmarking the Portuguese regulatory framework against a group of peer economies consisting of the Czech Republic, Estonia, Lithuania, Poland, the Slovak Republic and Spain. Differences in regulation between Portugal and these peer countries are assessed mainly from the perspective of foreign investors from outside the European Economic Area (EEA), as the treatment of intra-EEA investors is subject to a degree of harmonisation across the European Union (EU)'s Single Market. A dedicated section explores to what extent regional integration has reduced barriers for intra-EEA investors. Nonetheless, many aspects of the regulatory environment are applicable to foreign investors regardless of their origin and affect also domestic firms. Additionally, although EU-level regulation limits Portugal and the benchmarked countries' domestic policy making space in some areas, different approaches in areas not regulated at the EU level, as well as national differences in the transposition of EU directives into domestic law, result in some variation within the group of countries.

This chapter consists of four parts. First, it examines the main regulatory conditions applicable to foreign investors across all sectors of the economy and shaping the general business environment in Portugal. This horizontal analysis seeks to capture factors potentially holding back investment also in Portugal's priority industrial sectors for investment (e.g. life sciences, aerospace, automotive, food industry, smart materials). A second part assesses regulatory factors that might have an impact on foreign investment decisions in specific services sectors of strategic importance, namely professional services, transport services and logistics services, which provide essential inputs into global supply chains and are strongly integrated in other parts of the economy. A third part analyses Portugal's policy and regulatory environment affecting digital trade. Finally, a fourth part explores to what extent Portugal's regulatory framework is similar to other economies, and to which extent regulatory harmonisation within the Single Market has resulted in a more open regulatory environment in Portugal for foreign investors from within the EEA, compared to investors from third countries.

2.2. General regulatory environment for foreign investment

Portugal is considered one of the most open economies to FDI according to the OECD FDI Regulatory Restrictiveness Index (FDI RRI), having only a few discriminatory statutory restrictions on foreign investment in place. On average, across 22 sectors of the economy, Portugal's regulatory environment is the second most open to FDI among 84 countries covered in the FDI RRI (OECD, 2020[1]). The overall regulatory framework in Portugal is also more competition-friendly than the OECD average (see Section 2.2.3), and Portugal maintains fewer restrictions to services trade and foreign investment than the OECD average (Section 2.3). However, some barriers to competition and services trade remain present in Portugal, and the comparison to peer countries shows that there could be room for further improvements. The following sub-sections examine regulatory aspects that may affect investors across economic sectors and contribute to shaping Portugal's general business environment, such as rules pertaining to company establishment and operation, recruitment of foreign talent, barriers to competition and dispute settlement.

2.2.1. Foreign investors face comparatively few barriers to enter the Portuguese market

Company incorporation has been simplified in recent years

Overall, the administrative burden that domestic and foreign-owned firms face to start their business, in terms of number of private and public bodies that need to be involved and of the costs of complying with such requirements, is lighter in Portugal than in most benchmarked countries (OECD, 2018[2]). For example, the regulatory environment in Portugal is particularly favourable compared to that of the Slovak Republic, where the administrative burden faced by new firms is almost twice as high as the OECD average.

Examples of the main steps to incorporate a business in Portugal include requesting permits such as the certificate of admissibility for the company name (*certificado de admissibilidade*), submitting the statement of beginning of activity (*declaração de início de atividade*) for tax purposes, as well as registering in the commercial registry and in the social security system.[4]

As part of wider efforts to alleviate administrative burden for business, Portugal has implemented simplified company incorporation procedures and electronic registration services as alternatives to traditional company incorporation process. The *Empresa Online* initiative, launched in 2006, allows limited liability companies to be incorporated via an online service.[5] Recent legislation allows also branches of foreign companies to be registered online.[6] The creation of an "e-Residency" platform to allow foreign companies to incorporate in Portugal fully remotely, by using digital authentication, is also foreseen as part of the implementation of Portugal's Recovery and Resilience Plan (Portugal Government, 2021[3]).[7] Moreover, since the introduction of the *Empresa na Hora* programme in 2005, it is possible to create a limited liability company in less than 60 minutes at any of the one-stop-shops across the country.[8] Specific conditions apply to the *Empresa Online* and the *Empresa na Hora* regimes, including regarding the choice of company name and the company bylaws. These regimes increase options for investors regarding company incorporation procedures. Among the benchmark countries, Estonia has implemented tools for fast electronic incorporation of companies, including by foreign citizens.[9]

As part of a company incorporation process, shareholders (whether company or individual) must obtain a Portuguese tax identification number. This represents an additional administrative step for non-resident investors, who must appoint a tax representative that must be resident in the country. Foreign investors resident in another EU or EEA country are exempted from this obligation.[10] Following a recent communication of the Portuguese Tax and Customs Authority, non-EU/EEA residents who do not have any tax obligations in Portugal are also exempted from the obligation to appoint a representative, under certain conditions.[11]

Several initiatives have simplified business licensing and permit procedures

Foreign investors can set up operations in Portugal on the same conditions as domestic-owned businesses.[12] Obtaining the necessary licenses and permits for the planned economic activity, such as sector-specific operating licenses, environmental permits or construction permits, may however slow down investment projects if the related administrative procedures are complex and time-consuming.

Portugal has introduced several reforms and developed online services aimed at streamlining licensing and permit procedures. For instance, the *Licenciamento Zero* (Zero Licensing) initiative provides for simplified access to a number of commercial activities, including services, food and beverage activities.[13] New, consolidated legal frameworks for industrial licensing and environmental permits were approved in 2012 and 2015, respectively, and further simplification of the environmental licensing process is planned (Box 2.1). In line with the objectives of its 2020 Action Plan for Digital Transition,[14] including the increased digitisation of public services, Portugal has already implemented digital business licensing applications. Companies can access information on licensing of all economic activities and initiate licensing procedures with the relevant government agencies through a digital single point of contact (*Balcão do Empreendedor,* Entrepreneur's Desk).[15]

Nonetheless, there is room for Portugal to further develop online public services and increase their uptake. At 59%, the share of e-government users in Portugal is slightly below the EU average (65%), and the scope of online public services for starting a business and conducting regular business operations aligns with the EU average, indicating that yet more could be done by Portugal to position itself as a European frontrunner in digital public services (EC, 2022[4]). In fact, further investment in online procedures to reduce the administrative steps, costs and time to obtain sectoral licenses are foreseen as part of Portugal's Recovery and Resilience Plan (Portugal Government, 2021[3]).

Box 2.1. Industrial and environmental licensing have been simplified

To simplify industrial licensing in Portugal, several licensing or sectoral opinion issuing procedures related to the exercise of industrial activity were consolidated under a single legal act in 2012. A similar consolidation of various environmental permits under a single process was carried out in 2015.

Responsible Industry System for industrial licensing

Industrial licensing is regulated under the Responsible Industry System (*Sistema da Indústria Responsável*, SIR) framework.[1] The SIR applies to specified economic activities, such as extractive industries, manufacturing industries (including some of Portugal's priority industrial sectors, such as aerospace, automotive and food), accommodation, catering and similar activities. The SIR identifies three categories of establishments according to the degree of potential risk inherent to their operations:

- Category 1 establishments require an authorisation with prior inspection due to the high level of risk of the operations.
- Category 2 establishments are subject to authorisation without prior inspection.
- Category 3 establishments only require a prior communication to start the activity.

To diminish administrative hurdles in licensing procedure, the SIR includes a mechanism of institutional co-ordination. A public entity is appointed as the sole interlocutor of the industrialist, being also responsible for monitoring and streamlining the procedure and providing technical support to the applicant. To increase predictability for applicants, the SIR has time limits for authorities to respond to the authorisation requests on which the installation or operation of the establishment depends.[2] Tacit approval exists in case there is no response from the relevant authority within the prescribed timeline.

Moreover, the SIR established a new framework of Responsible Business Areas (*Zonas Empresariais Responsáveis,* ZERs) for simplified installation of new industries in pre-licensed areas. For instance, undergoing an environmental impact assessment is not necessary, if the environmental impact assessment of the ZER has included the relevant elements for the new installation.

Single environmental licensing

Under the Portuguese legal framework, multiple environmental licenses or authorisations may be required for a single installation, depending on the nature of activity. Under the new Single Environmental Licensing (*Licenciamento Único de Ambiente*) regime[3], a single application is submitted via an electronic platform to initiate the different licensing procedures[4], which are then advanced simultaneously under a framework of co-ordination between administrative entities in charge of environmental matters. The processing of the application is subject to payment of a single fee. At the end of the process, a Single Environmental Title (*Título Unico Ambiental*), incorporating all relevant licensing and prior control acts issued to the applicant under the various environmental regimes and all information on the environmental requirements applicable to the activity, is issued.

Further simplification measures to the environmental licensing regime are underway. After an extensive stakeholder consultation, the Government of Portugal approved in December 2022 a legislative package simplifying environmental licenses and procedures (see Chapter 4 for further information).[5]

Notes: 1. Decree-Law No. 169/2012. 2. These time limits depend on the applicable legal regime; in the context of an environmental impact assessment, for instance, the maximum time limit is 80 days. 3. Decree-Law No. 75/2015. 4. The scope of Single Environmental Licensing extends to 12 environmental regimes, including, among others, the environmental impact assessment regime, the industrial emissions regime, the waste management regime, and the water resources use regime. 5. Ministerial Council communication, 7 December 2022; DL 169/XXIII/2022, 2 August 2022. At the time of writing, the final text had not yet been published.

Moreover, despite the above-mentioned efforts to streamline licensing and permit procedures, investors across different sectors of the economy oftentimes still find them complex and excessively lengthy. Chapter 4 of this report discusses licensing and permits, as well as other administrative processes, from foreign companies' perspective.

Certain investment projects can also benefit from additional institutional co-ordination and monitoring in the licensing phase under special regulatory regimes for investment (Box 2.2). These regulatory incentives, but also initiatives like the Start-Up Visa programme (see Section 2.2.2), represent welcome support to FDI. Nonetheless, recent OECD analysis suggests that it will be important for Portugal to avoid inconsistencies and redundancies that may arise from operating too many regulatory incentives at too small a scale (OECD, 2022[5]). Portugal could thus potentially benefit from better differentiating support packages, including both financial support and technical assistance, to target specific types of FDI, e.g. large investors, start-ups or R&D.

Box 2.2. Examples of special regulatory regimes for investment

- Projects benefiting from the personalised follow-up of the Permanent Commission for Investor Support (*Comissão Permanente de Apoio ao Investidor;* CPAI). Monitored projects are those that may be of relevant importance for the dynamism of the Portuguese economy, through job creation or maintenance and other positive impacts on the economy.[1]
- Projects qualified as being of Potential National Interest (*Potencial Interesse Nacional;* PIN) or granted the Investment for the Interior (*Projeto de Investimento para o Interior*; PII) status. PIN projects are large-scale projects, which represent an investment of at least EUR 25 million and create at least 50 jobs.[2] PII status, in turn, can be granted to projects in the interior regions of Portugal, representing at least EUR 10 million in investment and creating at least 25 jobs.[3] PIN and PII projects are entitled to simplified licensing procedures, through priority assessments, simultaneous processing of different authorisations, a single public consultation period, and tacit approval, among other measures.

As of July 2022, a total of 68 finished projects, representing EUR 9 998 million of investment and 20 800 jobs, had benefited from CPAI's monitoring, PIN or PII status.[4] At the same time, 39 more projects (EUR 9 131 million in investment and 17 197 jobs) benefitting from support under these regimes were ongoing.

Notes: 1. Decree-Law No. 154/2013. In addition, other investment projects not fulfilling the eligibility criteria but that have already been waiting for a decision from the public administration for more than 12 months can benefit from monitoring.
2. Exceptionally, a project which does not meet the monetary value or job creation threshold may be recognised as a PIN project if it meets other requirements related to R&D activity, innovation, environmental interest, exports or production of tradeable goods and services. Decree-Law No. 154/2013.
3. Decree-Law No. 111/2018.
4. Figures were received in the context of consultations with Portuguese authorities in July 2022. The total number of 68 finished projects is comprised of three projects monitored by CPAI and 65 projects with PIN status.

Relatively high minimum capital requirement applies to public limited companies

Many countries have eliminated legal requirements for the minimum capital that must be deposited by shareholders before a new firm can commence business, as minimum capital requirements could act as barriers to entrepreneurship and have been shown to be inefficient in their intended purpose of protecting creditors.16 Since 2011, the capital of Portuguese private limited liability companies (sociedades por quotas) can be freely determined in the company bylaws.17 In this regard, the regulatory environment is less restrictive in Portugal than in many benchmark countries, where certain categories of private companies are subject to minimum capital requirements.

However, like all the peer countries, Portugal maintains a minimum capital requirement for public limited liability companies in line with an EU directive requiring all EU countries to impose on such firms a minimum capital of not less than EUR 25 000.18 Under Portuguese domestic legislation, public limited liability companies (sociedades anónimas) must have at least EUR 50 000 in share capital. This represents a stricter requirement than those found in some of the benchmarked countries. For instance, the minimum capital requirement is EUR 25 000 in Estonia and the SlovakRepublic.

Non-EEA acquisitions of strategic assets are subject to investment screening

As countries are increasingly concerned with balancing openness to FDI and managing risks that foreign investment may pose to their essential security interests, mechanisms that allow them to review specific transactions have become more common (OECD, 2020[6]). However, depending on how they are designed and implemented, investment screening mechanisms may have unintended consequences for prospective investment projects that present no potential security threat, in the form of increased transaction costs or legal uncertainty associated with the review process.

Portugal has a foreign investment screening mechanism since 2014 under Decree-Law No. 138/2014.[19] The legislation empowers the government to undertake, pursuant to a reasoned decision, an *ex post* review of any legal transaction where a non-EEA investor acquires any form of control over a strategic asset, to assess the risk of the operation for defence and national security or to the supply of essential services. Strategic assets are defined as the main infrastructures and assets assigned to defence and national security or to the supply of essential services in the areas of energy, transports and communications. In such cases, the government may block the transaction by means of a duly justified decision if it is determined that the transaction may jeopardise the interests of defence, national security or security of supply of services that the Decree-Law aims to safeguard. For the government to oppose the acquisition of control of a strategic asset, the threat posed by the transaction must be "real and sufficiently serious" according to the evaluation criteria specified in the Decree-Law.[20]

The review procedure under the Decree-Law is ad hoc in nature, i.e. there is no permanent entity or body in charge of foreign investment screening. The review procedure is led by the respective ministry associated with the strategic asset. As of September 2022, no transactions had yet been opposed under the Decree-Law.[21]

Scope of foreign investment screening in Portugal is narrower compared to peer countries

Many countries have adopted new review mechanisms or reformed their existing rules for investment screening in recent years.[22] The benchmark economies have also expanded their existing investment screening regimes or introduced new mechanisms in the last few years, or are planning to adopt legislation to enable screening.[23] In Portugal, there have been no amendments to the legal framework for FDI screening since its adoption in 2014, but an inter-ministerial working group has been established in 2020 to update the current legislation. Amendments could cover some technical aspects related to Regulation (EU) 2019/452, such as establishing a national contact point and aligning procedural deadlines between the domestic and EU mechanisms (EC, 2021[7]). Adopting rules that enable the compilation and sharing of information on the implementation of the domestic screening mechanism would also be important for Portugal's effective participation in the EU-level co-operation mechanism created by the EU Regulation (OECD, 2022[8]).

The Portuguese screening mechanism has a narrower scope than those currently in force in several other European countries, including some countries in the peer group.[24] Due to the definition of strategic assets that the Decree-Law safeguards, its sectoral scope of application is relatively limited. There is no systematic authorisation requirement, as acquisitions are only taken under scrutiny if the relevant ministry initiates a review procedure *ex officio*, within 30 days from the conclusion of the transaction or from the date when the transaction became public knowledge or following a voluntary notification by the foreign investor.[25] Moreover, some peer countries review also certain domestic investment projects, whereas the Portuguese mechanism applies only to non-EEA acquisitions.[26]

Flexibility in the implementation of screening process could be improved

Predictability of both the screening process and its outcomes, although inherently limited to some extent, matters for foreign investors. Regulated timelines for the screening process, the existence of tacit approvals and the possibility to request advance confirmation[27] are features of the Portuguese investment review mechanism that increase legal certainty for non-EEA investors looking to acquire assets in the Portuguese energy, transports and communications sectors. However, transparency and accountability in the implementation of the mechanism could be further improved by reporting (aggregated) information on screened transactions and outcomes (OECD, 2009[9]). Such information is currently not available to the public.

Moreover, under current rules, the only possible outcomes of a review process under the Decree-Law are either non-opposition or opposition. The latter entails that all acts and legal transactions referring to the operation in question (including those concerning the economic operation or the exercise of rights over the assets) are considered null and void. In some cases, negotiating or imposing obligations or conditions for the transaction may be a sufficient measure to address security concerns without blocking investment completely. Such mitigation measures, if applied with proportionality and consistently across projects, can help to increase predictability and ease investors' potential concerns with screening mechanisms.

The use of mitigation measures is not currently foreseen in the Portuguese legal framework for investment screening and may be a point to consider in the future. In the benchmark group, the review mechanisms in the Czech Republic and the Slovak Republic both enable the respective government to grant a conditional authorisation for investment.[28] Under the Czech mechanism, conditions may include, for instance, an obligation for the investor to initiate new consultations with the relevant ministry in the event of further increase in shareholding in the target entity or a change or expansion of the investor or target's business.

2.2.2. Entry of third-country nationals has been eased and special regimes put in place to attract foreign talent and investors

Maintaining firms' access to a pool of skilled labour is important to ensure Portugal's continued attractiveness to foreign investment. In Portugal, skill shortages are observed in certain fields, such as in information and communication technology (ICT) and science, technology, engineering and mathematics (OECD, 2021[10]). Fifty-one percent of jobs facing skill shortage are in high-skilled occupations and the remaining 49% in medium-skilled occupations (OECD, 2018[11]). In addition to boosting the domestic supply of qualified labour, attracting foreign skilled labour can contribute to mitigating skill shortages.

Measures that facilitate the entry of foreign workers improve firms' access to a pool of qualified labour and their ability to expand operations in Portugal. Foreign investors may want to source managers or specialists from headquarters abroad in the form of intra-corporate transferees or simply recruit them from overseas. Regulatory bottlenecks in the access to visas and residence permits can also discourage entrepreneurs from setting up their business in Portugal.

International talent from within the EU's Single Market enjoy freedom of movement in the area and their access to the Portuguese labour market is not restricted. In 2019, nationals of EU and EEA countries and Switzerland accounted for approximately 18% of Portugal's foreign workforce.[29] In comparison, investors, entrepreneurs and workers from third countries are generally required to obtain a visa to enter Portugal and, depending on the length of the stay, may also need to apply for a residence permit once in the country. The following sub-sections therefore focus on the regulatory framework for the entry of foreign talent from outside the Single Market. Foreign companies' perceptions of the regulatory framework are discussed in Chapter 4.

General framework for the entry of non-EU/EEA foreign talent

The Portuguese legal framework for the entry and stay of third-country (non-EU/EEA) workers, entrepreneurs and investors is based on the Foreigners Act of 2007 and its subsequent revisions.[30] Different categories of visas and residence permits exist for different purposes of entry and stay.[31] Foreign third-country nationals intending to stay in Portugal on a long-term basis need to first apply for a residence visa (*visto de residência*) in a Portuguese representation abroad. The Foreigners Act provides that the deadline for decisions on residence visa applications is generally 60 days from the submission of an application; 30 days in the case of a visa for highly qualified activity. The residence visa enables its holder to enter Portugal and request a residence permit (*autorização de residência*) once in the national territory. A residence visa for the purpose of employment, for instance, entitles the foreign national to begin work upon arrival in Portugal and while the residence permit application is pending. A recent 2022 amendment to the Foreigners Act created a new job-seeker visa type, which enables third-country nationals to enter Portugal for a duration of 120 days to look for work.[32]

Entry of certain foreign workers has been subject to quotas until recently

Until recently, the entry of third-country nationals for employment in Portugal was subject to labour market testing coupled with a quota system. Generally, a third-country national would be granted a residence visa for taking up employment only if there were job opportunities in the Portuguese labour market which had not been taken up by Portuguese or EU/EEA nationals.[33] An overall quota indicating the (presumed) availability of such employment opportunities for third-country nationals was fixed annually based on the estimated needs of the Portuguese labour market. However, the application of the quota system was suspended from 2020 to 2022,[34] and a 2022 amendment to the Foreigners Act fully abolished the quota system as well as the labour market testing system to facilitate the recruitment of foreign workers from third countries.[35] The amendments also facilitate the entry of nationals of Portuguese-speaking countries by easing their entry requirements.[36]

Validity of initial residence permits, including for highly skilled workers, has been extended recently

Holders of a residence visa may apply for a residence permit once they have completed certain necessary steps depending on the purpose of stay, such as concluding an employment contract and completing social security registration in the case of employees. Until 2020, a first residence permit was valid for one year and renewable for two years at a time. The same duration applied to residence permits for highly qualified workers seeking residence in Portugal under any of the special regimes available for them, namely the residence permit for highly qualified activity, the EU Blue Card or the Tech Visa (see the following sub-section).

From 2020 to 2022, temporary residence permit durations were extended on a temporary basis to two years for the initial permit and three years for renewed permits.[37] Following a 2022 amendment to the Foreigners Act, the extended residence permit durations have become a permanent rule.[38]

Extending the validity of the residence permit to two years contributes to reducing administrative burden and uncertainty associated with renewal processes. It also helps reduce the gap between Portugal and the benchmark countries, most of which already offered a duration of at least two years for highly qualified workers' initial residence permits. In Lithuania, the maximum duration is three years.[39] In Estonia, an EU Blue Card for a highly qualified employee can be granted for a maximum duration of two years and three months, renewable for a period of up to four years and three months, whereas residence permits for "top specialists" can be valid for up to five years, renewable for up to ten years.[40] Intra-corporate transferees in Portugal benefit from a flexible regime due to rules harmonised at the EU level, whereby a temporary residence permit may be granted for the duration of the transfer, up to a limit of three years in the case of managers and specialists (one year for trainees).[41]

Special entry and tax regimes are in place to attract foreign talent and investors

Portugal has implemented various initiatives to strengthen the acquisition of international talent. Several special visa and residence permit regimes within the legal framework of the Foreigners Act have been introduced within the last decade to facilitate the entry of certain categories of foreign workers and attract foreign investors and innovation to the country. Additionally, Portugal offers special tax treatment for incoming talent in specific activities with high value-added or bringing intellectual or industrial property or know-how into the country. Together these initiatives contribute to attracting foreign labour force to the Portuguese economy, including to its priority industrial sectors, such as aerospace and automotive industries, life sciences, smart materials and the food industry. Measures are in place to retain existing foreign talent in the country, such as international researchers or students after graduation, who can also contribute to increasing Portugal's pool of skilled workers.

Employee certification system to expedite recruitment of high-skilled workers

Launched in January 2019, Portugal's Tech Visa programme seeks to facilitate the recruitment of highly qualified and specialised staff from outside the EU/EEA by fast-tracking their visa and residence permit processes.[42] Originally, the scope of companies eligible for certification was those in the area of technology and innovation, but this has been extended to other firms producing goods and services for international markets.[43] To benefit from the scheme, a firm must have completed an employer pre-certification process with the Portuguese Agency for Competitiveness and Innovation (IAPMEI), and Tech Visa employees may not constitute more than 50% of the firm's workforce (80% in firms whose activity is mainly in inland territories). In early 2023, more than 400 companies had obtained certification.[44]

Start-up Visa to support Portugal's innovation ecosystem

Many OECD countries, including Estonia, Lithuania, Poland and Spain in the benchmark group, have introduced special entry programmes to attract start-ups and high potential entrepreneurs (OECD, 2022[12]). Portugal has also launched a technology and knowledge focused Start-up Visa programme in 2018 to attract foreign investment and highly qualified professionals and boost the country's innovation ecosystem.[45] Under this special regime, third-country nationals may apply for an entrepreneur's residence visa and permit based on launching a new innovative project in Portugal or relocating an already existing business to the country. Applicants must demonstrate that the project or business has potential to create employment and reach an annual turnover and/or asset value of more than EUR 325 000 within a five-year period, among other criteria. All projects must be hosted by a certified Portuguese business incubator, which will provide an individualised incubation plan and support for the project. The residence permit granted under the special regime can be periodically renewed until the holder qualifies for another status.

Special residence permit for foreign investors

Foreign investors who have entered Portugal with a short-stay visa may apply for the right to live and work in Portugal under a special residence permit regime for investors.[46] Investment projects that may entitle the foreign investor to reside in Portugal include, for instance, capital transfers of at least EUR 1.5 million, the creation of at least ten jobs and certain real estate acquisitions. The investment must be made for a period of at least five years. In addition, higher administrative fees are charged for the issue of the investor's residence permit than for other residence permit types.[47]

From its introduction in 2012 until December 2021, most of the investment brought to Portugal under this residence permit scheme (over EUR 5.5 billion of the total EUR 6 billion of investment) related to real estate investment.[48] Following a recent reform, in effect from 1 January 2022, the eligibility conditions are now more restrictive than under the original framework of 2012.[49] Among the amendments, residential real estate acquisitions entitling the acquirer to an investor's residence permit were limited to properties located in the Azores and Madeira and specified inland territories, thereby excluding real estate in the coastal mainland cities of Lisbon and Porto.

Special tax regime for international talent in priority sectors

Portugal has a special non-habitual resident tax regime to attract international talent to the country in activities providing high value-added or intellectual or industrial property or know-how. Under the Personal Income Tax Code, a person who becomes a Portuguese tax resident after not having been a resident taxpayer in the country in the prior five years is considered a non-habitual resident who can benefit from the special tax regime for a duration of ten years.[50] There is no nationality condition attached to the special tax treatment. Non-habitual residents enjoy the right to have their employment and business or professional income taxed at a flat rate of 20%, instead of the ordinary progressive personal income taxation, when said income derives from specified high value-added activities of a scientific, technical or artistic nature in Portugal.

New programme to support the return of Portuguese nationals

In 2019, Portugal introduced a new programme to attract Portuguese emigrants and support their return to the country as part of efforts to fulfil labour market needs and respond to demographic challenges.[51] Emigrants who left Portugal on or prior to 31 December 2015 can benefit from financial support and contribution to relocation expenses if they return to take up employment in mainland Portugal by the end of 2023.[52] An additional fiscal incentive applies to emigrants who returned to Portugal in 2019-23 after living abroad for at least three years.[53] Moreover, new rules for the recognition of foreign qualifications simplify the return of emigrants who have obtained an education abroad, but they also facilitate the entry of other foreign talent into Portugal.

International students and researchers may stay one more year to look for work or set up a company

The Foreigners Act incorporates special rules facilitating the retention of international researchers and students who have already benefitted from a residence permit or temporary visa to complete a research project or higher education diploma in Portugal. Both categories are eligible to apply for a one-year residence permit to look for work or start a business in Portugal after completing the diploma or research project in Portugal.[54] The one-year job-search extension applied in Portugal, Lithuania and Spain is longer than those observed in other countries of the benchmark group, but less favourable than conditions adopted in some other EU countries.[55] Retention remains low relative to other OECD countries, and former students accounted for only 2.5% of work permits issued in 2019, the lowest share among OECD countries for which this data was available (OECD, 2022[13]).

2.2.3. Pro-competitive regulation and regulatory policy practices could be further improved

Pro-competitive regulation is necessary for well-functioning markets and contributes to a country's business environment for both domestic and foreign investors. Overall, according to the OECD Product Market Regulation indicators, regulatory barriers to competition are slightly lower in Portugal than in the average OECD country, and the administrative burden that new businesses face is particularly light (see Section 2.2.1). Nonetheless, most benchmark countries have even more competition-friendly environments in several regulatory areas (Figure 2.1). The following sub-sections discuss certain policy areas in which the regulatory environment can cause distortions, including aspects where Portugal's product market regulation and regulatory policy practices could be improved.

Figure 2.1. Portugal could benefit from more pro-competitive regulation in certain areas

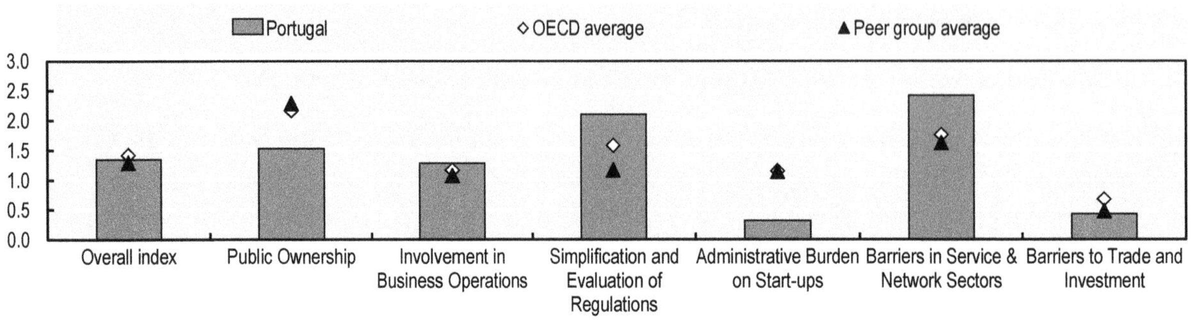

Note: The indicators refer to economy-wide regulation and are composed of the simple average of the sub-indicators on State involvement and Barriers to entry. The indicators range between 0 (most competitive) and 6 (least competitive environment).
Source: OECD (2018[2]), *Product Market Regulation indicators*, https://www.oecd.org/economy/reform/indicators-of-product-market-regulation/.

Public ownership of major firms is less prominent than in peer countries

State involvement in the economy through public ownership is relatively limited in Portugal compared to peer countries. Moreover, state-owned companies are subject to the same rules as private companies under Portuguese competition law,[56] and the coverage of sectors of the economy where the government controls at least one firm is narrower than in the benchmark countries, except for Spain (OECD, 2018[2]). At the end of 2020, 143 state-owned companies were active in Portugal in health, transport and storage, water management and financial sectors, among others (Conselho das Finanças Públicas, 2022[14]). In the case of Spain, limited public presence in network sectors (energy, transport and communications) contributes to the narrower scope of state-owned enterprises in the economy as compared to Portugal.[57]

A number of enterprises previously under state ownership were privatised as part of Portugal's privatisation programme, which was launched in 2011 following the financial crisis.[58] However, 2020 marked some increases in state ownership following the provisional nationalisation of a majority stake in energy and engineering company Efacec, with a view to re-privatise it in the shortest delay possible.[59] The re-privatisation process was concluded in February 2022.[60] In 2020, the Portuguese Government also increased its stake in airline TAP to help the company through the economic repercussions of the COVID-19 pandemic.[61]

Public procurement rules are relatively competition-friendly

Government procurement can represent an important source of revenues for both domestic and foreign-owned firms, particularly those engaged in sectors more exposed to government purchases, such as IT services and construction services. Consequently, shortcomings in public procurement can constitute behind-the-border barriers to trade and investment and be, at times, detrimental to welfare if a level playing field among potential suppliers is not ensured.

Portugal's Public Contracts Code and other domestic legislation for government purchasing follow the EU framework.[62] Overall, Portugal has a more competition-friendly legal framework for public procurement than other countries in the benchmark group, except for Lithuania and Estonia (OECD, 2018[2]). Portuguese procurement legislation is aligned with OECD best practices; for instance, contracting authorities must make tender documents available online, free of charge, and allow online submission of bids in all tenders. Moreover, tenderers from states parties to the World Trade Organisation (WTO)'s Government Procurement Agreement (GPA) benefit from the same procurement conditions as domestic and EU suppliers in accordance with the conditions laid down in preferential agreements.[63]

Simplification of public procurement of information and communication goods and services is foreseen as part of Portugal's 2020 Action Plan for Digital Transition, with a view to accelerate digital transition in the public sector and stimulate the market for small and medium-sized firms and start-ups.[64]

Regulatory impact assessment and stakeholder engagement could be strengthened

Regulatory policy plays a role in shaping a country's general business environment. Further involving businesses in the regulation-making process and systematically assessing the effects of both proposed and existing rules on companies help to ensure that business regulation meets its objectives, and with the minimum necessary regulatory burden for companies.

In 2016, Portugal launched a simplification and modernisation programme entitled Simplex+ as the continuation of Simplex (2006), with the aim to continue simplifying legislation and administrative processes, among other objectives. Reports evaluating the impact of Simplex+ indicate that Portugal has already taken successful simplification measures, which have reduced administrative burden and costs for businesses (NOVA IMS, 2017[15]; Ernst & Young, 2019[16]). Nevertheless, investors still find certain areas of regulation and administrative processes, such as tax regulation and compliance, burdensome (see Chapter 4 for further information on the perspective of foreign investors in this respect).

Portugal has also implemented several good regulatory practices aligned with the OECD (2012[17]) Recommendation on Regulatory Policy and Governance, but it remains below the average OECD country and tools of good regulatory practice could be further enriched in certain areas (OECD, 2021[18]).

According to the OECD (2021[18]) Indicators of Regulatory Policy and Governance, there is a formal requirement for the executive to undertake impact assessments for new regulation in Portugal, and reforms in recent years have expanded the scope of regulatory impact assessment (RIA).[65] Among these developments, a competition impact assessment for the evaluation of proposed regulation's impact on barriers to market entry and expansion is now a mandatory part of the executive branch's proposals for new regulation.[66] The competition impact assessment was developed following a joint project of the OECD and the Portuguese Competition Authority (OECD, 2018[70]; 2018[71]) and is based on the OECD Competition Assessment Toolkit.[67]

However, RIA of proposals for primary laws initiated by the parliament is not mandatory (OECD, 2021[19]). Impact assessment is also not used in consultation with stakeholders, and unlike in most benchmarked countries, RIA documents are not made publicly available online in Portugal.[68]

A public consultation procedure on draft regulation proposed by the executive is open to all interested persons, including businesses, through the online consultation portal ConsultaLEX.[69] In contrast, it is not mandatory to hold consultations with the general public regarding primary laws initiated by the parliament (OECD, 2021[19]). Systematically engaging with companies, and in earlier stages of drafting process, could improve the identification of alternative policy options and help ensure that business regulation works in practice. Moreover, Portugal could make more extensive use of *ex post* reviews to ensure that existing rules remain up to date and continue to deliver their policy objectives. Currently, *ex post* evaluations are not mandatory in Portugal (OECD, 2021[19]).

There is no requirement in Portugal to conduct stakeholder consultations at the negotiation stage of EU proposals, nor when transposing EU directives, and RIA is only required at the transposition stage (OECD, 2022[20]).[70] Strengthening RIA and stakeholder consultation not only in domestic law-making but also with regard to the development and transposition of EU legislation can help Portugal reap the potential benefits of EU legislation while reducing unnecessary regulatory burdens.

Additionally, there is room to improve regulatory transparency and predictability for both domestic and foreign businesses by ensuring a reasonable time between the publication and entry into force of new regulation (so-called *vacatio legis*). Currently, laws in Portugal enter into force five days after publication, unless otherwise specified. This period is shorter than international best practice, which often entails a period of at least 14 days after publication.[71] Most benchmarked countries have longer *vacatio legis* between the publication and entry into force of new legislation. In Spain, for instance, the minimum delay between publication and entry into force of laws is 20 days.[72] However, Portuguese legislation frequently establishes a transitional period after the publication and entry into force of new legislation to allow its addressees to adapt to new obligations.[73]

2.2.4. The efficiency of Portuguese courts has improved, but some challenges remain

Well-functioning justice systems are essential for business activity and contribute to a country's good investment climate. Alongside quality of justice and judicial independence, efficient court proceedings are part of an effective justice system. Although time efficiency is but one aspect of a well-performing judicial system, fast court proceedings help ensure effective contract enforcement and dispute resolution, while contributing to legal certainty for businesses. Moreover, effective appeal procedures against decisions made by regulatory authorities foster competition.

There have been improvements in the efficiency of Portuguese courts in recent years, but challenges remain in some areas. The estimated time to resolve litigious civil and commercial cases at first instance courts decreased from 369 days in 2012 to 200 days in 2019, but increased again to 280 days in 2020 (EC, 2022[21]). As such, the duration of proceedings is longer in Portugal than in most peer countries, with Lithuania being the best performer in the group at 117 days (Figure 2.2).[74] Portuguese courts fare comparatively better in the area of EU trademark infringement procedures, in which the average length of cases has remained stable in the recent years and was shorter in 2020 than in the benchmarked countries, except in Poland (EC, 2022[21]).

Figure 2.2. Estimated time needed to resolve civil and commercial cases increased in 2020

Disposition time (days) in litigious civil and commercial cases at first instance courts, 2012 and 2016-20

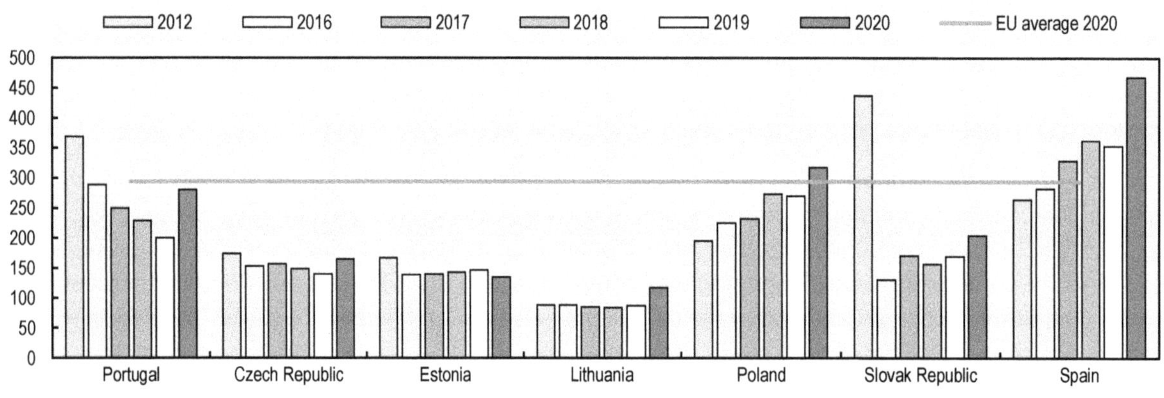

Note: Disposition time refers to the estimated number of days required to resolve a pending case in court. Due to changes in the structure of the caseload data, the number of cases for the Slovak Republic is not comparable between different cycles.
Source: CEPEJ (2022[22]), *Study on the functioning of judicial systems in the EU Member States. Facts and figures from the CEPEJ questionnaires 2012 to 2020*, https://ec.europa.eu/info/publications/two-studies-prepared-european-commission-cepej-european-commission-efficiency-justice-functioning-judicial-systems-eu-member-states-2022_en.

The clearance rate[75] decreased in civil and commercial cases from 109% in 2018 to 98% in 2020, but improved in administrative cases from 111% to 126% over the same period, indicating that civil and commercial courts were no longer able to resolve as many cases as the number of incoming cases, while administrative courts were increasingly able to cope with the caseload (EC, 2022[21]). Recent OECD analysis finds that enforcement cases (including contract enforcement and insolvency proceedings) still account for much of the backlog in courts, despite a declining number of cases. Although reforms in this area have already been implemented, it is recommended that Portugal continues improving the resolution of enforcement cases, which are particularly important for businesses (OECD, 2020[23]).

Moreover, administrative courts, particularly in first and second instances, continue to have long proceedings compared to benchmarked countries, as well as most other EU countries (EC, 2022[21]). Despite a decrease from 989 days in 2015 to 847 days in 2020, the estimated time to resolve a case in a first instance administrative court in Portugal remains more than seven times as long as in the group's best performer Lithuania (112 days) (CEPEJ, 2022[22]).[76] Lengthy proceedings in administrative courts can slow down investment if appeals against decisions regarding the necessary permits and licenses for new projects, such as environmental permits, take a long time to handle.

Reforms to increase the efficiency of the judicial system are planned as part of Portugal's Recovery and Resilience Plan (Portugal Government, 2021[3]). They include speeding up insolvency processes, increasing digitalisation in courts and reforming administrative and tax courts. Additionally, strengthening human resources in support functions would help Portugal address backlogs and improve court efficiency (OECD, 2020[23]).

The use of out-of-court procedures can also help ease the workload of courts, while offering advantages to the parties in commercial disputes. Overall, Portugal has undertaken relatively extensive efforts compared to other EU countries in the promotion of and incentives for using alternative dispute resolution (ADR) methods (EC, 2022[21]). Several arbitration centres offer ADR solutions, some of these centres specialising in areas such as intellectual property matters or even administrative and tax arbitration.[77] Mediation for civil and commercial disputes is also available.[78]

Yet, there is room for further efforts to encourage the use of out-of-court procedures and monitor their efficiency. For instance, in insolvency, increasing the take-up of out-of-court firm restructuring and introducing financially attractive out-of-court procedures for firm liquidation could help alleviate the pressure on courts and speed up procedures (OECD, 2021[10]).[79]

2.3. Sector-specific regulation

This section complements the assessment of Portugal's general regulatory and business environment by identifying regulatory aspects that might influence foreign investment decisions in some service sectors forming the backbone of well-functioning value chains and providing strategic support to Portugal's priority sectors for investment. These services sectors also greatly contribute to supporting the rest of the Portuguese economy, including companies engaged in agriculture or manufacturing. The OECD Services Trade Restrictiveness Index (STRI) is used to pinpoint sector-specific barriers to investment and trade and compare sectoral regulation with the peer group (Box 2.3). This tool provides a benchmark on the openness of the regulatory framework in a country regarding foreign services providers and is not meant to prejudge the legitimacy of restrictions put in place to attain specific public policy objectives.

Box 2.3. The OECD Services Trade Restrictiveness Index

The OECD STRI provides information on regulation affecting trade and investment in 22 services sectors across 50 countries, including OECD member countries, 24 EU/EEA countries and several emerging-market economies.

The index covers market access and national treatment provisions on all four Modes of Supply[1], as well as domestic regulation applicable to both resident companies (whether national or foreign) and to non-resident companies engaging with a given country. The indices are composed of several measures organised under five policy areas:

- **Restrictions to foreign entry:** foreign equity limits, nationality or residency requirements for the board of directors and managers, foreign investment screening, restrictions to cross-border mergers and acquisitions and other sector-specific measures
- **Restrictions on the movement of people:** quotas, economic needs tests, limitations to the duration of stay of foreign providers and the recognition of foreign qualifications in regulated professions
- **Other discriminatory measures:** discrimination of foreign providers with respect to taxes, subsidies and public procurement participation. Divergence between national and international standards is also covered
- **Barriers to competition:** information on anti-trust policy, government ownership of major firms and whether these are exempt from competition law and price regulation. Sector-specific pro-competitive regulation is also considered for network industries
- **Regulatory transparency:** consultation and publication of legislation prior to entry into force, administrative procedures to obtain a business visa.

The OECD STRI records laws and regulation in force in each country. It is compiled by qualified legal professionals according to a common and transparent methodology[2] and verified by each country's regulators and relevant authorities. The OECD STRI does not consider preferential trade agreements.

Notes: 1. The General Agreement on Trade in Services defines four Modes of Supply for services: 1) cross-border trade, where a service is provided from one territory to another; 2) consumption abroad, where a service is provided in the territory of the supplier to a consumer who has moved abroad to consume the service; 3) commercial presence abroad, where a service is supplied by a provider from one territory established in another one; 4) movement of natural persons, where a provider from one territory provides a service in another territory.
2. See Geloso Grosso et al. (2015[24]), *Services Trade Restrictiveness Index (STRI): Scoring and Weighting Methodology*, https://doi.org/10.1787/5js7n8wbtk9r-en.

The analysis focuses on policies that Portugal and the peer countries apply toward investors from outside the EU and EEA, as the restrictive measures captured by the STRI are based on Most Favoured Nation regulation. Therefore, they do not prejudice investment and trade between Portugal and the benchmarked countries, nor do they consider intra-EEA preferences. The extent to which regulatory harmonisation within the Single Market has resulted in lower barriers to investment and trade for intra-EEA investors is discussed in Section 2.5.

Portugal has a relatively open market compared to the peer group in several services sectors (Figure 2.3). However, foreign investors as well as domestic firms could benefit from further reduction of regulatory barriers in selected key services sectors, as discussed further below.

Figure 2.3. Comparatively high regulatory barriers remain in certain key services sectors

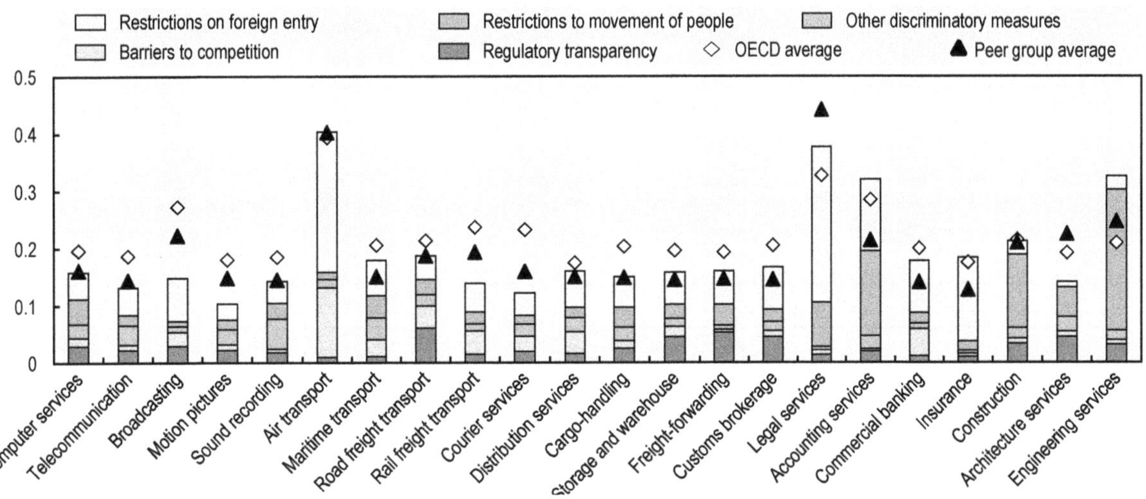

Note: The indices vary between zero and one, one being the most restrictive, and cover laws and regulation in force on 31 October 2022.
Source: OECD (2023[25]), *Services Trade Restrictiveness Index database*, https://www.oecd.org/trade/topics/services-trade/.

2.3.1. Professional services

Professional services sectors provide essential inputs, namely knowledge and skills, to support other businesses. In the area of professional services, the OECD STRIs capture laws and regulation in legal, accounting and auditing, architecture and engineering services. These services are generally subject to licensing conditions, thus typical regulatory barriers include, among others, nationality or residency requirements to obtain a license to practice the profession, equity limits based on licensing and license requirements for executive bodies and management.

Specific regulation and licensing requirements are common in professional services across the EU. However, the regulatory regime for accounting and auditing services and engineering services is more restrictive in Portugal than the EU average and more restrictive than in most peer countries (Figure 2.4). The OECD has previously conducted a comprehensive assessment of the impact of regulatory barriers to competition in 13 self-regulated professions in Portugal, providing recommendations to mitigate or eliminate these barriers (OECD, 2018[26]). According to the 2021 OECD Economic Survey of Portugal, some steps have been taken towards adopting these recommendations (OECD, 2021[10]). Nonetheless, in accounting and auditing, legal, architecture and engineering services, several regulatory barriers described in the 2018 review and captured in the OECD STRI remained in force at the time of writing of this report, as described below.

However, the Portuguese Parliament adopted on 22 December 2022 amendments that will require professional associations which currently limit the ownership and management of professional firms by persons other than members of the profession to lift such requirements, among other changes.[80] As of the moment of finalising this report, the amending Act had not yet been promulgated and hence not entered into force, and further amendments to the statutes of the relevant professional associations will be required to implement the changes. The Government of Portugal will have 120 days from the entry into force of the amending Act to present bills to amend the statutes and other relevant legislation. Nevertheless, the reform of the regulated professions is an important step towards addressing barriers in Portugal's professional services sectors and implementing its Recovery and Resilience Plan (Portugal Government, 2021[3]).

Figure 2.4. Professional services

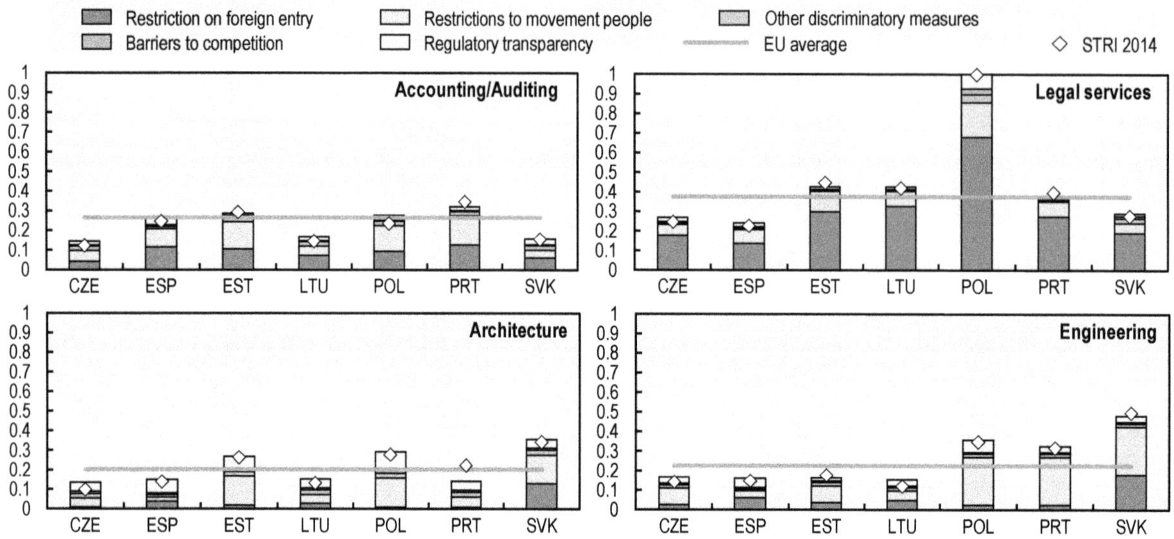

Note: The indices vary between zero and one, one being the most restrictive, and cover laws and regulation in force on 31 October 2022.
Source: OECD (2023[25]), *Services Trade Restrictiveness Index database*, https://www.oecd.org/trade/topics/services-trade/.

Legal services

Contributing to the relative restrictiveness of Portugal's regulatory set-up in the legal services sector are rules reserving equity participation in law firms and legal practice, understood as including the exercise of judicial mandate (*exercício do mandato forense*) and legal consultation (*consulta jurídica*), for lawyers (*advogados*) and solicitors (*solicitadores*) registered in the respective professional associations in Portugal. Although solicitors may also offer legal consultation and draft contracts, court representation is, in principle, reserved for lawyers who are members of the Portuguese Bar Association.[81] Only lawyers and law firms registered with the Bar can hold shares in law firms, and multidisciplinary practice in the form of commercial association between lawyers and other professionals is prohibited.[82] Additionally, directors and managers of law firms must be locally qualified lawyers.

Coupled with restrictive access to the profession of a lawyer, the above-mentioned restrictions effectively limit market access for foreign investors as regards the reserved activity of court representation, as well as their ability to appoint leadership of their choice. In the case of foreign lawyers from outside the EU, registration as a member of the Portuguese Bar Association is subject to reciprocal treatment of Portuguese lawyers in the home country of the foreign legal practitioner.[83] In comparison, the rules regulating access to the profession and/or ownership of law firms are more liberal in peer countries such as Spain, the Czech Republic and the Slovak Republic.[84]

Moreover, restrictions on advertising represent a barrier to competition in the Portuguese legal services sector. Neither individual lawyers nor law firms are entitled to engage in comparative advertising or mention the quality of the office in advertising.[85] Limitations on advertising might be particularly harmful for new entrants, including foreign law firms, and consequently to competition, which can ultimately be detrimental to a broader access to quality legal services by individuals and firms.

Accounting and auditing

Equity restrictions coupled with restricted access to the accounting profession contribute to the relative restrictiveness of Portugal's regulatory framework for accounting services. In Portugal, at least 51% of the capital of accounting firms must belong to locally certified accountants, and 51% of the board of directors must be certified accountants.[86] Non-EU nationals may register as a certified accountant only if their home country law offers reciprocal rights to Portuguese nationals. By contrast, accounting is not a regulated profession in any of the peer countries, nor do they impose any limitations on ownership in accounting firms.

In auditing, the minimum conditions for the approval of statutory auditors and audit firms are harmonised at EU level by a directive[87] and are therefore similar across the peer group. In compliance with the Directive, Portuguese domestic legislation provides that most of the capital and voting rights in audit firms must belong to Portuguese or EU-licensed auditors or other audit firms, and a majority of the board of directors of an audit firm must be composed of auditors or audit firms from EU countries.[88]

To become a licensed auditor, a professional must fulfil the conditions required by the Directive with regard to e.g. educational qualifications and practical training.[89] In addition, third-country auditors must pass a local exam and have a domicile, permanent professional establishment or a representative in Portugal to obtain a local license.[90] Until a recent liberalising reform, in effect from 30 January 2022, an additional barrier to access the profession applied, as third-country nationals were required to reside in Portugal for at least three years before a local license could be granted.[91]

Architecture and engineering

Portugal's STRI scores in the architecture and engineering services sectors are driven by restrictions to the movement of professionals. In the field of architecture, foreign professionals from outside the EEA have to complete a 12-month professional traineeship to become members of the professional association and hence obtain the right to practice the profession in Portugal.[92] In engineering services, non-EEA nationals can be registered with the Portuguese professional bodies and practice the profession of engineer or technical engineer only on the basis of reciprocity.[93]

In contrast to the regulatory framework for legal, accounting and auditing services, ownership in architecture and engineering firms is not restricted. Therefore, investors from outside the profession, including foreign investors, are free to hold shares in architecture and engineering companies. In fact, there are fewer restrictions on foreign entry in the Portuguese architecture and engineering sectors than in peer countries. Nonetheless, the above-mentioned limitations to the movement of professionals may impact both domestic and foreign-owned companies' ability to source talent from abroad.

2.3.2. Transport services

In the transport sector, the OECD STRI measures the trade restrictiveness of regulation in air transport, maritime freight transport, rail freight transport and road freight transport services. Overall, Portugal's regulatory framework for transport services is liberal compared to some peer countries, and the gap between Portugal and the best performers in the group is small (Figure 2.5). Many restrictive policy measures are also similar across the benchmark group due to EU-level harmonisation of sectoral regulation. To regulate the sector and promote competition in the Portuguese transport sector, the Mobility and Transport Authority (*Autoridade da Mobilidade e dos Transportes*), an independent regulatory authority, was created in 2014.[94] Nonetheless, some barriers to services trade and investment remain in Portugal's domestic legislation, which affect competition and foreign establishment in the sector.

Figure 2.5. Transport services

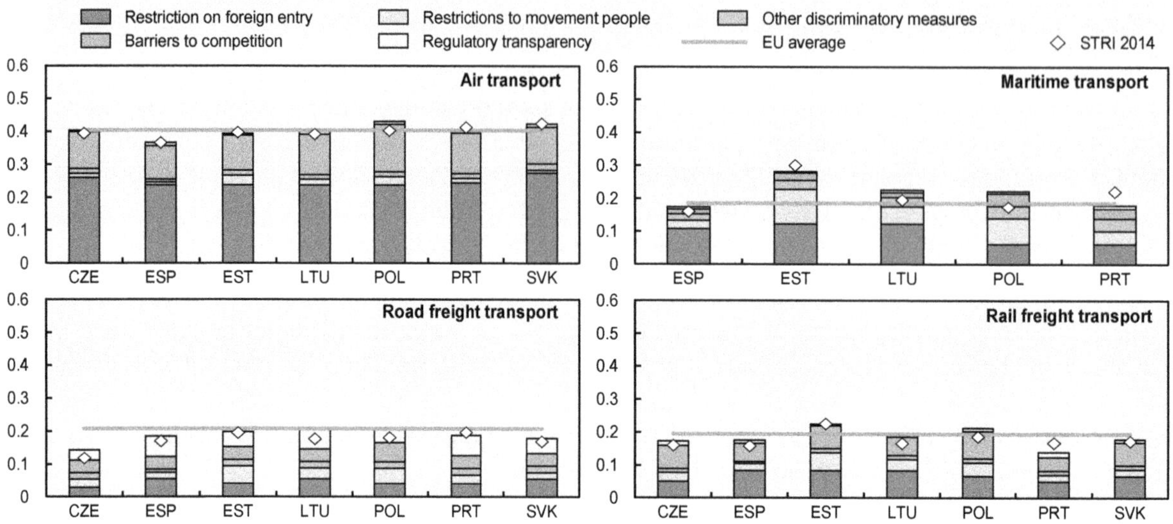

Note: The indices vary between zero and one, one being the most restrictive, and cover laws and regulation in force on 31 October 2022.
Source: OECD (2023[27]), *Services Trade Restrictiveness Index database*, https://www.oecd.org/trade/topics/services-trade/.

Air transport

Regulation of air transport services is largely harmonised at EU level, leaving limited domestic policy making space for Portugal. Due to Single Market harmonisation, restrictive policy measures in this sector are also very similar across the benchmark group, consisting mainly of barriers to market entry and competition. For instance, under EU aviation regulation, foreign investment in EU-incorporated airlines is capped at 49% of share capital.[95] Moreover, EU-wide rules for the administration of take-off and landing slots at airports favour incumbent air carriers over new entrants.[96]

In Portugal, domestic rules impose a general prohibition of airport use between midnight and 6:00, except for reasons of force majeure.[97] Night-time use may, however, be authorised by ordinance setting a maximum number of take-offs and landings during the period between midnight and 6:00.[98] Time limits for airport use may be imposed for a variety of reasons, including to reduce noise pollution, but lengthy curfew periods could significantly inhibit the complex time schedule of airlines, especially for all-cargo carriers and integrated express operators, which tend to travel at night and face tight delivery deadlines (e.g. due to the carriage of perishable goods). Among the benchmark group, Poland is the only other country to maintain schedules for airport use.[99]

Maritime freight transport

Portugal has a relatively liberal regulatory framework for maritime freight transport services compared to non-landlocked peer countries. Among the remaining regulatory barriers, foreign-flagged ships from outside the EU may be authorised to provide maritime cabotage services in Portugal only if no Portuguese or EU-flagged vessels are available.[100] However, as part of a new, simplified registration process, ship registration under the Portuguese flag does not depend on the applicant's nationality or headquarters, thereby allowing vessels under foreign ownership to be registered in Portugal and to provide cabotage services.[101] In comparison, benchmarked countries maintain restrictions to the registration of foreign-owned vessels under the national flag, in addition to limiting the provision of cabotage services by foreign-flagged ships.[102] However, several other EU countries (e.g. Denmark, Ireland, Latvia, the Netherlands and Norway) allow foreign-flagged vessels to provide maritime cabotage services (OECD, 2023[25]).

Pursuant to rules adopted at EU level, Member States may issue state aid to EU shipping companies, such as tax relief or subsidies for the manning costs of vessels, to increase the competitiveness of EU shipping companies with respect to non-EU companies.[103] In Portugal, so-called tonnage tax and seafarer incentive schemes were introduced in 2018.[104] Only shipping companies which have their head office or effective management in Portugal may opt for the tonnage tax regime. Income from activities carried out through non-EU/EEA-flagged vessels may be taxed under the special regime, on the condition that these vessels constitute no more than 40% of the net tonnage of the fleet and the management of all ships is carried out within the EEA. Additionally, at least half of the crew of all vessels benefitting from tonnage taxation must be EU/EEA nationals or nationals of a Portuguese-speaking country. The special tax and social security benefits for crew members apply exclusively to the crew of EU/EEA-flagged ships.[105] Similar support measures whereby foreign suppliers are treated less favourably than domestic ones are common among the non-landlocked peer group countries.[106]

Moreover, nationality requirements for ship crew and captain limit the ability of maritime transport service providers to recruit crew members from third countries. As a rule, the captain and at least 60% of the crew of a vessel flying the Portuguese flag must be EU/EEA nationals or nationals of a Portuguese-speaking country.[107] Additionally, both domestic and foreign maritime transport companies must hire a shipping agent to represent them in ports other than those where they are headquartered, or constitute themselves as shipping agents according to the respective administrative procedure, increasing operational costs.[108]

Finally, non-competitive market regulation regarding the provision of port services, such as cargo-handling, pilotage and towage services, can negatively affect both foreign and domestic providers in the sector. In the Competition Assessment of Portugal, the OECD identified various domestic legal provisions restricting competition in Portuguese ports and made recommendations to amend them (OECD, 2018[27]). For instance, the length of concession contracts is not systematically linked to the level of investment by the concessionaire, and concessions can be renewed without opening a new public tender (OECD, 2018[27]).[109] Non-competitive rules for the award of concessions and unnecessary barriers to market entry can contribute to increased port tariffs for users and reduced quality of port services.

Rail freight transport

The regulatory framework for rail freight transport services is largely harmonised at EU level. EU legislation imposes certain regulatory barriers in the sector which are shared across the jurisdictions in the peer group.[110] Due to the existence of comparatively few barriers arising from domestic legislation, the Portuguese legal framework for rail freight transport is more liberal than those of the benchmark countries.

Among the remaining relatively stricter requirements in Portuguese legislation, railway undertakings may not freely choose the legal form in which they are established in the country, as they are governed by the legal framework of public limited companies.[111]

Road freight transport

Sector-specific regulatory barriers captured by the OECD STRI for Portugal in the road freight transport sector respond to EU-wide rules. Regulation (EC) 1071/2009 lays down directly applicable rules regulating the licensing of road freight transport operators[112] and imposes certain barriers to market entry in the sector. Under the Regulation, EU countries are required to demand that operators hold a minimum amount of capital and reserves per vehicle during the financial year.[113] Each road transport firm must also designate a transport manager, who must be an EU resident. The transport manager may manage activities of up to four transport companies with a combined maximum total fleet of 50 vehicles.

The above-mentioned rules of the EU Regulation are applied across the benchmark group. However, in some areas, Portuguese domestic legislation imposes some additional requirements. For instance, in addition to the requirement to hold a minimum amount of capital and reserves during the financial year,

Portuguese legislation also requires a minimum capital of EUR 125 000 (or EUR 50 000 in case of operators using exclusively light vehicles) for starting a business as a condition for the issuance of a road transport operating license.[114] Moreover, more stringent requirements apply to the activity of transport manager in mainland Portugal under domestic legislation, limiting transport managers to the management of one company or, in some conditions, up to three companies.[115] Although the EU Regulation explicitly allows member states to impose a lower number of transport companies managed by a transport manager, the more stringent requirements applied in Portugal might prevent transport managers from expanding their business to a greater extent than in most other EU countries and rise costs for Portuguese transport companies (OECD, 2018[27]).

2.3.3. Logistics services

Logistics services play a crucial role in the development of global value chains, connecting production sites, manufacturers and consumers. In logistics, the OECD STRI records regulation in cargo-handling, freight forwarding, customs brokerage and storage and warehouse services. Additionally, it assesses whether countries have put in place certain customs simplification measures, affecting not only logistics service providers, but also operators in courier and distribution sectors (Box 2.4). Portugal's regulatory framework for logistics services is more liberal than the EU average but not on par with the most liberal regulatory settings in the peer group (Figure 2.6), indicating that there is still room to improve sector-specific regulation and streamline border procedures.

Figure 2.6. Logistics services

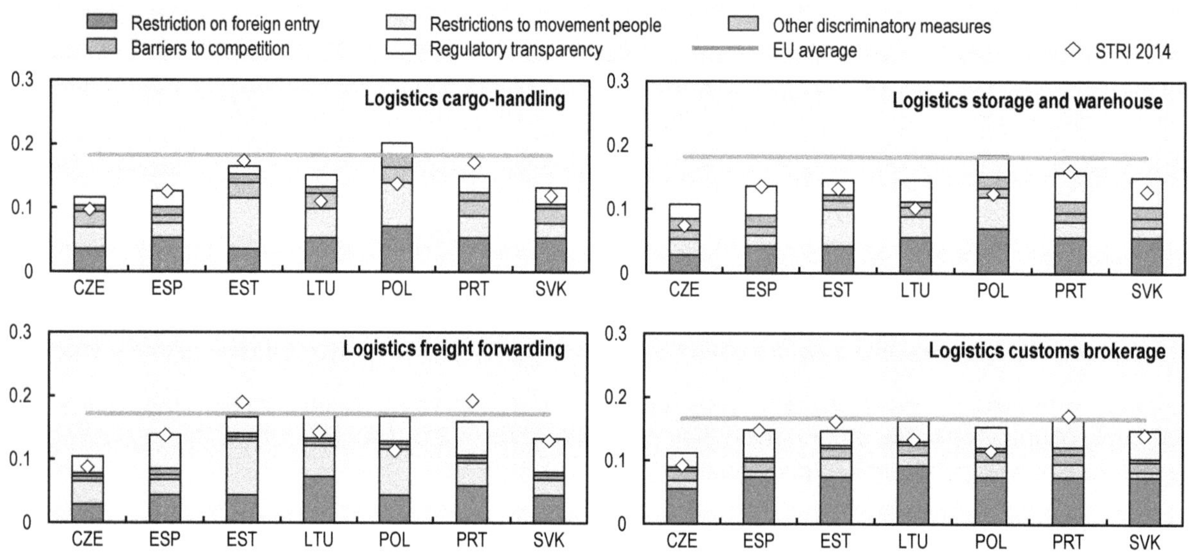

Note: The indices vary between zero and one, one being the most restrictive, and cover laws and regulation in force on 31 October 2022.
Source: OECD (2023[25]), *Services Trade Restrictiveness Index database*, https://www.oecd.org/trade/topics/services-trade/.

In cargo-handling and storage and warehousing services, Portugal could reduce the gap with the best-performing peer country, the Czech Republic, by adopting more competition-friendly rules regarding the award of contracts for port services. The non-competitive aspects of the award procedure have been discussed above under maritime freight transport. Namely, the OECD has previously recommended for Portugal to amend domestic legislation so that cargo-handling concessions at ports cannot be renewed without opening a new public tender for the provision of the service, and to establish objective criteria to determine the length of concessions based on the level of investment by the concessionaire (OECD, 2018[27]).

Box 2.4. The efficiency of customs procedures could be improved

Border barriers related to customs procedures can impact both domestic and foreign firms operating in transport, logistics, distribution and courier sectors. The overall efficiency of customs procedures, measured by the speed, simplicity and predictability of formalities at the border, matter for providers engaged in the import or export of goods.

According to international surveys, Portugal's customs regime is efficient compared to some countries in the benchmark group, but not on par with European best performers,[1] indicating that border procedures could be further streamlined and simplified. Moreover, the OECD Trade Facilitation Indicators suggest that certain other aspects of border procedures could also be reformed for the benefit of courier service providers, cargo carriers, logistics firms and distributors in Portugal.[2] For instance, electronic payment is currently not available for all duties, taxes, fees and charges. There is also room to improve information availability by making a minimal set of information available on the national customs website in one of the official WTO languages, such as in English. For information on foreign investors' perspectives on customs procedures in Portugal, see Chapter 4.

The OECD STRI captures several general customs procedure simplification principles via additional measures in logistics, courier and distribution sectors. These principles relate to the processing of shipment information ahead of shipment arrival at the border, the release of goods before determination and payment of duties, and the existence of a *de minimis* regime, where goods not exceeding a certain value or weight are exempted from import duties, internal taxes or full declaration procedures. Due to regulatory harmonisation in the EU, these principles are applied in Portugal and across the benchmark group, apart from a value added tax (VAT) *de minimis* regime.[3] Portugal also maintains an advance ruling system and a single window for customs procedures, which contribute to the transparency, predictability and efficiency of border procedures.[4]

Additionally, promoters of certain investment projects in Portugal may benefit from simplified customs procedures, such as an exemption from providing a guarantee of certain import duties and other taxes, under a special regime of contractual tax benefits.[5] Eligibility conditions include that the investment project must be connected to one of the specified economic activities[6] and its relevant investment must be equal to or higher than EUR 3 million.

Notes: 1. Portuguese customs procedures were perceived by business executives as the second most efficient in the benchmark group, after Estonia. Other better performing EU countries include Finland, the Netherlands and Sweden. World Economic Forum (2017[28]), *Global Competitiveness Report. Burden of Customs Procedure*, https://tcdata360.worldbank.org/indicators/IQ.WEF.CUST.XQ. Portugal ranks 35th globally as regards the efficiency of border clearance processes, falling behind Spain, Estonia, the Czech Republic and Poland, as well as several other EU countries. World Bank (2018[29]), *International Logistics Performance Index*, https://lpi.worldbank.org/international/global.

2. OECD (2019[30]), *Trade Facilitation Indicators*, https://www.oecd.org/trade/topics/trade-facilitation/. Currently, the Tax and Customs Authority only provides information related to taxation in English. Tax and Customs Authority, consulted on 29 April 2022.

3. Regulation (EU) 952/2013, Articles 171, 194 and 195. Due to the implementation of the EU's new VAT e-commerce rules, member countries have abolished any previously existing VAT *de minimis* rules (Directive (EU) 2017/2455). A *de minimis* regime with respect to import duties continues to apply under Regulation (EC) 1186/2009, Article 23, whereby goods valued up to EUR 150 are exempted.

4. Regulation (EU) 952/2013, Article 33. Decree-Law No. 158/2019.

5. Investment Tax Code (Decree-Law No. 162/2014), Article 12.

6. Investment projects connected to the following economic activities may be eligible: extractive industry and manufacturing industry; tourism, including activities of interest to tourism; IT and related activities and services; agricultural, aquaculture, fish, livestock and forestry activities; research and development and high technological intensity activities; information technologies and audio-visual and multimedia production; defence, environment, energy and telecommunications; shared service centre activities.

Additionally, individual licensing requirements are imposed on warehousing and freight forwarding, thereby limiting the ability of logistics services providers to integrate their activities.[116] In the benchmark group, the

Czech Republic and Estonia do not impose license requirements on either activity.[117] As regards customs warehouses, EU-wide rules constitute an entry barrier by subjecting operating licenses to an economic needs test in all member countries.[118]

Unlike in most benchmarked countries, customs broker is a regulated profession in Portugal, and access by third-country nationals to the profession is restricted. Customs brokers from outside the EU/EEA may register with the Portuguese professional association only if Portugal has signed a reciprocity agreement with their country of origin.[119] Coupled with a requirement that the majority of capital with voting rights in customs brokerage companies must be owned by licensed customs brokers, the reciprocity requirement limits the ability of foreign investors to own shares in customs brokerage firms incorporated in Portugal.[120] Additionally, at least one member of the management or administrative entity in the firm must be a licensed professional.[121]

Moreover, provisions restricting how customs brokers can advertise their services represent a barrier to competition in the sector.[122] A previous OECD assessment has also identified various other provisions in Portuguese legislation which may have competition-distorting effects in the customs brokerage sub-sector (OECD, 2018[26]). For instance, customs brokers' exclusive right to certain professional activities, such as representing economic operators before tax and customs authorities, excludes other, potentially equally capable, professionals from the market.[123] The financial requirements to register with the professional association, namely obligations to provide a financial guarantee and hold professional insurance, may also cause customs brokers to incur unnecessary costs, as the requirements address similar kinds of risks and the minimum values prescribed by law may not be appropriate for the level of risk.[124]

2.4. Digital trade

Digital trade involves digitally enabled or digitally ordered cross-border transactions in goods and services, which can be either digitally or physically delivered (López González and Jouanjean, 2017[31]). Declining costs of sharing information are powering a digital trade revolution that is changing traditional trade patterns. Access to cheaper, more sophisticated and diverse digital inputs – including productivity enhancing software, communications technology or e-payment services – can help firms deliver their outputs to a wider customer base across different countries and overcome existing trade cost disadvantages.

Portugal has actively designed and implemented policies to embrace the digital transformation in recent years (Box 2.5). The regulatory framework for digital trade is an important leverage to facilitate and enhance the objectives defined in these policies and to fully benefit from the digital transformation. Portugal already has a comprehensive regulatory environment for digital trade, composed of general rules that apply irrespective of the use of electronic or analogic means (such as industrial property and intellectual property laws,[125] competition law,[126] consumer protection laws[127] and data protection regulation[128]) and other provisions that specifically target interchanges that usually take place electronically (e.g. law regulating electronic communications,[129] decree-law regulating information society services, in particular e-commerce,[130] and decree-law regulating distant sales contracts[131]).

The Portuguese regulatory framework for digital trade, as measured by the OECD's Digital Services Trade Restrictiveness Index, is on par with the EU average but slightly more restrictive than most peer countries' (Figure 2.7). This indicator measures cross-cutting barriers that affect trade in digitally enabled services.

Improvements could be introduced in some areas to better align Portugal's regulatory environment for digital trade with more open peer countries. For instance, lifting the requirement for a permanent representative in Portugal for those foreign companies that exercise activities for more than one year in the country could help ease cross-border digital sales for firms established abroad. Among the benchmark group, only the Czech Republic maintains a similar requirement. The requirement in Portugal's domestic regulation couples with the EU-wide requirement for digital services providers not established in the EU but offering digital services within the Union to designate a representative in the Union.[132] Portugal could also deepen its participation in international efforts to facilitate the use of electronic communications in international trade by signing the United Nations (UN) Convention on the use of Electronic Communications in international contracts (2005). Portugal is not party either to the UN Commission on International Trade Law (UNCITRAL) Model Law on Electronic Commerce (1996) or the UNCITRAL Model Law on Electronic Signatures (2001).

Figure 2.7. Economy-wide barriers to trade in digital services are relatively low in Portugal

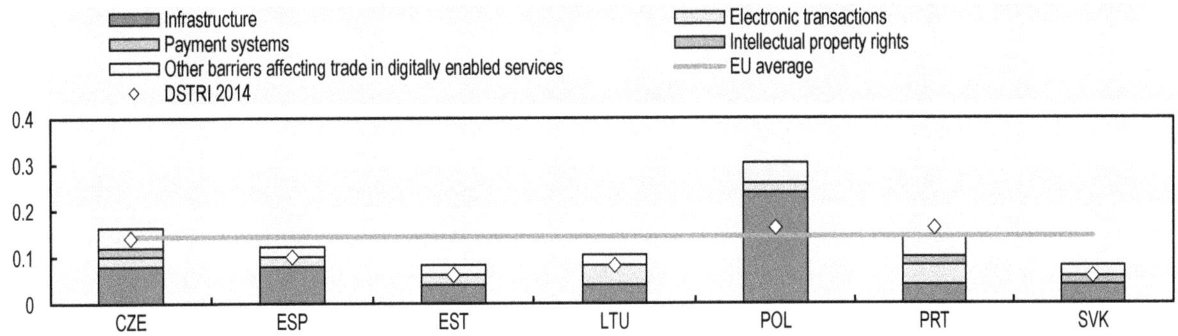

Note: Digital STRI scores range between 0 and 1, where 1 indicates the most restrictive regulatory environment. Scale adjusted to 0.4. The indices cover laws and regulation in force on 31 October 2022.
Source: OECD (2023[25]), *Digital Services Trade Restrictiveness Index database*, https://www.oecd.org/trade/topics/services-trade/.

In recent years, barriers to digital trade have been increasing worldwide with some slowdown identified in the aftermath of the COVID-19 pandemic (OECD, 2023[25]). Compared to peer countries, Portugal has been the only country to lower economy-wide barriers to trade in digital services in the recent years (Figure 2.8). This results from a 2015 policy reform introduced by the National Telecommunications Authority (ANACOM) reducing the requirements on vertical separation in the mobile segment of the telecommunications sector.[133]

Figure 2.8. Portugal has lowered economy-wide barriers to trade in digital services in recent years

Changes in the OECD Digital STRI index values in 2022 compared to the values in 2014

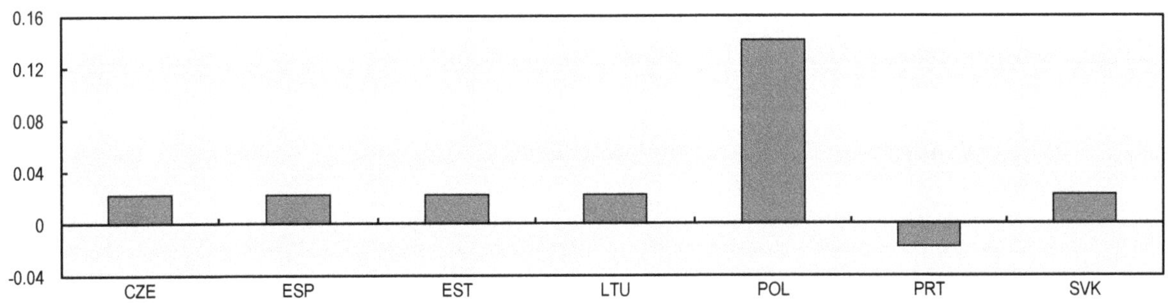

Note: Negative changes indicate trade liberalising reforms; positive changes indicate the introduction of regulatory barriers to digital trade.
Source: OECD (2023[25]), *Digital Services Trade Restrictiveness Index database*, https://www.oecd.org/trade/topics/services-trade/.

Other regulation, such as that restricting FDI and access to public procurement markets, can also importantly impact the development of the ICT sector. Furthermore, restrictions to the cross-border movement of computer professionals can hinder other efforts to develop an information knowledge society, as it could impact the transmission of knowledge. In this regard, the OECD STRI for computer services is a useful tool to analyse sector-specific barriers affecting ICT services.

In Portugal, the regulatory barriers for computer services appear slightly lower than in some peer countries and below EU average levels (Figure 2.9). Nonetheless, despite the 2022 amendments to the entry framework of third-country nationals, residence permits for contractual services suppliers and independent services suppliers remain shorter than those recommended by international best practice (see Section 2.2.2).[134] This creates administrative obstacles for companies to benefit from the services of third-country computer professionals. Other remaining obstacles include long visa processing times and cumbersome number of documents required for business visitor visa applicants.

Box 2.5. Strategies and initiatives for Portugal's digital transformation

Among the various policy instruments for Portugal's digital transformation, the 2012 Portugal Digital Agenda[1] sets out priority areas of intervention to reinforce the competitiveness of the country's ICT sector and to enhance the information and knowledge society: including, for instance, broadband access, investment in R&D and innovation, improving digital literacy and internationalisation of the ICT sector.

The 2020 Action Plan for Digital Transition[2] has three main pillars of action: digital empowerment of citizens, businesses' digital transformation and digitisation of public services. A cross-cutting dimension encompasses various "catalysts" of digital transition, such as regulation and disruptive technologies[3].

In public administration, Portugal plans to leverage digitalisation to provide simpler, more efficient and more transparent services through six strategic lines of action, defined in the recent Strategy for the Digital Transformation of Public Administration 2021-26 and to be initiated according to the corresponding Action Plan for years 2021-23.

Notes: 1. Ministerial Council Resolutions 112/2012 and 22/2015. 2. Ministerial Council Resolution 30/2020. The co-ordination and monitoring of the Action Plan is entrusted to the Portugal Digital Mission Structure (Portugal Digital), created by Ministerial Council Resolution 31/2020. 3. Portugal has also developed technology-specific strategies supporting its digital transformation, such as the 2019 national strategy for artificial intelligence (AI). See Portugal INCoDe.2030 (2019), *AI Portugal 2030*, https://www.incode2030.gov.pt/en/ai-portugal-2030. 4. The strategic lines of action are digital public services, valorisation of data, reference architectures, ICT skills, ICT infrastructure and services, security and trust. Ministerial Council Resolution 131/2021.

Figure 2.9. Barriers to trade in computer services could be further lowered in Portugal

OECD Services Trade Restrictiveness Index for computer services, 2022

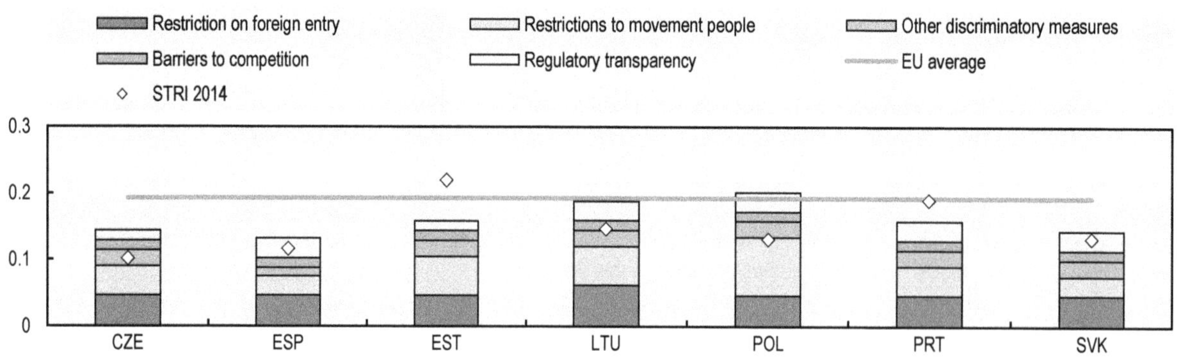

Note: The computer services STRI scores range from 0 to 1, where 1 indicates the most restrictive regulatory environment. Scale adjusted to 0.4. The indices cover laws and regulation in force on 31 October 2022.
Source: OECD (2023[25]), *Services Trade Restrictiveness Index database*, https://www.oecd.org/trade/topics/services-trade/.

In terms of trends, Portugal has eased barriers on computer services in recent years (Figure 2.9). In particular, in 2017, Portugal extended the duration of stay for services suppliers from four months to 12 months.

Adequate regulatory frameworks can enhance the adoption of new technologies while ensuring the protection of other policy objectives. Trade policies are particularly important to allow access to and development of these new technologies (Ferencz, 2022[32]). Further efforts to strengthen the regulatory environment for trade in digitally enabled services could be a good complement to Portugal's ongoing efforts to support the development and experimentation of technologies-based innovations, such as with its network of Digital Innovation Hubs and the recently established legal framework of Technology Free Zones (Box 2.6).

Box 2.6. Digital Innovation Hubs and Technology Free Zones support business innovation

Portugal has developed a network of 17 Digital Innovation Hubs as part of its Action Plan for Digital Transition (see Box 2.5). Digital Innovation Hubs allow SMEs to test digital solutions, provide assistance for obtaining funding and offer training for firms' digital transition. The Hubs also support start-up incubation and promote SMEs and public administration's relationships with partners in enterprises and entities from the research and innovation ecosystem.

Legislation adopted in 2021 establishes the regulatory framework for Technology Free Zones (*Zonas Livres Tecnológicas*; ZLTs) and defines the governance model for promoting technology-based innovation through the creation of these zones. As with "regulatory sandboxes", ZLTs are expected to provide a structure for companies to test new technologies and business models in the market within a controlled environment, monitored by the competent authorities and with safeguards to contain the consequences of failures. A distinctive feature of Portugal's ZLTs with respect to regulatory sandbox experiences of other countries is that Portuguese legislation provides for a cross-sector framework, while regimes in other countries tend to apply to a certain sector (e.g. fintech).

Coupled with Digital Innovation Hubs, the ZLTs are a welcome development to boost innovation and technological developments, as they should help to reduce regulatory uncertainties for new digitally enabled businesses that are not governed and monitored by current legislation and institutions.

Source: Portugal Digital, accessed on 6 January 2023; Decree-Law No. 67/2021.

2.5. Regulatory similarity to selected peer countries

High degrees of regulatory heterogeneity, i.e. large regulatory differences between jurisdictions, represent additional compliance costs for firms operating in several countries, who must adapt their business model to conform with varying local rules. Regulatory coherence between countries has been shown to benefit trade and investment: on average, even a very small reduction in regulatory heterogeneity between a country pair is associated with 2.5% higher services exports, with the impact of improved coherence being larger in relatively liberal markets (Nordås, 2016[33]). This section assesses which OECD and EEA countries share the most similar rulebooks with Portugal in the economic sectors covered in this chapter, and to which extent regulatory harmonisation within the Single Market has resulted in a more open regulatory environment in Portugal for foreign investors from within the EEA, compared to investors from third countries.

Of all OECD countries, Portugal's regulatory framework for services trade and investment is most similar to that of the Czech Republic in the majority of economic sectors covered in this chapter (Table 2.1).[135] In addition to similarities in sector-specific regulation, there are commonalities in the rules that apply to services providers and investors across all sectors of the economy in Portugal and the Czech Republic. For instance, both countries maintain mechanisms to screen certain foreign investment projects. Some similarities are due to absence of restrictions: for example, neither country imposes limitations on the acquisition of land or real estate by foreign buyers. The similarity of rules applicable economy-wide contributes to regulatory homogeneity between the country pair in each sector.

Table 2.1. The Czech Republic has the most similar regulation to Portugal's in most sectors

Sector	Most similar regulation (all OECD countries)	Most similar regulation (benchmark group)
	Professional services	
Architecture	Czech Republic	Czech Republic
Engineering	Lithuania	Lithuania
Legal	Netherlands	Czech Republic
Accounting & auditing	Czech Republic	Czech Republic
	Transport services	
Air	Slovenia	Czech Republic
Maritime	France	Lithuania
Rail	Czech Republic	Czech Republic
Road	Czech Republic	Czech Republic
	Logistics services	
Cargo-handling	Lithuania	Lithuania
Storage & warehousing	Czech Republic	Czech Republic
Freight forwarding	Czech Republic	Czech Republic
Customs brokerage	Czech Republic	Czech Republic
	ICT services	
Computer services	Czech Republic	Czech Republic
Digital services	Japan	Lithuania

Source: OECD (2023[25]), *Services Trade Restrictiveness Index and Regulatory Heterogeneity databases*, https://www.oecd.org/trade/topics/services-trade/.

Due to a high degree of regulatory harmonisation within the Single Market, services providers and investors within the EEA benefit from a substantially more open regulatory environment than under multilateral rules applicable to third countries. Yet, there is potential for further market integration within the Single Market, as obstacles to trade and investment have not been completely eliminated.

Figure 2.10 shows to what extent investors and trading companies from within and outside the EEA face regulatory barriers in Portugal. Regional integration has lowered barriers for EEA investors in all sectors, particularly in sectors such as air transport, professional services and construction.[136] Yet, despite this harmonisation, air transport remains a relatively strictly regulated sector also for EEA carriers.[137] Other sectors with relatively high barriers for EEA investors, but in which Portugal has more extensive domestic policy making space, include accounting services and legal services.

Moreover, Portugal's regulatory set-up with respect to EEA investors is slightly tighter than the benchmark group average in 12 of the 22 sectors. This indicates that there is still room to further lower regulatory barriers for intra-EEA investment and align Portugal's regulatory framework to peer countries' more open regulatory landscapes.

Figure 2.10. Regional integration has reduced barriers for EEA investors in Portugal in all sectors

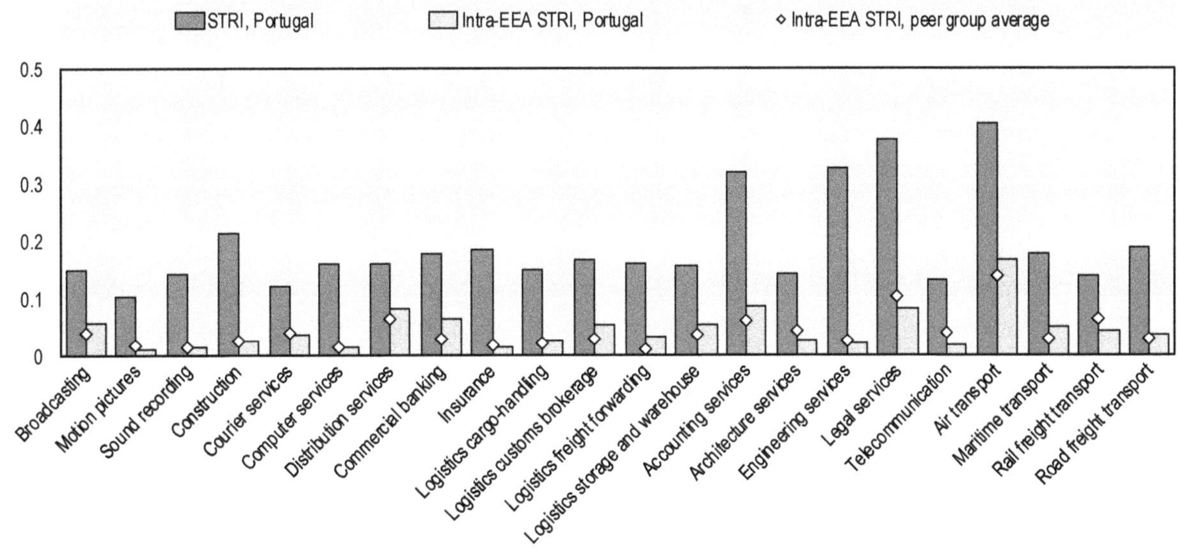

Note: The OECD STRI reports restrictions to trade and investment on a Most Favoured Nation basis, while the OECD Intra-EEA STRI captures the level of restrictions applicable to all EEA countries. Peer group average is the average Intra-EEA STRI score per sector of the benchmarked countries. The indices cover laws and regulation in force on 31 October 2022.

Source: OECD (2023[25]), *Services Trade Restrictiveness Index and Intra-EEA Services Trade Restrictiveness Index databases*, https://www.oecd.org/trade/topics/services-trade/.

2.6. Conclusions

This chapter has highlighted regulatory factors that might influence foreign investment decisions in Portugal, benchmarking them to regulation in a group of peer countries. Some of these regulatory aspects have potential impacts on FDI and business operations across many sectors of the economy. For instance, there is room to strengthen business involvement in the regulation-making process and systematically assess the effects of proposed and existing rules on companies to ensure that business regulation economy-wide meets its objectives, while reducing unnecessary administrative burden for companies. The efficiency of judicial procedures, particularly in administrative courts, is another area impacting Portugal's business environment and investment climate in which the benchmarking exercise indicates room for improvement. Finally, although the scope of transactions potentially scrutinised under Portugal's foreign investment screening mechanism is more limited than in peer countries, flexibility in the implementation of the mechanism could be enhanced by enabling risk mitigation agreements.

This chapter has also identified areas that could benefit from targeted reforms in selected services sectors providing strategic support to the economy. Among professional services, engineering, accounting and auditing services remain relatively strictly regulated in Portugal and could be further assessed to verify whether alternative, less restrictive and non-discriminatory measures can address the regulator's concerns in a more efficient manner. Rules regarding third-country professionals' access to exercise the profession, coupled with restrictions on the ownership and management of professional firms by non-licensed professionals, act as a possible barrier to foreign investment in legal services and accounting and auditing services sectors.

In transport services, although some limitations arise from EU-wide regulation, there is still space for Portugal to ease certain rules. Examples of domestic regulatory barriers include the imposition of schedules for airport use, discriminatory conditions to receive state aid in the maritime transport sector, nationality conditions for ship crew and captain, non-competitive regulation in port services and additional minimum capital requirements for road transport undertakings.

In logistics services, individual licensing requirements are imposed on warehousing and freight forwarding, restricting the ability of providers to integrate their activities. Limited access by third-country nationals to the profession of customs broker is coupled with restrictions to ownership of customs brokerage firms by non-licensed professionals. Additionally, the efficiency of customs procedures could be improved for the benefit of both domestic and foreign firms operating in transport, logistics, distribution and courier sectors.

Trade is an essential vehicle to enable digital transformation, which relies heavily on access to digital networks and equipment, seamless transfer of data across borders and movement of skilled workers and knowledge. Portugal's Digital Agenda, Action Plan for Digital Transition and AI strategy underline the importance of digitalisation for business environment in Portugal. A comprehensive regulatory environment is currently in place for digital trade; however, reduction of barriers, in particular to the movement of professionals, could improve Portugal's development of an information and knowledge society.

This chapter has also shown that although Single Market harmonisation has reduced regulatory barriers for foreign investors from within the EEA in all sectors, they continue to face slightly higher barriers in Portugal than the peer country average in most services sectors. Further liberalisation of Portugal's domestic regulatory environment to reduce gap with the benchmark group could attract more EEA and non-EEA investors to the country.

The following Chapter 3 assesses the impact of regulatory restrictions on FDI through an econometric analysis of cross-border mergers and acquisitions and greenfield investment projects, to estimate to what extent foreign investment projects respond to the removal of unnecessary regulatory obstacles. Chapter 4, in turn, discusses foreign investors' perspectives on the various regulatory aspects analysed in the present chapter and certain additional regulatory areas, such as labour regulation and tax compliance.

References

Benz, S. and F. Gonzales (2019), "Intra-EEA STRI Database: Methodology and Results", *OECD Trade Policy Papers*, No. 223, OECD Publishing, Paris, https://doi.org/10.1787/2aac6d21-en. [41]

CEPEJ (2022), *Study on the functioning of judicial systems in the EU Member States. Facts and figures from the CEPEJ questionnaires 2012 to 2020*, https://ec.europa.eu/info/publications/two-studies-prepared-european-commission-cepej-european-commission-efficiency-justice-functioning-judicial-systems-eu-member-states-2022_en. [22]

Conselho das Finanças Públicas (2022), "Sector Empresarial do Estado 2019-2020", *Relatório n.º 04/2022*, https://www.cfp.pt/en/publications/general-government-sectors/state-owned-enterprises-2019-2020. [14]

EC (2022), *Digital Economy and Society Index (DESI) 2022. Portugal*, https://digital-strategy.ec.europa.eu/en/policies/countries-digitisation-performance. [4]

EC (2022), *The 2022 EU Justice Scoreboard*, Publications Office of the European Union, https://ec.europa.eu/info/policies/justice-and-fundamental-rights/upholding-rule-law/eu-justice-scoreboard_en. [21]

EC (2021), "Screening of FDI into the Union and its Member States", *Commission Staff Working Document SWD(2021) 334 final*, Brussels, 23.11.2021, https://trade.ec.europa.eu/doclib/docs/2021/november/tradoc_159939.pdf. [7]

Ernst & Young (2019), *Assessment of Simplex+ Programme. Final report*, Ernst & Young, European Commission Structural Reform Support Service. [16]

Ferencz, J. (2022), "Artificial Intelligence and international trade: Some preliminary implications", *OECD Trade Policy Papers* 260, https://doi.org/10.1787/13212d3e-en. [32]

Fournier, J. (2015), "The negative effect of regulatory divergence on foreign direct investment", *OECD Economics Department Working Papers*, No. 1268, OECD Publishing, Paris, https://doi.org/10.1787/5jrqgvg0dw27-en. [36]

Geloso Grosso, M. et al. (2015), "Services Trade Restrictiveness Index (STRI): Scoring and Weighting Methodology", *OECD Trade Policy Papers*, No. 177, OECD Publishing, Paris, https://doi.org/10.1787/5js7n8wbtk9r-en. [24]

López González, J. and M. Jouanjean (2017), "Digital Trade: Developing a Framework for Analysis", *OECD Trade Policy Papers*, No. 205, OECD Publishing, Paris, https://doi.org/10.1787/524c8c83-en. [31]

Mistura, F. and C. Roulet (2019), "The determinants of Foreign Direct Investment: Do statutory restrictions matter?", *OECD Working Papers on International Investment*, No. 2019/01, OECD Publishing, Paris, https://doi.org/10.1787/641507ce-en. [34]

Nordås, H. (2016), "Services Trade Restrictiveness Index (STRI): The Trade Effect of Regulatory Differences", *OECD Trade Policy Papers*, No. 189, OECD Publishing, Paris, https://doi.org/10.1787/5jlz9z022plp-en. [33]

NOVA IMS (2017), *Avaliação das Medidas do Programa Simplex+2016. Relatório Final*, Nova Information Management School, Universidade Nova de Lisboa. [15]

OECD (2022), *Better Regulation Practices across the European Union 2022*, OECD Publishing, Paris, https://doi.org/10.1787/6e4b095d-en. [20]

OECD (2022), *Framework for Screening Foreign Direct Investment into the EU. Assessing effectiveness and efficiency*, OECD Publishing, Paris, https://www.oecd.org/investment/investment-policy/oecd-eu-fdi-screening-assessment.pdf. [8]

OECD (2022), *International Migration Outlook 2022*, OECD Publishing, Paris, https://doi.org/10.1787/30fe16d2-en. [13]

OECD (2022), *Services Trade Restrictiveness Index*, https://www.oecd.org/trade/topics/services-trade/. [25]

OECD (2022), *Strengthening FDI and SME Linkages in Portugal*, OECD Publishing, Paris, https://doi.org/10.1787/d718823d-en. [5]

OECD (2022), *What are the risks and rewards of start-up visas?*, https://www.oecd.org/migration/mig/MPD-28-What-are-the-risks-and-rewards-of-start-up-visas.pdf. [12]

OECD (2021), *Indicators of Regulatory Policy and Governance Survey 2021*, https://www.oecd.org/gov/regulatory-policy/indicators-regulatory-policy-and-governance.htm. [18]

OECD (2021), *OECD Economic Surveys: Portugal 2021*, OECD Publishing, Paris, https://doi.org/10.1787/13b842d6-en. [10]

OECD (2021), *OECD Regulatory Policy Outlook 2021*, OECD Publishing, Paris, https://doi.org/10.1787/38b0fdb1-en. [19]

OECD (2020), *Acquisition- and ownership-related policies to safeguard essential security interests. Current and emerging trends, observed designs, and policy practice in 62 economies*, https://www.oecd.org/investment/OECD-Acquisition-ownership-policies-security-May2020.pdf. [6]

OECD (2020), *FDI Regulatory Restrictiveness Index*, https://www.oecd.org/investment/fdiindex.htm. [1]

OECD (2020), *Investment screening in times of COVID-19–and beyond*, OECD Publishing, Paris, https://doi.org/10.1787/aa60af47-en. [39]

OECD (2020), *Justice Transformation in Portugal: Building on Successes and Challenges*, OECD Publishing, Paris, https://doi.org/10.1787/184acf59-en. [23]

OECD (2019), *Trade Facilitation Indicators*, https://www.oecd.org/trade/topics/trade-facilitation/. [30]

OECD (2018), *OECD Competition Assessment Reviews: Portugal: Volume I - Inland and Maritime Transports and Ports*, OECD Competition Assessment Reviews, OECD Publishing, Paris, https://doi.org/10.1787/9789264300026-en. [27]

OECD (2018), *OECD Competition Assessment Reviews: Portugal: Volume II - Self-Regulated Professions*, OECD Competition Assessment Reviews, OECD Publishing, Paris, https://doi.org/10.1787/9789264300606-en. [26]

OECD (2018), *Product Market Regulation database*, https://www.oecd.org/economy/reform/indicators-of-product-market-regulation/. [2]

OECD (2018), *Skills for Jobs. Portugal country note*, https://www.oecdskillsforjobsdatabase.org/data/country_notes/Portugal%20country%20note.pdf. [11]

OECD (2012), *Recommendation of the Council on Regulatory Policy and Governance*, OECD Publishing, Paris, https://doi.org/10.1787/9789264209022-en. [17]

OECD (2009), *Recommendation of the Council on Guidelines for Recipient Country Investment Policies relating to National Security*, https://legalinstruments.oecd.org/en/instruments/OECD-LEGAL-0372. [9]

Portugal Government (2021), *PRR – Plano de Recuperação e Resiliência*, República Portuguesa, XXII Governo, https://recuperarportugal.gov.pt/documentacao/. [3]

Rouzet, D., S. Benz and F. Spinelli (2017), “Trading firms and trading costs in services: Firm-level analysis”, *OECD Trade Policy Papers*, No. 210, OECD Publishing, Paris, https://doi.org/10.1787/b1c1a0e9-en. [35]

Vitale, C., C. Moiso and I. Wanner (2020), *A detailed explanation of the methodology used to build the OECD PMR indicators*, OECD, Economics department, https://www.oecd.org/economy/reform/OECD-PMR-detailed-explanation-methodology-used-to-build-PMR-indicators.pdf. [40]

WEF (2017), *Global Competitiveness Report. Burden of Customs Procedure*, https://tcdata360.worldbank.org/indicators/IQ.WEF.CUST.XQ. [28]

World Bank (2019), *Doing Business 2020: Comparing Business Regulation in 190 Economies*, Washington, DC: World Bank, https://doi.org/10.1596/978-1-4648-1440-2. [38]

World Bank (2018), *International Logistics Performance Index*, https://lpi.worldbank.org/international/global. [29]

World Bank (2013), *Why are minimum capital requirements a concern for entrepreneurs?*, World Bank, https://doi.org/10.1596/978-0-8213-9984-2_Case_studies_1. [37]

Notes

[1] Mistura and Roulet (2019[34]) estimate that the introduction of reforms liberalising FDI restrictions by about 10% as measured by the OECD FDI Regulatory Restrictiveness Index could increase bilateral FDI inward stocks by around 2.1% on average.

[2] Rouzet, Benz and Spinelli (2017[35]) also find that if multinational firms do set up establishments in countries with a more restrictive regulatory environment for services, as measured by the OECD Services Trade Restrictiveness Index (STRI), the foreign affiliates tend to realise lower sales than in host countries with a more liberal regulatory framework. The OECD STRI captures also behind-the-border factors.

[3] Fournier (2015[36]) finds that reforms reducing the divergence of product market regulation by one-fifth could increase FDI by about 15%.

[4] ePortugal.gov.pt, Guide to create a business, consulted on 15 June 2022.

[5] Decree-Law No. 125/2006.

[6] Decree-Law No. 109-D/2021.

[7] The attribution of "e-Residency" in Portugal would give the foreign national or company access to Portuguese online public services, company registration, opening a bank account, as well as assigning a tax identification number and social security number. According to information received in consultation with Portuguese authorities in April 2022, the launch of a first version of the e-Residency platform is scheduled for the end of 2022, with all functionalities scheduled to be operational by the end of 2023.

[8] Decree-Law No. 111/2005.

[9] Estonia State Portal, Registering a company, consulted on 28 June 2022.

[10] Decree-Law No. 398/98 and Decree-Law No. 14/2013. Portuguese Tax and Customs Authority, "Registo Contribuinte > Identific > Atrib/Alter NIF-Singulares", consulted on 15 June 2022.

[11] According to the Tax and Customs Authority's ruling (Ofício Circulado No. 90054 of 6 June 2022), a person who, cumulatively, i) has no tax domicile in Portugal, the EU or the EEA, ii) does not meet the legal requirements to have the tax status of resident, iii) is not a taxable person in the sense of Article 18(3) of Decree-Law No. 398/98, iv) is not subject to the fulfilment of obligations nor intends to exercise any rights with the Tax Administration, is not required to designate a tax representative. The appointment of a representative becomes mandatory if the person owns a vehicle or property in Portugal, signs an employment contract in Portugal or carries out a self-employed activity in Portugal.

[12] Foreign acquisitions of control of certain strategic assets constitute a notable exception, as they are subject to a specific investment screening regime to protect Portugal's essential security interests.

[13] Decree-Law No. 10/2015.

[14] *Plano de Ação para a Transição Digital* (Ministerial Council Resolution No. 30/2020).

[15] ePortugal.gov.pt, consulted on 15 June 2022.

[16] Some of the shortcomings associated with minimum capital requirements are that fixed minimum amounts do not account for differences in business size, activity and risk; creditors typically rely more on other metrics to evaluate credit risk; and the funds used to meet minimum capital requirements could be put to other productive use (World Bank, 2013[37]; 2019[38]).

[17] Commercial Companies Code (Decree-Law No. 262/86).

[18] Directive EU 2017/1132.

[19] The legal regime for investment screening, as enacted in the implementing Decree-Law No. 138/2014, is based on legislative authorisation granted by Law No. 9/2014. Unofficial English translations of both legal texts are annexed to Portugal's notification to the OECD of its investment policy ([DAF/INV/RD(2019)7] of 22July 2019).

[20] The Decree-Law expressly provides the evaluation criteria for the real and sufficiently serious nature of the threat, namely: physical security and integrity of the assets; permanent availability and operability of the assets; continuity, regularity and quality of services of general interest; and preservation of the confidentiality of data and information obtained in the exercise of the activity and the technologic resources needed for the management of the assets. Additionally, a non-exhaustive list indicates situations that are susceptible of posing a threat, such as the existence of connections between the investor and third countries that do not recognise or respect democracy and the rule of law.

[21] Information obtained in the context of consultations with Portuguese authorities in September 2022.

[22] A growing number of transactions are potentially subject to review, as many mechanisms now cover a broader section of the economy or include lower trigger thresholds than before (OECD, 2020[6]). In the first half of 2020, the COVID-19 pandemic further accelerated reforms by attracting attention to the protection of health-related industries and infrastructure in many countries (OECD, 2020[39]).

[23] Lithuania, Poland and Spain have recently amended or expanded the scope of their review mechanisms, while the Czech Republic and the Slovak Republic have adopted completely new rulesets for investment screening (EC, 2021[7]). Estonia is in the process of legislating a foreign investment screening mechanism (Bill 639 SE of 13 June 2022).

[24] Spain, for instance, broadened the scope of its investment screening as a response to the COVID-19 pandemic and its economic impact through a number of amendments to Law 19/2003 in 2020 and 2021 (Royal Decree-Laws 8/2020, 11/2020, 34/2020, 12/2021 and 27/2021).

[25] In comparison, under a new regime for the screening of non-EU investment in the Czech Republic (Act No. 34/2021), investment in particularly sensitive areas, including critical infrastructure, are subject to mandatory prior approval. Investment in other sectors of the economy may be voluntarily notified by the investors, or a review can be initiated by the responsible ministry up to five years after completion.

[26] Lithuania applies a review with regard to transactions in specified assets deemed important for essential security interests, irrespective of investor nationality, under its Act No. IX-1132 of 10October 2002.

Under Poland's investment review mechanism (Act of 24July 2015), certain investment in a closed list of strategic companies may be reviewed regardless of the nationality of the investor, including those by domestic investors. In 2020, Poland made temporary amendments to the Act in connection with the COVID-19 pandemic, adding mandatory reviews for certain investment from non-EU/EEA/OECD countries in specific categories of companies. The temporary mechanism was to cease to apply on 25 July 2022, but its validity has since been extended until 24 July 2025 (Act of 12May 2022).

In the Slovak Republic, a 2021 amendment to Act No. 45/2011 established a sector-specific investment screening mechanism to safeguard critical infrastructure elements in mining, electricity, gas, oil and petroleum products, pharmaceutical, metallurgical and chemical industries. The review mechanism applies irrespective of the nationality of the investor. Additional legislation for the screening of foreign investment in other sectors is under preparation.

Spain's merger review regime under Law 15/2007 empowers the Council of Ministers to prohibit a merger based on reasons of general interest, including defence and national security. This review is not specific to foreign investment.

[27] Reviews under Portugal's investment screening framework are conducted *ex post* and can be initiated by the relevant ministry within 30 days of the conclusion of the transaction or from the day that it becomes publicly known. After the investor has provided the necessary information and documents related to the transaction, the Council of Ministers has 60 days to emit an opposing decision. It is also possible for the acquirer to voluntarily request confirmation that the government will not oppose the transaction. In the absence of an opposing decision by the Council of Ministers within the 60-day time limit, or if no screening procedure has been triggered within 30 days of the investor's request, a tacit decision of non-opposition is presumed to exist.

[28] The Czech Republic's Act No. 34/2021 and the SlovakRepublic's Act No. 45/2011, as amended by Act No. 72/2021.

[29] In 2019, the total share of foreign nationals in Portugal's workforce was 6.7%, of which 17.8% were nationals of other countries participating in the EU's Single Market. Statistics Portugal (INE), *Quadros de Pessoal* (2019). Data do not cover the financial sector.

[30] Law No. 23/2007.

[31] Business travellers, such as prospective investors, may apply for a short-stay visa according to rules harmonised under the Schengen framework to visit Portugal for a maximum of 90 days during any 180-day period (Regulation (EC) No 810/2009). Temporary visas can be issued for stays of less than one year, for instance for the purpose of independent contractor work or scientific research, higher education teaching or other highly qualified activity.

[32] Law No. 18/2022 (25 August 2022) introducing a new Article 57-A to Law No. 23/2007.

[33] However, several categories of workers, such as intra-corporate transferees and highly skilled workers were exempted from labour market testing.

[34] Law No. 2/2020, Law No. 75-B/2020 and Law No. 12/2022.

[35] Law No. 18/2022 (25 August 2022) amending Article 59 of Law No. 23/2007.

[36] Law No. 18/2022 (25 August 2022) introducing a new Article 52-A to Law No. 23/2007, according to which a specific framework applies to nationals of the Community of Portuguese Speaking Countries, whereby it is not mandatory for the Portuguese Immigration and Borders Service to produce a prior opinion concerning the attribution of a residence permit, reducing the associated time constraints.

[37] Article 183 of Law No. 2/2020, Article 192 of Law No. 75-B/2020 and Article 153 of Law No. 12/2022.

[38] Law No. 18/2022 (25 August 2022) amending Article 75 of Law No. 23/2007.

[39] Lithuania's Act No. IX-2206 of 29April 2004.

[40] Estonia's Aliens Act (9 December 2009). Top specialists must earn at least twice the annual average gross monthly salary in Estonia.

[41] Directive 2014/66/EU.

[42] Ordinance No. 328/2018.

[43] Initially, only firms in high-technology and innovation areas could benefit from employer certification under the Tech Visa programme, but this eligibility requirement was removed already in April 2019 to allow also for other types of companies in need of highly-skilled workers to apply for certification. A further 2022 amendment eliminated the need for applicant firms to obtain a positive evaluation with regard to market potential and orientation towards foreign markets. Instead, it is required that the company produces goods or services in sectors that are exposed to international competition. Ordinances No. 99/2019 and No. 59-A/2022 amending Ordinance No. 328/2018.

[44] IAPMEI, TechVisa Programme - List of certified companies, 6 February 2023.

[45] Ordinance No. 344/2017 and Legislative Order No. 4/2018.

[46] Article 90-A of the Foreigners Act (Law No. 23/2007).

[47] For instance, the administrative fee for issuing the initial residence permit for investment is EUR 5 325. The same rate applies to initial residence permits granted to the investor's family members on the basis of family reunification. Ordinance No. 1 334-E/2010, as amended by Ordinance No. 204/2020.

[48] AICEP Portugal Global,"Investment from golden residence permits totalled EUR42.1M in December", 14 January 2022.

[49] Decree-Law No. 14/2021.

[50] Law No. 82-E/2014.

[51] *Programa Regressar* was introduced by Ministerial Council Resolution No. 60/2019.

[52] Ordinance No. 214/2019, as last amended by Ordinance No. 23/2021.

[53] Law No. 71/2018 and Law No. 12/2022.

[54] Article 122 of the Foreigners Act (Law No. 23/2007).

[55] Several EU countries have adopted a job-search extension policy or extended the stay period as part of national transposition of Directive (EU) 2016/801, which establishes a minimum period of nine months for the stay for the purpose of seeking employment or setting up a business after the completion of research or studies (OECD, 2022[13]). Finland recently extended the maximum stay period from one year to two years (Act 719/2018, as amended by Act 277/2022 from 15 April 2022).

[56] The competition regime established by Law No. 19/2012 applies to all types of economic activities regardless of whether they are carried out by public or private undertakings.

[57] The OECD Product Market Regulation (PMR) indicators capture the extent of state-owned enterprises in the economy by measuring whether the government controls at least one firm in specified sectors. A higher weight is given to key network sectors consisting of electricity, natural gas, air transport, rail transport, road transport, water transport and fixed and mobile e-communications. For more details regarding the OECD PMR indicators methodology, see Vitale, Moiso and Wanner (2020[40]). Although Portugal had no public presence in the energy sector at the end of 2020, the transport and storage sector had one of the highest concentrations of state-owned enterprises (Conselho das Finanças Públicas, 2022[14]). The OECD PMR indicators also show that government involvement in network sectors was more extensive in Portugal than in Spain, as measured by the size of the government's stake in the largest firm in key network sectors (OECD, 2018[2]).

[58] The legal framework for privatisations is established in Law No. 11/90, as amended by Law No. 50/2011.

[59] Decree-Law No. 33-A/2020 on the nationalisation of Winterfell 2 Limited's shareholding in Efacec Power Solutions, SGPS, S. A.

[60] República Portuguesa, XXII Governo, 24 February 2022.

[61] The government increased its shareholding in TAP from 50% to 72.5%. República Portuguesa, XXII Governo, press release, 2 July 2020. TAP has since been subject to further aid measures due to the pandemic. See European Commission, press release, 22 December 2021.

[62] The Public Contracts Code (Decree-Law No. 18/2008) and the Law regulating the access and use of electronic platforms for public procurement (Law No. 96/2015) implement Directive 2014/24/EU on public procurement, Directive 2014/23/EU on the award of concession contracts and Directive 2014/25/EU on procurement by entities operating in the water, energy, transport and postal services sectors.

[63] Article 6 B of the Public Contracts Code (PCC) stipulates that in areas covered by Annexes 1, 2, 4 and 5 (central government entities, sub-central government entities, goods, services) of the EU's schedule under the GPA and other international agreements to which the EU is bound, suppliers from states parties to those agreements are given the same treatment under the PCC as is accorded to EU suppliers.

[64] *Plano de Ação para a Transição Digital* (Ministerial Council Resolution No. 30/2020).

[65] A new model for systematic RIA was introduced by Ministerial Council Resolution No. 44/2017 and made permanent by Ministerial Council Resolution No. 74/2018, whereby it is mandatory for ministries in Portugal to undertake an assessment of the impacts of new primary laws and subordinate legislation on citizens

and businesses. RIA was further reinforced by Decree-Laws No. 169-B/2019 and No. 32/2022, establishing impact assessment as mandatory for all governmental norms as part of the legislative process. Other legal acts also foresee RIA, namely Law No. 4/2018, which establishes the framework for gender impact assessment of legal acts.

66 See Article 57 of Decree-Law No. 169-B/2019 and Article 55 of Decree-Law No. 32/2022.

67 See OECD, Competition Assessment Toolkit, consulted on 20 February 2023, and Recommendation of the Council on Competition Assessment (OECD/LEGAL/0455), adopted on 11 December 2019.

68 In Estonia, Poland, the Slovak Republic and Spain, it is systematically required to make regulatory impact assessment documents available for consultation with the general public with regard to both primary laws and subordinate regulation (OECD, 2021[19]).

69 Ministerial Council Resolution No. 77/2010. ConsultaLEX was launched in July 2019 (Portugal Government, Press release, 4 July 2019).

70 In contrast, among the peer group, Estonia and Poland (in the case of some EU directives/regulation), and the Slovak Republic (in the case of major EU directives/regulation) require stakeholder engagement at the negotiation stage of EU proposals. All benchmarked countries also require stakeholder engagement in the transposition stage (in the Czech Republic and Lithuania, only for some EU proposals). RIA is required at the negotiation stage of EU proposals in Estonia, Lithuania, Poland (for some EU proposals), and the Slovak Republic. (OECD, 2022[20]) Nonetheless, according to information obtained from Portuguese authorities in February 2023, the Technical Unit for Impact Assessment in Portugal has been involved in the RIA of EU proposals during the negotiation phase since the introduction of Decree-Law No. 169-B/2019.

71 Law No. 74/98. International best practice is to publish new regulation within a specified timeframe prior to its entry into force. In the context of the OECD Services Trade Restrictiveness Index, a period of 14 days is considered to be a reasonable time between publication and entry into force of regulation.

72 Spain's Civil Code (Royal Decree of 24July 1889). The minimum delay between publication and effective date of laws is 14 days in Poland (Act of 20July 2000) and 15 days in the Czech Republic (Act No. 309/1999).

73 Moreover, Article 77 of Decree-Law No. 32/2022 provides that, as a general rule, normative acts that change the legal framework of legal persons can only enter into force every six months, on 1 January or 1 July each year.

74 Lithuania, Estonia, the Czech Republic and the Slovak Republic had faster proceedings than Portugal in civil and commercial cases in 2020 (EC, 2022[21]). In Portugal, the estimated time needed to resolve a litigious civil or commercial case was 280 days in the first instance, 99 days in the second instance and 126 days in the Supreme Court in 2020 (CEPEJ, 2022[22]).

75 Clearance rate refers to the ratio of the number of resolved cases over the number of incoming cases.

76 In 2020, the estimated time needed to resolve administrative cases in Portugal was 847 days in the first instance, 877 days in the second instance and 291 days in the Supreme Court (CEPEJ, 2022[22]). In comparison, in Lithuania (the best performer in the benchmark group), the lengths of proceedings were 112 days in first instance administrative courts and 282 days in the second instance.

[77] Directorate-General for Justice Policy, List of authorised arbitration centres, consulted on 15 March 2022. Arbitration in commercial matters is regulated by Law No. 63/2011 and Decree-Law No. 425/86. The Code of Procedure of Administrative Tribunals (Law No. 15/2002, Article 180) enables, among others, the use of arbitration to judge the validity of administrative acts, unless otherwise specified by law. The use of tax arbitration is regulated by Decree-Law No. 10/2011.

[78] The commercial mediation regime is foreseen in Law No. 29/2013.

[79] Portugal has already taken steps to improve the insolvency framework. An out-of-court regime for firm restructuring was established by Law No. 8/2018, and an early warning mechanism was introduced under Decree-Law No. 47/2019.

[80] Draft law No. 108/XV/1 of 1 June 2022, approved on 22 December 2022.

[81] Law No. 49/2004 and Law No. 145/2015. Parties may be represented by solicitors in cases where the appointment of a lawyer is not mandatory under the Code of Civil Procedure (Law No. 41/2013).

[82] Law No. 145/2015. Law firms may not undertake their activity in association or integration with entities whose purpose is not exclusively the rendering of legal services. Similarly, professional societies of solicitors and enforcement agents may be formed by licensed solicitors and enforcement agents or other such professional societies registered with the Chamber (Law No. 154/2015).

[83] Law No. 145/2015. By contrast, lawyers from other EU and EEA countries may exercise in Portugal under their home country title provided that they register with the Bar. EU/EEA lawyers may represent parties in court only in association with a Portuguese lawyer, unless they pass the Portuguese Bar exam in order to practice under the Portuguese title of lawyer.

[84] For instance, Spain requires that in the area of domestic law, the majority of shares must be owned by locally licensed lawyers, the remaining equity participation being open to non-lawyers and foreign investors (Law 2/2007, Royal Decree 135/2021 and Law 34/2006). In the Czech Republic and the Slovak Republic, although ownership of law firms is fully reserved for licensed professionals in both domestic and international law, the recognition of foreign qualifications and hence obtaining a local license is not subject to a reciprocity condition (the Czech Republic's Acts 85/1996 and 111/1998, and the Slovak Republic's Acts 586/2003 and 422/2015).

[85] Law No. 145/2015.

[86] Decree-Law No. 425/99 with subsequent amendments.

[87] Directive 2006/43/EC.

[88] Law No. 140/2015.

[89] For instance, due to requirements imposed by the EU Directive, auditors must have completed at least three years of practical training, of which at least two-thirds shall be completed with a statutory auditor or an audit firm approved in any EU country. The requirement to complete training with an EU-approved auditor or audit firm represents a barrier for third-country professionals.

[90] In addition, auditors registered with similar professional bodies in their home country may be admitted in the Portuguese Order of Chartered Accountants on a reciprocity basis.

[91] The amendment was brought by Law No. 99-A/2021, in effect from 30 January 2022.

[92] Decree-Law No. 176/98, as amended by Law No. 113/2015, Articles 5 to 9. Regulation 350/2016, Article 4 and Annexes I and II. In theory, an applicant may be exempted of the traineeship requirement based on a reciprocity agreement between Portugal and the country of origin.

[93] Decree-Laws No. 119/92 and No. 349/99 with their respective subsequent amendments.

[94] Decree-Law No. 78/2014.

[95] The issuance of an operating license for an air carrier established in the EU is conditional on majority ownership and effective control of the air carrier by EU countries or nationals of EU countries. Regulation (EC) No 1008/2008.

[96] Incumbent air carriers that operate at least 80% of their allocated take-off and landing slots are allowed to retain the same slots from one season to another. New entrants only have access to the remaining slot pool. However, secondary trading of slots between air carriers is authorised. Council Regulation (EEC) No 95/93.

[97] Decree-Law No. 9/2007.

[98] At the Lisbon airport, for instance, the maximum number of night-time slots is 91 per week (Ordinance No. 259/2005). For information regarding other airports, see Portuguese Civil Aviation Authority, Operating Restrictions Related to Noise at Airports and Aerodromes.

[99] In 2018, Warsaw airport introduced a prohibition of flights between 23:30 and 5:30. Warsaw Chopin Airport, consulted on 15 June 2022.

[100] Decree-Law No. 7/2006.

[101] Decree-Law No. 92/2018. The new provisions regulating ship registration, contained in chapter IV of the Decree-Law, entered into force on 1 January 2019.

[102] In Estonia and Poland, the registration of a ship under the national flag is conditional on it being majority-owned by nationals or legal persons of EU/EEA countries (Estonia's Act of 11February 1998 and Poland's Act No. 138/2001). Under Spanish law, individuals and legal entities residing or domiciled in an EEA country are entitled to register a vessel in the national registry (Royal Legislative Decree 2/2011). In Lithuania, ships owned by Lithuanian citizens and companies registered in Lithuania can register a ship under the national flag (Act No. I-1513 of 12September 1996). Under Estonia's Act of 9December 1991 and Lithuania's Act No. I-1513, the provision of cabotage services is fully reserved for national or EU/EEA-flagged vessels, whereas Polish and Spanish legislation provide for the possibility to authorise foreign, non-EU/EEA flagged vessels to perform cabotage under specified, exceptional circumstances (Poland's Act No. 138/2001 and Spain's Royal Decree 1516/2007).

[103] Commission communication C(2004) 43, Community guidelines on State aid to maritime transport.

[104] Decree-Law No. 92/2018, Annex. Under the tonnage tax regime, taxable income is determined according to fixed rates based on the eligible ship's net tonnage, instead of ordinary corporate income tax rules. The Decree-Law also provides for an additional reduction of taxable income by 10%-20% in the case of vessels with a tonnage exceeding 50 000 net tons that use mechanisms to preserve the marine environment and reduce the effects of climate change. The seafarer scheme refers to the special tax and social security benefits for crew members, introduced in the same Decree-Law to reduce labour costs for eligible ships.

[105] For instance, under Decree-Law No. 92/2018, the remuneration of crew members of ships considered for the purposes of the tonnage tax regime is exempt from personal income taxation. In the case of vessels carrying out regular passenger services between EEA ports, only crew members who are EU/EEA nationals can benefit from the tax exemption.

[106] See C(2019) 8917 final (16 December 2019) on the Estonian tonnage tax scheme and seafarer scheme; C(2017) 2840 final (24 April 2017) on the Lithuanian tonnage tax scheme; C (2009) 10376 final (18 December 2009) on the Polish tonnage tax scheme; C (2019) 9217 final (16 December 2019) on the Polish seafarer scheme; C (2004) 1931 final (2 June 2004) on the Spanish tonnage tax scheme.

[107] The share of crew members from other countries may exceed 40% in duly justified, exceptional cases. Decree-Law No. 166/2019, Article 68. The rules of the Decree-Law do not apply to vessels registered in the International Ship Registry of Madeira.

[108] Decree-Law No. 264/2012. See also OECD (2018[27]).

[109] In addition, cumulative financial requirements imposed on private operators increase entry costs and may prevent particularly smaller providers from accessing the market (OECD, 2018[27]). Financial obligations imposed on service providers can consist of financial guarantees, minimum capital requirements and insurance requirements. See, for instance, Article 11 of Decree-Law No. 75/2001 regulating towing activity, and Articles 9 and 11 of Decree-Law No. 298/93 imposing financial requirements for cargo-handling operators.

[110] Namely, once allocated, the transfer or trading of railway infrastructure capacity between operators is prohibited (Directive 2012/34/EU) and certain rail transportation agreements are exempted from the prohibitions on cartel agreements (Regulation (EC) No 169/2009).

[111] Decree-Law No. 217/2015.

[112] Regulation (EC) 1071/2009. Operators using solely vehicles with a laden mass not exceeding 2.5 tonnes, as well as operators engaging exclusively in national transport operation in their country of establishment by using solely vehicles with a laden mass not exceeding 3.5 tonnes, are exempted from the EU-level licensing requirement under the Regulation.

[113] Regulation (EC) 1071/2009, Article 7. For each financial year, road transport operators must have at their disposal capital and reserves totalling at least EUR 9 000 for the first vehicle used, EUR 5 000 for each additional vehicle with a laden mass exceeding 3.5 tonnes and EUR 900 for each additional vehicle with a laden mass between 2.5 and 3.5 tonnes. Operators using exclusively light truck vehicles (between 2.5 and 3.5 tonnes) are subject to less stringent requirements: EUR 1 800 for the first vehicle and EUR 900 for each additional vehicle.

[114] Decree-Law No. 257/2007, as amended by Decree-Laws No. 137/2008 and 136/2009, Article 9.

[115] Decree-Law No. 257/2007, as amended by Decree-Laws No. 137/2008 and 136/2009, Article 6 provides that a transport manager may serve only one company, unless at least 50% of the share capital of each company belongs to the same shareholder. The scope of the criterion has been enlarged by Deliberation No. 1065/2012 of the Institute for Mobility and Transport, allowing operators to hire a transport manager in the capacity of owner, shareholder, manager, director or employee, in which case the transport manager can serve up to three companies; or hire an independent third party, in which case the third party transport manager can serve up to three companies with a combined maximum total fleet of 50 vehicles.

Specific rules apply in the regions of Azores and Madeira by virtue of Regional Legislative Decrees No. 7/2010/A and 10/2009/M.

116 Decree-Law No. 255/99, as amended by Law No. 5/2013, Article 2 (freight forwarding). Decree-Law No. 152/2008, Article 16 (warehousing).

117 The Czech Republic's Act No. 455/1991 Coll. Estonian Classification of Economic Activities database (consulted on 19 December 2022).

118 Under Regulation (EU) 952/2013, Article 211(2), the issuance of a license for the operation of storage facilities for customs warehousing is conditional on the existence of a proven economic need.

119 Law No. 112/2015, Article 102. Candidates from third countries may also be required to prove their knowledge of Portuguese language and take a local exam in order to register with the professional association, which is a prerequisite to practicing the profession.

120 Law No. 112/2015, Article 95.

121 Law No. 112/2015, Article 97.

122 Law No. 112/2015, Article 41. Customs brokers can advertise their professional activity, as long as advertising is carried out in an objective, truthful and dignified manner. The Law provides for a list of forms of advertising considered objective, truthful and dignified, such as contact information or areas of specialisation of the customs broker. Mentioning the quality of the custom's broker's services or promising certain results is considered illegal advertising.

123 Law No. 112/2015, Article 66.

124 Law No. 112/2015, Article 67. A security deposit, bank guarantee or insurance guarantee of EUR 49 879.79, and holding a professional civil liability insurance of at least EUR 50 000 is required. See OECD (2018[26]) for further details.

125 Decree-Law No. 110/2018 and Decree-Law No. 63/85.

126 Law No. 19/2012.

127 Law No. 24/96 and Decree-Law No. 84/2021.

128 Regulation (EU) 2016/679 and Law No. 58/2019.

129 Law No. 5/2004.

130 Decree-Law No. 7/2004.

131 Decree-Law No. 24/2014.

132 Article 18(2) of Directive (EU) 2016/1148, transposed by Article 2(3) of Law No. 46/2018.

133 ANACOM (2015) wholesale markets for voice call termination on individual mobile networks.

134 In the context of the OECD STRI, a duration of more than 36 months of the initial work or residence permit is considered international best practice.

[135] The similarity of regulatory frameworks is assessed with the OECD STRI Regulatory Heterogeneity Indices, which measure the extent to which regulation, as recorded in the OECD STRI database, is similar in two countries. The lower these indices, the more similar are the rules in force in each country pair. The Regulatory Heterogeneity Indices do not indicate the level of openness to services trade and investment, but only the degree of similarity between the rulebooks of one country to those of another. For details, see Nordås (2016[33]).

[136] The OECD Intra-EEA STRI Indices capture restrictions to trade and investment in services sectors within the Single Market. The indices illustrate the generalised level of homogeneity across EEA countries' regulatory set-ups, arising from EU regulation. Differences in the indices across EEA countries are due to aspects regulated by domestic legislation, rather than at the EU level. The indices do not fully reflect differences in the degree to which EU countries transpose directives in their national legislation. For details regarding the methodology, see Benz and Gonzales (2019[41]).

[137] The relative restrictiveness of the air transport sector for EEA air carriers might reflect the scope of the OECD STRI in air transport services. The STRI does not currently cover cross-border air transport, as the market segment is regulated via bilateral air transport agreements, which are not always publicly available. At the same time, cross-border air transport is the area where most liberalisation has focused.

3 The impact of the regulatory framework on FDI

This chapter explores the impact of regulatory restrictions on foreign direct investment flows through an econometric analysis of data on cross-border mergers and acquisitions and greenfield investment projects. Several policy measures are considered, including economy-wide and sector-specific restrictions, regulatory differences between the host and the country of origin, restrictions to digital trade and other types of business costs.

Key findings

- Portugal's relatively open regulatory stance creates favourable conditions for foreign direct investment (FDI). Nonetheless, there are still some regulatory hurdles to trade and investment which, if removed, could further increase Portugal's FDI attractiveness, particularly in a time of tightened worldwide competition for foreign investment and widespread uncertainty over the post-pandemic recovery and Russia's war of aggression against Ukraine.
- Countries with higher barriers to trade and investment in services sectors receive, on average, fewer FDI projects overall, partly because services provide essential inputs into several other industries and also because some measures affecting services are cross-sectoral in nature, i.e. affect other sectors too. If Portugal were to implement reforms that would reduce its level of services regulatory restrictiveness – as measured by the OECD Services Trade Restrictiveness Index – and put it on par with the most open economy in the Single Market, it could see 13% more cross-border mergers and acquisitions (M&As) and 6% more greenfield projects.
- Accounting for sectoral differences and variations in investor motivations, mode of entry and firm characteristics, the highest gains are estimated to come from the removal of regulatory hurdles to trade and investment in professional services. Reforms that would allow Portugal to align itself to the best performing economy in the European Economic Area (EEA) in professional services could boost the number of foreign M&As and greenfield projects in these sectors by 30% and 19%, respectively.
- Beyond the degree of regulatory restrictiveness, similarities between home and host country regulatory environments are also found to be conducive to more FDI. This partly explains the high number of FDI projects from Spain and France, which have relatively similar regulatory frameworks to Portugal. Reducing Portugal's average level of regulatory divergence with other countries to Lithuania's average divergence level (the lowest observed among the benchmarked economies) could increase the number of cross-border M&A deals by 4%. Strengthening regulatory coherence in a similar fashion with EEA countries alone could boost the number of cross-border M&A deals by an extra 1%. Regulatory co-operation can, therefore, be critical to facilitate FDI, as harmonised rules and regulation lower compliance costs for investors.
- Foreign firms are also found to privilege investment in countries with limited obstacles to digitally enabled services, suggesting that Portugal's relatively open regulatory environment for digital trade adds to its international competitiveness. Further efforts to bring Portugal's level of digital restrictiveness on par with that of the "frontier" country in the Single Market (Estonia) could give it an extra boost: 19% more cross-border M&A deals and 7% more greenfield projects.
- Foreign investors are also more prone to invest in countries where it is easier to start a company, suggesting that lowering the administrative burden related to setting up businesses and reducing red tape for business overall could further contribute to attracting more FDI.
- Countries with better logistics services and port infrastructure also generally host more FDI projects, at least in some sectors, indicating that improved efficiency of logistics and ports has potential to strengthen Portugal's attractiveness to foreign investment.

3.1. Introduction

Portugal has long recognised the importance of foreign direct investment (FDI), stepping up efforts to promote and open the economy to foreign investors over time. Currently, Portugal enjoys one of the highest stocks of inward FDI in proportion to its gross domestic product (GDP) among OECD countries, but further increasing the level of international investment remains high in Portugal's priorities for the next decade (see the *Internacionalizar 2030* and the *Acordo de Parceria Portugal 2030* programmes). This seems a timely endeavour in light of the consequences of Russia's war against Ukraine and the uncertainties surrounding the global economic outlook, which tends to negatively weigh on investor sentiment and intensify the competition for FDI. Ensuring that Portugal remains attractive for investors becomes an ever more critical challenge in this context.

Several factors are known to influence a country's attractiveness for FDI, but not that many can be shaped or modified by government policy in the short-to-medium term as its own regulatory environment. Beyond the more direct effect of discriminatory measures against foreign investors regulating market access and national treatment, other non-discriminatory measures can influence FDI indirectly by raising the relative costs of doing business in one location versus another, notably if the rules are excessively stringent compared to regulatory frameworks observed elsewhere. As FDI can play a vital role in addressing Portugal's productivity challenge, supporting economic recovery and progressing on several areas of the Sustainable Development Goals (see Chapter 1), understanding the interplay between domestic regulation and FDI becomes particularly important.

Addressing policy constraints to trade and investment is not an end in itself. Certain policies may sometimes be necessary to achieve intended public goals, but where such regulatory measures are overly strict, they may entail disproportional costs to society (e.g. foregone investment and tax; higher costs and lower product and services differentiation among others). For this reason, countries should regularly assess the extent to which applied regulation is proportional to the risks it is intended to address and if there are alternative and more efficient ways to achieve the same objectives (OECD, 2015[1]).[1]

As is shown by the OECD Services Trade Restrictiveness Index (STRI; see Chapter 2), some countries have adopted comparatively less burdensome policies for regulating business activity in their jurisdictions. There is certainly no "one-size-fits-all" policy regime that would work adequately for all countries, as that depends on a country's political and economic context, but the experience of other countries shows that alternative approaches may sometimes be feasible.

The comparative regulatory assessment carried out in Chapter 2 and the empirical analysis of the potential effects of the domestic regulatory environment on FDI, discussed in this chapter, serve the objective of informing policy making and discussions in this regard. The empirical assessment builds on a number of possible reform scenarios derived from regulatory settings observed in peer economies to simulate, and put into the perspective, the potential impact of such reforms in the case of Portugal. But it does not consider the social-political-economic particularities of the Portuguese economy. This is an assessment which the Government of Portugal is best placed to undertake. Some more qualitative and contextualised elements complementing and supporting a more comprehensive assessment are provided in Chapter 4, which investigates the perception of foreign investors about Portugal's business environment.

This chapter is structured as follows: the next section provides a non-technical explanation of the applied empirical approach, while the subsequent section presents the main findings; a short conclusion follows. The methodology used for the analysis is outlined in Annex 3.A.

3.2. Empirical approach

The empirical approach uses transaction-level data on cross-border M&As and greenfield investment into 48 countries between 2012 and 2022.[2] Including a large set of countries in the analysis allows one to evaluate how different regulatory settings shape FDI occurrence. The estimated effects are interpreted in relation to the Portuguese context, that is, in what manner FDI activity in Portugal is expected to be impacted if Portugal were to reform its regulatory framework so as to resemble that of the "least restrictive"/best performing country in the Single Market, as measured by the STRI and other indicators (see below).[3] The estimation is performed separately for cross-border M&A deals and greenfield projects to better understand how these two types of FDI respond to changes in the regulatory environment.

In examining the effect of the regulatory setting on FDI, the analysis takes into account several factors that have been found to influence investment. These factors include the geographical distance between investing and host countries, their respective market sizes, as well as the existence of a common border and of a common official language (see Box 3.2 further below). Data on foreign greenfield investment used in this chapter did not distinguish among investors' origin, hence, the analysis of greenfield investment patterns exploits only the information about host countries.[4]

The link between the regulatory framework and FDI is evaluated using the OECD STRI (see Chapter 2) – a comprehensive policy-based indicator capturing both "at the border" and "behind the border" obstacles to trade and investment – and other complementary indicators from the World Economic Forum and the World Bank, capturing some other important non-regulatory aspects of the business environment (see Annex 3.B for a description of the data).

The following effects are assessed in the analysis:

- The economy-wide impact on FDI of regulatory barriers to trade and investment in services sectors, as services provide essential inputs to every segment of the economy and as some regulatory measures contributing to services sector restrictions stem from horizontal regulation which is equally applied in other sectors
- The impact of such barriers on FDI in their respective services sectors
- The channels behind the impact of these policy measures on FDI, i.e. sector-specific effects, the role of different categories of regulatory restrictiveness and the impact of regulatory divergence between the host and the country of origin
- The effect of regulatory restrictions on digital trade
- The role of other types of hurdles to business operation, such as performance of logistics services and ports, as well as administrative burden to start a business.

3.3. The impact of regulation on FDI

This section discusses the main findings on the link between various regulatory measures and FDI. Tables with the estimation results are reported in Annex 3.B.

3.3.1. Countries with higher regulatory hurdles attract less FDI

Restrictions to trade and investment in services sectors, as measured by the aggregate STRI score (average across 22 services sectors), are found to be negatively related to the total number of FDI projects a country receives across sectors, both in terms of the cross-border M&A deals and greenfield projects. This result shows the importance of the regulatory landscape for an investor's location choice.[5] For example, implementing reforms that would bring Portugal's aggregate STRI score on par with that of the Netherlands, the best performing country from the Single Market in the STRI, could increase the total number of M&As in the Portuguese economy by 13% and the number of greenfield projects by 6% (Figure 3.1). As the uncertainty surrounding the global economic outlook may continue to delay investment projects worldwide, addressing the existing regulatory hurdles might be opportune to remain competitive and be better positioned for when investor confidence is restored.

The estimated growth in FDI projects in services sectors as a whole could amount 15% for M&As and 10% for greenfield investment; in manufacturing, to 11% and 3% respectively. The sizeable impact of regulatory hurdles to trade and investment in services on FDI in the whole economy, including manufacturing, is consistent with the increased use of services inputs in productive activities economy-wide. This is observed, for instance, in their substantial contribution to the value added exported by Portugal (see Chapter 1, Section 1.4.4). By deterring entry of foreign firms and restraining competition, excessive regulation of services sectors can limit the ability of all businesses to access high-quality services at the best price, reducing the competitiveness of the whole economy.[6]

Figure 3.1. Estimated change in the number of FDI projects in all sectors

Percentage change in the number of M&A deals or greenfield projects

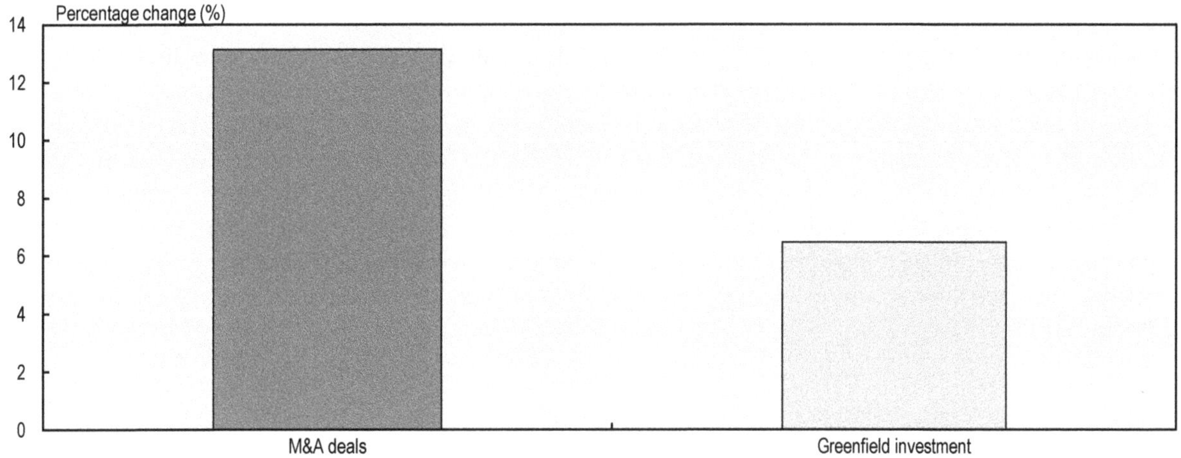

Note: Estimated impact of a reduction in the STRI score from Portugal's average to the least restrictive level in the EEA.
Source: Own elaborations on data from Refinitiv M&A database and Financial Times fDi Markets database.

Several factors might contribute to explaining why the predicted increases in the number of FDI projects differ between cross-border M&As and greenfield investment. First, some dimensions of policy restrictiveness can affect one FDI type more heavily than the other (see Section 3.3.3). Secondly, sectoral distribution of M&As and greenfield investment might play a role, as FDI flows into some economic activities might be more responsive to regulatory obstacles in their own or the supplying sectors. Furthermore, the relevance of regulatory costs can vary between M&A and greenfield investment due to the difference in their nature, motivation behind the investment and characteristics of the investing firms (Box 3.1).[7]

3.3.2. FDI flows less freely to countries with restrictive services sectors

When looking at the direct impact of barriers to trade and investment within the 22 individual services sectors covered by the STRI, one can observe some important variations in the way FDI responds to the regulatory environment in those sectors. On average, across these sectors, reforms that would allow Portugal to align with the STRI of the Netherlands are predicted to give a boost to the number of foreign M&A deals by 6% and of greenfield projects by 5% (Figure 3.2).[8]

Across the various assessed services, professional services are those from which the impact of reforms streamlining the regulatory environment could be the largest. For consumer protection purposes, professional services have often been somewhat strictly regulated to ensure the quality and optimal provision of these services. In particular, information asymmetries between the average consumer (who typically does not possess technical knowledge on the matter) and suppliers would typically prevent the former from adequately evaluating the quality of such services. Negative externalities have equally been a concern: poorly provided engineering and architectural services, for instance, may put public safety at risk; low-quality legal services can have a negative impact on judicial procedure efficiency, etc. Hence, governments and professional associations have a legitimate interest in regulating such activities to ensure the proper qualification of professionals and the optimal provision of services.

Countries' experience shows, nonetheless, a wide variation in how governments have addressed such risks. Some countries have found equilibrium in balancing such objectives with relatively less restrictive rules, being able to keep some level of competitive pressure on services providers while still protecting consumers and society from the potential problems that could stem from fully unregulated services.

Increasingly so, professional services provide key inputs to business operations. Companies use legal advice and accounting services to enforce contracts and perform financial transactions. Businesses require engineers and architects when setting up new facilities and developing infrastructure projects.

Where excessively stringent, regulatory restrictions on professional services might unnecessarily deter qualified foreign firms and professionals from entering these sectors, contributing potentially to higher services inputs costs for all firms in the economy. The estimated impact of reforms that would allow Portugal's regulatory environment for professional services, as measured by the STRI score, to align with that of more open countries, such as Netherlands, could boost the number of M&As and greenfield projects by 30% and 19%, respectively. In legal services, for instance, such a reduction in the score could be achieved by removing the equity restrictions applying to non-licensed individuals.[9] In engineering and architectural services, this reduction could be achieved, for example, by easing sector-specific licensing requirements for non-EEA nationals and lifting the economy-wide requirement for foreign companies wishing to exercise their activity in Portugal for more than one year to establish a permanent representation in Portugal.[10,11]

Figure 3.2. Estimated change in the number of FDI projects in services sectors

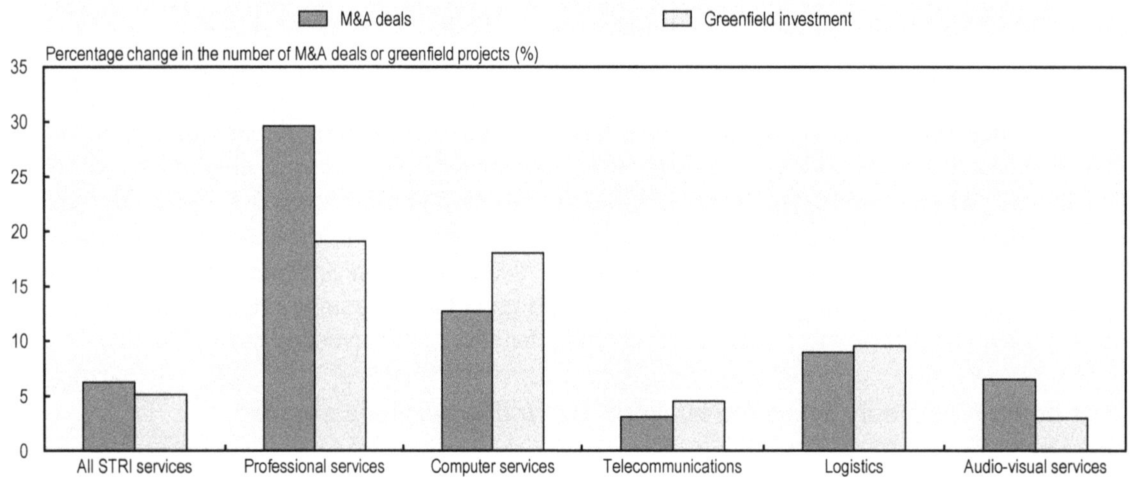

Note: Estimated impact of a reduction in the STRI score in a given services sector from Portugal's current level to the least restrictive level in the EEA. The first two bars ('All STRI services') refer to the results for all services included in the STRI database pooled together. Other bars represent the results for individual sectors. Professional services include accounting and auditing, legal, architectural and engineering services. Only selected statistically significant estimations are reported.
Source: Own elaborations on data from Refinitiv M&A database and Financial Times fDi Markets database.

FDI in computer and telecommunication services is also negatively affected by more restrictive regulatory environments, which may further hinder the uptake of digital technologies and prevent firms from exploiting the potential of digitalisation. The number of cross-border M&As and the number of greenfield projects in computer services is predicted to rise by 13% and 18%, respectively, if Portugal's STRI score in computer services declines from its current level to the lowest level observed in Spain.[12] Telecommunications could attract 3% more cross-border M&A deals and 5% more greenfield projects if Portugal were to lift existing regulatory hurdles so as to align itself with the regulatory framework present in Spain, the country with the lowest STRI score among EU economies. Such a reduction in the score could be achieved, for instance, by removing the horizontal restriction on commercial presence to provide cross-border services.[13]

Well-functioning logistics are essential for delivering intermediate inputs and final products to local and international markets. By supporting the transportation sector, logistics services play a crucial part in operations of firms with a global footprint. Lowering regulatory hurdles in logistics services to match best practice in the EEA (the Netherlands) could attract about 9% more cross-border M&A deals and greenfield projects. The removal of individual licensing requirements to provide warehousing and freight forwarding services could be a step in the direction of narrowing the difference in restrictiveness.

Box 3.1. The cost of regulatory restrictions can differ between M&A and greenfield investors

Entry costs can depend on the mode of entry

Foreign investors' perception of regulatory restrictions might depend on the type of FDI. Firms undertaking cross-border M&As enter the destination country by transferring ownership of existing assets, whereas greenfield investors often set up their operations from scratch or expand their own existing investment projects in the host economy. These modes of entry involve different kinds of costs and investors' capabilities. For instance, lengthy approval processes of construction permits might be more discouraging for foreign firms seeking to establish a new facility abroad, whereas uncertainty around the investment screening mechanisms might have a stronger deterring effect on businesses seeking to undertake a cross-border M&A. Investors who have already established their presence in the country might be less affected by various regulatory costs, as they have already incurred the sunk costs related to entry.

The costs of restrictiveness can depend on investor's motivation

The motivation behind the entry can also influence the relevance of regulatory costs. Foreign investors might be less sensitive to entry barriers when they intend to access a particular market. Market access is a common driver of greenfield investment, which is in line with the findings that greenfield projects are often less sensitive to the destination country's institutional quality and cultural barriers than cross-border M&As (Davies, Desbordes and Ray, 2018[2]). Similarly, the intent to access a specific asset – such as technology or knowledge – might play a role in weakening the relevance of these barriers to some foreign investors. For instance, availability of an attractive target might render regulatory obstacles less important for M&A investors (Hebous, 2011[3]). When access to a market or an asset is not a primary objective, the relevance of regulatory costs might depend on the pool of potential locations: if an investor chooses between a large set of countries, even small regulatory hurdles can tilt the location choice towards a destination with a more efficient regulatory environment.

The burden of regulation can vary depending on firm characteristics

Investors' characteristics might also diminish the importance of some policy obstacles. Larger, more productive firms tend to have more resources to bear the costs of complying with the host country's regulation. They might be also better equipped to pass the regulatory costs on final prices. For instance, Rouzet, Benz and Spinelli (2017[4]) find that companies with larger turnover are less sensitive to regulatory restrictions, whereas Spinelli, Rouzet and Zhang (2020[5]) show that more productive investors are less responsive to measures restricting commercial presence.

The audio-visual sector is another sector where FDI is expected to respond to further liberalisation reforms. Efficient audio-visual services can facilitate creation of digital content and the additional competitive pressure brought by foreign investors can help to spur such environment. The number of cross-border M&As in audio-visual services, for instance, is expected to grow by 7% if Portugal were to implement reforms that would reduce its average STRI score in audio-visual services from the current level to "best practice" in the Czech Republic. The corresponding rise in the number of greenfield projects is 3%. Example of measures contributing to such a difference in the scores are the quota for domestic music in radio broadcasting time and the existence of music creation subsidies for Portuguese work.

No significant relationship between FDI and regulatory restrictions could be consistently established for some other services sectors, such as construction, finance and distribution, suggesting that even if policy conditions in these sectors were to influence investors' location choice, they do so in a non-systematic manner. As even a more granular analysis of narrowly defined economic activities within these sectors reveals no significant association between FDI and regulatory restrictions, it is plausible that differences in the profiles of firms investing in these sectors or in the motives behind the investment projects might mask the effect (see Box 3.1). It is also possible that the applied regulatory regimes in these sectors in the countries assessed are already quite enabling and, thus, do not deter FDI. Regulatory compliance measures, for instance, might be relatively less costly for firms in some of the more capital-intensive activities, such as construction and transport.

3.3.3. Different dimensions of policy hurdles matter

Regulatory restrictions to trade and investment can be grouped into several policy areas that could help identify priorities for reforms and design targeted policy interventions. These groupings can reveal how FDI responds to different types of restrictions.

Barriers to entry and competition are most deterring

Results show that the number of FDI projects is lower in countries with higher barriers to foreign entry, for instance in the form of foreign equity restrictions or limitations on the legal forms of new ventures.[14] Although Portugal maintains one of the lowest levels of restriction to foreign entry within the EEA, reforms that would further reduce its score from the current average level to the lowest level observed in the Netherlands could still lead to a modest growth in the number of FDI projects – a 3% increase in the number of greenfield projects. No significant results were obtained for cross-border M&A deals in this respect.

Barriers to competition appear to have a strong deterring effect on foreign investment. Although Portugal's average score in this domain is relatively low on average across sectors, lifting existing obstacles could raise the number of cross-border M&As by 6% and the number of greenfield projects by over 2%.

Obstacles to ongoing operations supress FDI, as do barriers to all modes of supply

Evidence shows that FDI projects are also sensitive to "behind-the-border" regulation affecting day-to-day business operations, which confirms that in addition to costs associated with the establishment of operations, investors also weigh in the costs of doing business in a location when choosing where to invest.[15] The number of foreign M&As and greenfield projects could go up by 6% and 5% respectively if Portugal's level of restrictiveness associated with "behind-the-border" measures would decrease from its average level across services sectors to the lowest level in the EEA observed in Spain.[16]

In terms of mode of supply,[17] barriers to all modes are negatively associated with the number of FDI projects, highlighting the interdependencies between trade and investment decisions of global firms. Cross-border M&As are expected to rise by 12% and greenfield projects by 7% if restrictions affecting all modes of supply are reduced to the "best practice" level observed in Spain.

FDI responds negatively to both discriminatory and non-discriminatory policies

Discriminatory measures, i.e. measures that raise costs disproportionately for foreign enterprises as defined in the STRI database, are found to act as a more important hurdle to greenfield projects. Achieving the Czech Republic's average level of discriminatory restrictions could lead to a 4% growth in greenfield projects to Portugal. Revisiting equity restrictions applying to not locally licensed providers of accounting and legal services would be a step towards reducing Portugal's level of discriminatory restrictions to the level observed in the Czech Republic.[18]

Cross-border M&As appear, in turn, more sensitive to non-discriminatory obstacles, i.e. measures that raise costs uniformly for domestic and foreign companies. A reduction in Portugal's current level of non-discriminatory barriers to the one observed in the Netherlands, the least restrictive country in the Single Market in this respect, could bring 5% more foreign deals.

3.3.4. Regulatory heterogeneity holds back FDI within the EEA

Whereas continued diversification of the investor base to attract more FDI from outside the Single Market could broaden Portugal's economic opportunities (see Chapter 1), enhancing regulatory co-operation and coherence with EEA countries could further contribute to boosting FDI from investors operating in such markets. Although restrictions on trade and investment within the Single Market are considerably lower than towards third countries, they are still found to negatively affect FDI, being associated with fewer FDI projects from EEA investors. Reducing regulatory hurdles as measured by the intra-EEA STRI score (which accounts for preferential treatment accorded to EEA investors with respect to the applied most-favoured nation regime) from Portugal's average level to the lowest average level observed in the Netherlands could increase the number of cross-border M&A deals from within the Single Market by 15% and of greenfield projects by 11%.

Beyond the absolute degree of restrictiveness of policy barriers, substantial differences in the regulatory framework across countries can also act as a deterring factor to FDI by imposing additional compliance costs for investors present in multiple foreign markets. Evidence shows that foreign firms are less likely to undertake M&As in countries with more dissimilar regulatory environments, as measured by the STRI heterogeneity score, which implies that lack of regulatory co-operation and coherence between countries can be a drag to FDI.[19] In turn, improved regulatory coherence could boost FDI activity.[20] This finding is in line with the substantial number of FDI projects in Portugal originating from Spain and France, which have fairly similar regulatory frameworks. Reducing Portugal's average level of regulatory differences with other countries to the average divergence level of Lithuania, the lowest level observed among the benchmarked economies, could potentially increase the number of cross-border M&A deals by 4% (Figure 3.3).

Figure 3.3. Estimated change in the number of cross-border M&As, regulatory heterogeneity

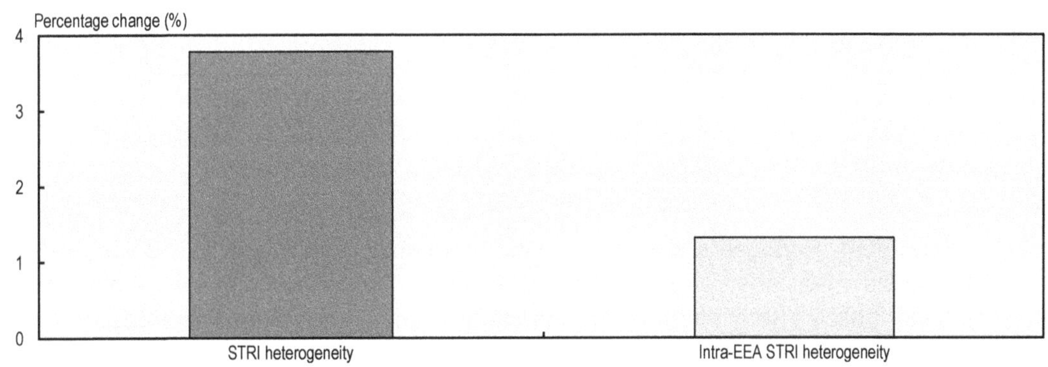

Note: Estimated impact of a reduction in the heterogeneity score in services sectors from Portugal's current average level towards all partner countries to the lowest average level in the EEA.
Source: Own elaborations on data from Refinitiv M&A database.

Similarly, strengthening regulatory coherence with EEA countries can also stimulate further investment from these countries. Although market integration within the Single Market has led to significant regulatory harmonisation among its members, policy regimes can still differ among countries depending on how they transpose EU directives and how they govern policy areas that are not covered at the EU level. The existing regulatory differences are negatively correlated with the number of FDI projects. While Portugal has already transposed most of the Single Market directives, being the Member State with the lowest deficit according to the EU Single Market Scoreboard, it can still benefit from further harmonisation.[21] Reducing regulatory divergence within the Single Market from Portugal's average level to the level observed in Lithuania could lead to an extra 1% in the number of cross-border M&A deals (Figure 3.3).

3.3.5. Less FDI goes to countries with restrictive digital services

With the growing digitisation of information, efficient digital services can be vital for a country's ability to attract FDI in all sectors. The digital transformation enables new types of transactions, helping companies optimise resource management, access new markets and develop novel business models. However, regulatory hurdles inhibiting firms' ability to supply services using electronic networks may present an obstacle to enterprises with a global footprint.

Regulatory restrictions to digital trade, as measured by the Digital STRI (DGSTRI) score, are negatively associated with the number of FDI projects flowing into economies.[22] Implementing reforms that could help lower Portugal's average level of digital restrictiveness under the DGSTRI to the lowest level in Switzerland could raise the number of cross-border M&As by 19% and the number of greenfield projects by over 7% (Figure 3.4). Making online tax registration and declaration available to all non-resident foreign providers and removing commercial presence requirements for cross-border services provider are examples of measures that could help reduce Portugal's digital restrictiveness.[23]

Figure 3.4. Estimated change in the number of FDI projects, digital restrictiveness

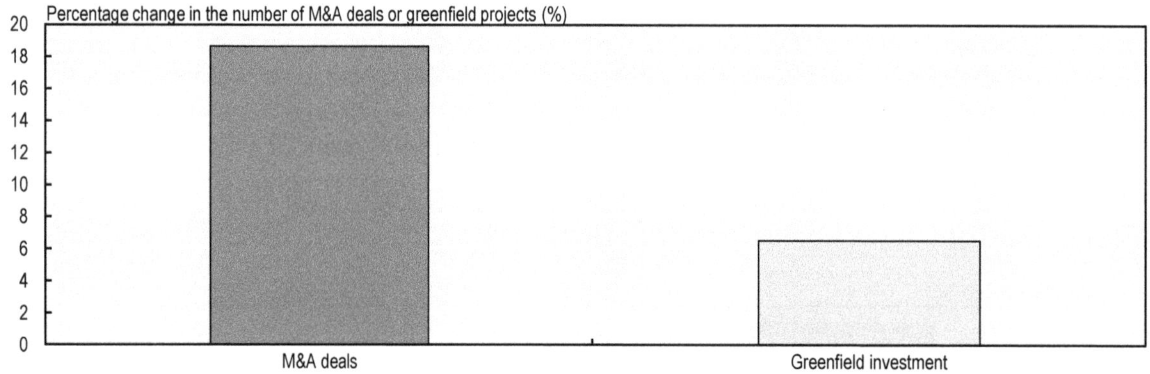

Note: Estimated impact of a reduction in the DGSTRI score from Portugal's current level to the lowest average level in the EEA.
Source: Own elaborations on data from Refinitiv M&A database and Financial Times fDi Markets database.

According to the DGSTRI, Portugal is more restrictive than some of its peers in the area of payment systems (which include measures related to the accessibility of various payment methods and the alignment of security policies with international standards), as it maintains discriminatory access to payment settlement methods. Removing such restrictions associated with payment systems could boost the number of cross-border M&As by nearly 4% and the number of greenfield projects by roughly 1.5%.[24]

3.3.6. Other types of business costs and hurdles for foreign investors

Beyond regulatory barriers and other more structural factors (see Box 3.2), investors' location choices also depend on a range of other factors affecting the cost of doing of business. A few of these factors are assessed below, notably those more directly associated with Portugal's objective to attract investment that can spur further integration into global and regional value chains, taxes and labour regulation.[25]

Box 3.2. Non-regulatory determinants of FDI

Beyond regulatory aspects, other country-level factors can influence FDI flows. Evidence from the transaction-level data confirm that larger countries receive more FDI projects, indicating that market potential attracts FDI.[1] The number of cross-border M&As is also found to decrease the greater is the distance to the host country. Greater distance often entails higher information and transaction costs for foreign investors, which can be particularly dissuading for market-driven investors.

Similarly, sharing a border and an official language typically increases the number of M&As between countries. The importance of these two factors is consistent with the idea that common background facilitates cross-border investment, as a common border and language often indicate strong historical and cultural ties between the economies. Foreign M&As are also more likely between countries within the Single Market, suggesting that economic integration encourages investment flows. These findings confirm the key results of the literature examining the determinants of FDI (e.g. di Giovanni (2005[6]), Hijzen et al. (2008[7]), de Sousa and Lochard (2011[8]) and Bloningen and Piger (2014[9])).

[1] These results are reported in Annex Table 3.B.2 and Annex Table 3.B.3.

Evidence shows that countries that perform better in trade logistics infrastructure tend to attract more cross-border M&A deals in manufacturing sectors, for instance, which underlines the overall importance of trade activities for many of such firms, be it for intra-and-extra firm input trade or simply final product exports. According to the latest World Bank Logistics Performance Index (LPI) (2018[10]), which assesses the overall efficiency of customs, the ease of arranging shipments and the quality of logistics services and transport infrastructure, Portugal ranked 23rd out of 160 economies in the world. Despite Portugal's overall good performance, implementing reforms that would allow it to move further up to Spain's 17th place could boost the number of cross-border M&A deals in manufacturing by 6%.[26] Improving logistics efficiency to match the score in best-performing Germany could lead to a 19% rise in cross-border activity in the sector. While Portugal's logistic performance may have already evolved since the release of the latest LPI in 2018, the estimated result gives an idea of the magnitude of the impact that reforms in this area can have on foreign investment activity.

Interestingly, for greenfield projects, efficiency of logistics matters only for the distribution sector, likely reflecting the importance of well-functioning logistical services for the sector's principal activities. Reforms that would place Portugal in the top LPI position could bring as much as 27% more announced greenfield projects in the distribution sector. The insignificant result for other sectors is likely driven by a combination of factors described in Box 3.1.

Similarly to the findings above, the evidence also suggests that more cross-border M&As take place in countries with efficient ports. According to the latest Quality of Port Infrastructure index (2017-18), which measures business executives' perception of their country's port facilities, Portugal was ranked 25th (WEF, 2018[11]). Moving up in the ranking to reach Estonia's eleventh position was estimated to potentially lead to a 4% increase in cross-border M&A activity. Raising the quality of port infrastructure to reach the leading place in the ranking held by the Netherlands could potentially boost foreign M&A deals by 19%. While based in 2017-18 data, these results point to the potentially significant impacts that improvements in seaport services and infrastructure can have on foreign investment activity in Portugal.

Entry costs, as measured by the number of procedures required to register a business (World Bank, 2019[12]), may represent a barrier for new investment if procedures are excessive and complex. Similarly, burdensome construction-related procedures may add to investors' entry and expansion costs. Albeit limited in scope, these measures can also sometimes be seen as partly indicative of the overall efficiency of the public bureaucracy in dealing with businesses, as entry requirements and permit procedures often rank high in most investment climate reform efforts.

In this assessment, entry costs are found to play a particularly significant role for the number of greenfield projects in information and communication technologies (ICT) and professional services, possibly because the relatively low capital intensity of many firms in these sectors (e.g. software and information technology consultancy firms, law firms, accounting and auditing firms) makes them less dependent on geographical aspects of host countries (than, for instance, firms in energy or heavy manufacturing sectors) and possibly more susceptible to red tape.[27] The predicted growth in the number of greenfield projects in these sectors is 11% in ICT and 12% in professional services if Portugal were to halve the number of procedures required (6 in 2019) to the level in Estonia and Slovenia (3).

Interestingly, the number of cross-border M&As is also negatively associated with entry costs even if, in principle, foreign M&A investors are not subject to such measures, which seems to support the idea that such measures capture more than just entry costs and tend to somewhat also reflect countries' overall level of business red tape. In this respect, implementing reforms that would allow for a reduction in business red tape in a manner correlated with the halving of the number of procedures, as mentioned above, could generate 14% more cross-border M&As. Similarly, the time needed to complete all required procedures for obtaining a permit for building a simple commercial warehouse is also found to be negatively associated with the number of FDI projects (both greenfield and M&A) a country receives.

Corporate taxes can sometimes be seen as a cost for businesses, especially when investors consider it to be incommensurable with the offer and quality of existing public services. This has been somewhat a concern for businesses in Portugal (INE, 2022[13]). But where taxes contribute to financing good quality public services that are critical for a healthy business environment, such as education and infrastructure, they should matter less (Bénassy-Quéré, Fontagné and Lahrèche-Révil, 2005[14]).

In this assessment, statutory corporate income tax (CIT) rates are not found to affect foreign investors' location choices in a statistically significant manner. Besides being partly related to the quality of public services, as mentioned above, the result might be explained by the fact that they do not reflect the real expected tax burden on business. This is better revealed in the effective average tax rate (EATR), which is found to be negatively associated with the number of cross-border M&A deals a country receives.[28] Labour tax and contributions paid by companies are also negatively associated with both the number of greenfield and cross-border M&A projects. These results show that keeping corporate taxes relatively low is likely relevant for attracting FDI, but a truly competitive tax system needs to take into consideration tax distributional effects and tax administration burdens.

Stringent employment protection legislation (EPL) has also been reported by investors to be an obstacle for conducting business in Portugal (see Chapter 4). While stricter rules may potentially raise labour adjustment costs for firms, they are central for productivity growth and social equity, including by providing incentives for firms and workers to invest in long-term training and by ensuring that the social costs associated with unemployment are partly shared by economic actors. In this report, the OECD's EPL indicator is found to be negatively associated with greenfield FDI, meaning that on average more stringent regimes contribute to deter FDI.[29] Striking the right balance between job protection and labour market flexibility is therefore critical to keep an attractive environment for FDI.

3.4. Conclusion

This chapter has provided evidence on the potential impact that liberalising reforms could have on foreign investment in Portugal. Several possible reform scenarios were derived from actual regulatory practices applied in some of Portugal's peer economies or in EEA countries and their potential impact was estimated using transaction-level data on cross-border M&As and foreign greenfield investment into 48 countries between 2012 and 2022. Other countries' policy experiences show that alternative regulatory approaches are sometimes possible and can be effective in addressing public interests.

As mentioned in the introduction, regulatory liberalisation is not an end in itself. Countries have legitimate concerns when choosing to regulate business activities, and the most suitable regulatory framework for a country is likely one that adequately captures its own political and economic context. The extent to which the simulated regulatory regimes are suitable to Portugal is thus an assessment that the Government of Portugal is best placed to undertake. This chapter can only support such an exercise by providing evidence on the expected impact of potential liberalising reforms. The analysis, however, does not consider any social-political-economic particularities of the Portuguese economy. Knowledge about potential gains in FDI may represent only part of the information needed to adequately assess the suitability of a regulatory reform in a specific context, but it is a critical one to sustain informed policy making and discussions.

There may also be other complementary issues not captured in the above indicators that might be affecting the degree of restrictiveness of the regulatory framework. Implementation aspects, such as the transparency and predictability of rules and decision making processes, can influence compliance costs and weigh on investment attraction and retention as well. The next chapter seeks precisely to complement this rules-based empirical assessment by investigating how Portugal's regulatory framework is perceived by foreign investors, which allows for broader considerations of the context and the manner with which measures are implanted.

References

Bénassy-Quéré, A., L. Fontagné and A. Lahrèche-Révil (2005), "How Does FDI React to Corporate Taxation?", *International Tax and Public Finance* 12, pp. 583-603, https://doi.org/10.1007/s10797-005-2652-4. [14]

Blonigen, B. and J. Piger (2014), "Determinants of foreign direct investment", *Canadian Journal of Economics/Revue canadienne d'économique*, Vol. 47/3, pp. 775-812, https://doi.org/10.1111/caje.12091. [9]

Davies, R., R. Desbordes and A. Ray (2018), "Greenfield versus merger and acquisition FDI: Same wine, different bottles?", *Canadian Journal of Economics*, Vol. 51/4, pp. 1151–1190, https://doi.org/10.1111/caje.12353. [2]

de Sousa, J. and J. Lochard (2011), "Does the Single Currency Affect Foreign Direct Investment?", *The Scandinavian Journal of Economics*, Vol. 113/3, pp. 553-578, https://doi.org/10.1111/J.1467-9442.2011.01656.X. [8]

di Giovanni, J. (2005), "What drives capital flows? The case of cross-border M&A activity and financial deepening", *Journal of International Economics*, Vol. 65/1, pp. 127-149, https://doi.org/10.1016/j.jinteco.2003.11.007. [6]

Geloso Grosso, M. et al. (2015), "Services Trade Restrictiveness Index (STRI): Scoring and Weighting Methodology", *OECD Trade Policy Papers* No. 177, https://doi.org/10.1787/5js7n8wbtk9r-en. [18]

Hebous, S. (2011), "The effects of taxation on the location decision of multinational firms: M&a vs. greenfield investments", *National Tax Journal*, Vol. 64/3, pp. 817-838. [3]

Herger, N., C. Kotsogiannis and S. McCorriston (2016), "Multiple taxes and alternative forms of FDI: evidence from cross-border acquisitions", *International Tax and Public Finance*, Vol. 23/1, pp. 82-113, https://doi.org/10.1007/S10797-015-9351-6. [15]

Hijzen, A., H. Görg and M. Manchin (2008), "Cross-border mergers and acquisitions and the role of trade costs", *European Economic Review*, Vol. 52/5, pp. 849-866, https://doi.org/10.1016/j.euroecorev.2007.07.002. [7]

INE (2022), *Inquérito aos Custos de Contexto 2021*, https://www.ine.pt/xportal/xmain?xpid=INE&xpgid=ine_destaques&DESTAQUESdest_boui=540898022&DESTAQUESmodo=2. [13]

Nocke, V. and S. Yeaple (2007), "Cross-border mergers and acquisitions vs. greenfield", *Journal of International Economics* 72, pp. 336-365, https://doi.org/10.1016/j.jinteco.2006.09.003. [19]

Nordås, H. (2016), "Services Trade Restrictiveness Index (STRI): The Trade Effect of Regulatory Differences", *OECD Trade Policy Papers*, No. 189, OECD Publishing, Paris, https://doi.org/10.1787/5jlz9z022plp-en. [17]

OECD (2018), "Trade and investment interdependencies in global value chains: Insights from new OECD analysis", *COM/DAF/INV/TAD/TC(2018)1*. [16]

OECD (2015), *Policy Framework for Investment, 2015 Edition*, OECD Publishing, Paris, https://doi.org/10.1787/9789264208667-en. [1]

Rouzet, D., S. Benz and F. Spinelli (2017), "Trading firms and trading costs in services: Firm-level analysis", *OECD Trade Policy Papers*, No. 210, OECD Publishing, Paris, https://doi.org/10.1787/b1c1a0e9-en. [4]

Spinelli, F., D. Rouzet and H. Zhang (2020), "Networks of Foreign Affiliates: Evidence from Japanese Micro-Data", *The World Economy*, p. twec.12963, https://doi.org/10.1111/twec.12963. [5]

WEF (2018), *The Global Competitiveness Report 2017-2018*, World Economic Forum, https://www3.weforum.org/docs/GCR2017-2018/05FullReport/TheGlobalCompetitivenessReport2017%E2%80%932018.pdf. [11]

World Bank (2019), *Start-up procedures to register a business*, https://data.worldbank.org/indicator/IC.REG.PROC. [12]

World Bank (2018), *International Logistics Performance Index*, https://lpi.worldbank.org/about. [10]

Annex 3.A. Methodology

The econometric analysis estimates the effect of regulatory obstacles on foreign investment into 48 economies, including Portugal. For cross-border M&As, the estimation approach builds on the gravity model, which has a strong explanatory power in the context of international investment and trade flows.[30] As required by the gravity framework, where no cross-border M&A deal from an investing country has been recorded in the database for a given destination country-sector in a given year, it is assumed that no investment has occurred and zero deals are thus imputed to such home-destination country-sector pair, provided that the investing country has engaged in at least one cross-border transaction in the same sector. As the greenfield project data used in this assessment were not suitable to gravity analysis, the related regressions exploit only sectoral and country-level information of the destination countries.

A count model is used to estimate the number of investment projects that were to be expected in a given country and sector at a given point in time, as this model is well suited to deal with the underlying data and its suitability for the analysis of FDI determinants has been confirmed by several studies (see, for instance, Hijzen et al. (2008[7]), Herger et al. (2016[15]) and Bloningen and Piger (2014[9])). First, a common issue in the empirical analysis of M&A, a large share of deal values is undisclosed, which increases the number of missing values. The imputation of zero investment flows required by the gravity framework aggravates this problem. While this limitation of M&A data decreases the explanatory power of models based on investment values, count models tend to have a good fit to data as they exploit the number of deals instead of values. Secondly, for greenfield projects, a large portion of capital values are estimated by the data provider, which might result in some measurement error. Since count models do not take investment values into account, this shortcoming of greenfield data does not affect the analysis either.

A negative binomial regression is used to model FDI counts, as this model is well suited for the over-dispersion observed in the data, i.e. the sample variance of count data greatly exceeds the sample mean. The model is specified as follows:

$$n_{ijklt} = \beta_o + \beta_1 X_{jlt} + \beta_2 Y_{kt} + \beta_3 Z_{lt} + \beta_4 G_{klt} + \delta_i + \theta_j + \mu_k + \tau_t + \varepsilon_{oct}^s$$

where n_{ijklt} is the number of cross-border FDI projects undertaken by investors coming from industry *i* in country *k* with the investment project taking place in industry *j* in country *l* at time *t*. X_{jlt} is a vector of host country regulatory variables, as measured by the various indices. Y_{kt} and Z_{lt} measure market size of the origin and host economies, measured by their GDP. G_{klt} includes bilateral variables (the distance between the two countries; binary variables for whether the two countries have a common border, share a common language, belong to the EEA). The model includes source-industry (δ_i) and destination-industry (θ_j) fixed effects to control for time-invariant properties of sectors; source-country (μ_k) fixed effects account for time-invariant characteristics of investor's countries; time fixed effects τ_t are included to control for global economic trends. For greenfield specifications, only the control variables describing the host country and sector are retained (i.e. those indexed by *j*, *l* and *t*). As the key objective of the empirical analysis is to estimate the effects of country and sector-specific policy measures with no or little variation over time, host-country fixed effects are not included in this specification. By controlling for known determinants of FDI, this estimation strategy gives good estimates of the correlation between investment and the policy measures of interest, but cannot ensure that the correlation implies a causal relationship.

Marginal effects are used to report the predicted change in the number of inward FDI projects in response to a given change in the policy variables. These effects are calculated from the fitted model, where all control variables are at their mean level and two levels of the policy variable are considered – Portugal's average level and best practice in the EEA.

Annex 3.B. Supplementary tables

Annex Table 3.B.1. Definition of variables and data sources

Variable	Definition	Source
Ln(Distance)	Distance between capitals in km, expressed in logarithms.	CEPII Gravity
Ln(GDP, origin), Ln(GDP, host)	GDP of origin and host countries in current USD, million; expressed in logs. The variables are used as a proxy for the market size. Estimates for the year 2022 were included in the estimations involving the policy variables available for that year.	IMF, World Economic Outlook (WEO), October 2022
Common border	Binary variable taking a value of 1 if the origin and host countries share a common border.	CEPII Gravity
Common language	Binary variable taking a value of 1 if the origin and host countries share an official language.	CEPII Gravity
EEA	Binary variable taking a value of 1 if the origin and host countries belong to the European Economic Area.	OECD STRI Regulatory Database
STRI	The OECD Services Trade Restrictiveness Index measures regulatory restrictions to services trade and investment in 22 services sectors. The indices take values between zero (a sector is completely open to trade and investment) and one (a sector is completely closed to foreign services providers). The STRI score for all sectors is calculated as a geometric weighted average of the sector-specific STRI indices, with sectoral weights derived from the OECD Trade in Value-Added database. The indices are available for 2014-22.	OECD STRI Regulatory Database
STRI heterogeneity	The OECD STRI heterogeneity indices measure regulatory heterogeneity between countries on sectoral level. For each country-sector pair, the indices capture the share of measures for which the two countries have dissimilar regulation. The indices take values between zero (same regulatory measures) to one (completely different regulation) and come in two versions: one based on the qualitative answers in the STRI database (Heterogeneity Answer), the other on the scores (Heterogeneity Score). The indices are available for 2014-22.	OECD STRI Regulatory Database
Intra-EEA STRI	The OECD Intra-EEA Services Trade Restrictiveness Index covers policy measures that restrict trade and investment within the EEA. The indices take values between zero and one, where a higher value represents a sector with more restrictive barriers to services trade and investment. The indices are available for 2014-22.	OECD Intra-EEA STRI Regulatory Database
Intra-EEA STRI heterogeneity	Intra-EEA STRI heterogeneity indices measure regulatory heterogeneity within the EEA. For each country-sector pair, the indices reflect the share of measures for which the two countries have different regulation. The indices are available for 2014-22.	OECD STRI Regulatory Database
DGSTRI	The OECD Digital Services Trade Restrictiveness Index measures barriers to services traded digitally. The indices take values between zero (an economy with a regulatory framework completely open to digitally enabled services) and one (an economy closed to digital trade). The indices are available for 2014-22.	OECD DGSTRI Regulatory Database
Logistics Performance Index (LPI)	The index measures the overall quality of trade-related infrastructure and procedures (customs performance, simplicity of arranging and tracking shipments, timeliness of shipments, quality of logistics services and transport infrastructure, etc.). The values range from 1 to 5, with a higher score indicating greater efficiency. The measure is available for 2012-18.	World Bank, Logistic Performance Indicators
Quality of Port Infrastructure	The Quality of Port Infrastructure reflects business executives' perception of their country's port facilities. The values range from 1 to 7, with a higher score representing more efficient infrastructure. The measure is available for 2012-17.	World Economic Forum
Costs of entry and to obtain construction-related permits	The number of procedures to register a business. The covered procedures include those required to set up a business, such as interactions to obtain necessary permits and licenses and to complete all documents to begin operations. The measure is available for 2012-19. Time required to build a warehouse is measured as the number of calendar days needed to complete the required procedures for building a warehouse. If a procedure can be speeded up at additional cost, the fastest procedure, independent of cost, is chosen. The measure is available for 2012-19.	World Bank, Doing Business
Tax measures	Corporate Income Tax (CIT) refers to the combined central and sub-central (statutory) statutory CIT measured as the central government rate (less deductions for sub-national taxes) plus the sub-central rate. The measure is available for 2012-22. EATR refers to the forward-looking effective tax rate impinging on a profit-making investment project when a set of base tax provisions, beyond the CIT rate, are considered (e.g. capital	OECD, Corporate Tax Statistics OECD, Corporate Tax Statistics World Bank, Doing

Variable	Definition	Source
	allowances, inventory valuation methods, etc.). Country-specific real interest and inflation rates are used. The measure is available for 2017-21. Labor tax and contributions refers to the amount of taxes and mandatory contributions on labour paid by businesses. It is measured as a percentage of a company's commercial profits. The measure is available for 2012-19.	Business
Employment Protection Legislation (EPL)	EPL indicators reflect the strictness of regulation on individual and collective dismissals of workers under regular contracts. For each year, indicators refer to regulation in force on the 1st of January. Version 4 of the indicator is used. The measure is available for 2013-19.	OECD, Employment Protection Indicators

Source: Based on CEPII, OECD, World Economic Forum and World Bank databases.

Annex Table 3.B.2. Regulatory hurdles and cross-border M&As

	All sectors	Services sectors	Professional services	Computer services	Telecommunications	Logistics	Audio-visual services
STRI, level	-3.130***	-1.533***	-1.535***	-4.502***	-2.066***	-1.361**	-3.096***
	(0.620)	(0.413)	(0.363)	(0.660)	(0.514)	(0.611)	(0.573)
Ln(GDP_d)	0.644***	0.603***	0.685***	0.649***	0.432***	0.587***	0.664***
	(0.033)	(0.034)	(0.041)	(0.038)	(0.042)	(0.040)	(0.052)
Ln(GDP_o)	0.052	0.141	0.118	0.092	0.118	0.101	0.260
	(0.112)	(0.151)	(0.356)	(0.288)	(0.623)	(0.514)	(0.583)
Ln(Distance)	-0.286***	-0.344***	-0.192**	-0.278***	-0.369***	-0.374***	-0.275**
	(0.078)	(0.083)	(0.088)	(0.089)	(0.111)	(0.085)	(0.121)
Common border	0.466***	0.427**	0.283	0.389*	0.687***	0.586***	0.154
	(0.160)	(0.177)	(0.200)	(0.207)	(0.199)	(0.194)	(0.264)
Common language	1.046***	1.161***	1.264***	1.235***	1.100***	0.815***	1.330***
	(0.102)	(0.114)	(0.147)	(0.118)	(0.131)	(0.149)	(0.178)
EEA	0.303**	0.305*	0.687***	0.412**	-0.203	0.316*	0.520*
	(0.154)	(0.173)	(0.176)	(0.161)	(0.305)	(0.191)	(0.302)
Observations	2 009 472	558 336	71 237	121 401	27 458	42 675	32 305
Likelihood-ratio test	1.138***	1.062***	0.490	0.650***	0.759*	0.778***	0.379
	(0.160)	(0.174)	(0.301)	(0.178)	(0.449)	(0.277)	(0.383)
Pseudo R-squared	0.161	0.160	0.179	0.206	0.138	0.155	0.170

Note: The table reports estimated coefficients from the negative binomial regressions. The dependent variable is a number of cross-border M&A. In the specification in the first column, the STRI for all sectors is used. All specifications include a constant, source-country, source-industry, destination-industry and year fixed effects. Robust standard errors are reported in the parentheses. ***, ** and * denote statistical significance at 1%, 5% and 10% levels respectively. The period of analysis is from 2014 to 2022.
Source: Own elaborations on data from Refinitiv M&A database.

Annex Table 3.B.3. Regulatory hurdles and greenfield investment

	All sectors	Services sectors	Professional services	Computer services	Telecommunications	Logistics	Audio-visual services
STRI, level	-1.590***	-1.268***	-1.033***	-6.231***	-3.008***	-1.446***	-1.432***
	(0.113)	(0.357)	(0.206)	(0.668)	(0.340)	(0.031)	(0.483)
Ln(GDP_d)	0.489***	0.449***	0.515***	0.489***	0.445***	0.524***	0.395***
	(0.006)	(0.028)	(0.045)	(0.033)	(0.024)	(0.046)	(0.137)
Observations	14 164	3 971	538	697	342	424	296
Likelihood-ratio test	-0.863***	-0.689***	-0.983***	-0.433***	-1.814***	-0.836***	-2.246***
	(0.020)	(0.158)	(0.082)	(0.069)	(0.188)	(0.046)	(0.272)

	All sectors	Services sectors	Professional services	Computer services	Telecommunications	Logistics	Audio-visual services
Pseudo R-squared	0.167	0.122	0.118	0.094	0.151	0.122	0.125

Note: The table reports estimated coefficients from the negative binomial regressions. The dependent variable is a number of greenfield investment projects. In the specification in the first column, the STRI for all sectors is used. All specifications include a constant, destination-industry and year fixed effects. Robust standard errors are reported in the parentheses. ***, ** and * denote statistical significance at 1%, 5% and 10% levels respectively. The period of analysis is from 2014 to 2022.
Source: Own elaborations on data from Financial Times fDi Markets database.

Annex Table 3.B.4. Regulatory hurdles (by types) and cross-border M&As

	(1)	(2)	(3)	(4)	(5)
STRI, Restrictions on foreign entry	-0.419				
	(0.563)				
STRI, Restrictions to movement of people	0.644				
	(1.350)				
STRI, Other discriminatory measures	-8.435***				
	(2.574)				
STRI, Barriers to competition	-3.167***				
	(0.838)				
STRI, Regulatory transparency	-6.155***				
	(1.378)				
STRI, Mode 1		-4.734**			
		(2.206)			
STRI, Mode 3		0.363			
		(0.574)			
STRI, Mode 4		0.936			
		(1.535)			
STRI, All modes		-4.850***			
		(0.996)			
STRI, DR & other			-4.080***		
			(1.076)		
STRI, MA & NT			-0.088		
			(0.406)		
STRI, Establishment				-0.666	
				(0.661)	
STRI, Operations				-2.350***	
				(0.718)	
STRI, Discriminatory					-0.510
					(0.485)
STRI, Non-discriminatory					-3.182***
					(1.100)
Observations	558 336	508 806	526 031	558 336	526 031
Likelihood-ratio test	1.046***	1.063***	1.069***	1.062***	1.071***
	(0.173)	(0.170)	(0.174)	(0.173)	(0.173)
Pseudo R-squared	0.161	0.163	0.161	0.160	0.161

Note: The table reports estimated coefficients from the negative binomial regressions. The dependent variable is a number of cross-border M&A. All control variables reported in Annex Table 3.B.2 are also included in these regressions, but not displayed for brevity. All specifications include a constant, source-country, source-industry, destination-industry and year fixed effects. Robust standard errors are reported in the parentheses. ***, ** and * denote statistical significance at 1%, 5% and 10% levels respectively. The period of analysis is from 2014 to 2022.
Source: Own elaborations on data from Refinitiv M&A database.

Annex Table 3.B.5. Regulatory hurdles (by types) and greenfield investment

	(1)	(2)	(3)	(4)	(5)
STRI, Restrictions on foreign entry	-0.877*				
	(0.468)				
STRI, Restrictions to movement of people	0.588				
	(2.247)				
STRI, Other discriminatory measures	-8.521***				
	(2.539)				
STRI, Barriers to competition	-2.874***				
	(0.776)				
STRI, Regulatory transparency	2.798				
	(1.901)				
STRI, Mode 1		-4.872			
		(3.055)			
STRI, Mode 3		-0.493			
		(0.573)			
STRI, Mode 4		-0.101			
		(1.422)			
STRI, All modes		-2.923**			
		(1.395)			
STRI, DR & other			-2.592***		
			(0.571)		
STRI, MA & NT			-0.793		
			(0.539)		
STRI, Establishment				-0.793	
				(0.649)	
STRI, Operations				-1.947***	
				(0.437)	
STRI, Discriminatory					-1.072**
					(0.515)
STRI, Non-discriminatory					-1.975**
					(0.820)
Observations	3 971	3 455	3 675	3 971	3 675
Likelihood-ratio test	-0.724***	-0.633***	-0.657***	-0.692***	-0.655***
	(0.159)	(0.155)	(0.156)	(0.158)	(0.154)
Pseudo R-squared	0.125	0.112	0.116	0.122	0.116

Note: The table reports estimated coefficients from the negative binomial regressions. The dependent variable is a number of greenfield investment projects. All specifications include a constant, destination-industry and year fixed effects and a logarithm of GDP of the destination country. Robust standard errors are reported in the parentheses. ***, ** and * denote statistical significance at 1%, 5% and 10% levels respectively. The period of analysis is from 2014 to 2022.
Source: Own elaborations on data from Financial Times fDi Markets database.

Annex Table 3.B.6. Regulatory heterogeneity and FDI

	MA	GI	MA	MA
Intra EEA STRI, level	-9.492***	-6.825*		-7.058***
	(2.128)	(3.788)		(1.903)
STRI, level			-1.333***	

			(0.507)	
STRI, Heterogeneity Score			-1.379***	
			(0.464)	
Intra-EEA STRI, Heterogeneity Score				-4.194**
				(1.700)
Observations	136 432	1 960	484 058	117 156
Likelihood-ratio test	0.654***	-0.799***	0.768***	0.464***
	(0.155)	(0.196)	(0.131)	(0.154)
Pseudo R-squared	0.120	0.138	0.177	0.135

Note: The table reports estimated coefficients from the negative binomial regressions. The dependent variable is a number of FDI projects, the type of FDI is reported in the column name. The control variables and fixed effects are as in Annex Table 3.B.2-Annex Table 3.B.3. Robust standard errors are reported in the parentheses. ***, ** and * denote statistical significance at 1%, 5% and 10% levels respectively. The period of analysis is from 2014 to 2022.
Source: Own elaborations on data from Refinitiv M&A database and Financial Times fDi Markets database.

Annex Table 3.B.7. Restrictions to digital services and FDI

	MA	GI
Digital STRI	-2.030***	-0.755***
	(0.401)	(0.204)
Observations	2 005 305	14 164
Likelihood-ratio test	1.201***	-0.846***
	(0.132)	(0.075)
Pseudo R-squared	0.152	0.165

Note: The table reports estimated coefficients from the negative binomial regressions. The dependent variable is a number of FDI projects, the type of FDI is reported in the column name. The control variables and fixed effects are as in Annex Table 3.B.2-Annex Table 3.B.3. Robust standard errors are reported in the parentheses. ***, ** and * denote statistical significance at 1%, 5% and 10% levels respectively. The period of analysis is from 2014 to 2022.
Source: Own elaborations on data from Refinitiv M&A database and Financial Times fDi Markets database.

Annex Table 3.B.8. Other types of business costs and FDI

	MA, manuf.	GI, distribution	MA	MA	GI, Prof. Services & ICT)	MA	GI	MA	GI	MA	GI	MA	GI	GI
LPI	0.304*	0.424***												
	(0.158)	(0.032)												
Quality of Port Infrastructure			0.109**											
			(0.049)											
No. procedures to start a business				-0.044***	-0.036***									
				(0.012)	(0.010)									
Time required to build a warehouse						-0.001**	-0.001***							
						(0.001)	(0.000)							
CIT rate								-0.005	-0.002					
								(0.006)	(0.002)					
Labor tax and contributions										-0.006*	-0.002**			
										(0.003)	(0.001)			
EATR												-0.011*	-0.003	
												(0.006)	(0.003)	
EPL														-0.092**
														(0.036)
Observations	292 098	141	1 271 616	1 698 480	2 903	1 698 480	12 439	2 331,158	17 006	1 698 480	12 439	1 050 505	7 517	8 613
Likelihood-ratio test	0.679***	-1.111***	1.155***	1.121***	-0.902***	1.121***	-0.961***	1.184***	-0.861***	1.127***	-0.947***	1.095***	-0.826***	-0.902***
	(0.205)	(0.098)	(0.181)	(0.162)	(0.127)	(0.168)	(0.073)	(0.156)	(0.072)	(0.167)	(0.072)	(0.153)	(0.077)	(0.082)
Pseudo R-squared	0.163	0.122	0.152	0.155	0.185	0.154	0.175	0.153	0.165	0.154	0.173	0.161	0.164	0.175

Note: The table reports estimated coefficients from the negative binomial regressions. The dependent variable is a number of FDI projects, the type of FDI is reported in the column name. The control variables and fixed effects are as in Annex Table 3.B.2-Annex Table 3.B.3. Robust standard errors are reported in the parentheses. ***, ** and * denote statistical significance at 1%, 5% and 10% levels respectively.
Source: Own elaborations on data from Refinitiv M&A database and Financial Times fDi Markets database. The period of analysis varies depending on the availability of the independent variables (see Annex Table 3.B.1 for such information).

Notes

[1] Potential benefits and costs to upstream and downstream sectors and end consumers should also be considered. Such a broader cost-benefit assessment of specific measures of the regulatory framework lies beyond the scope of this chapter.

[2] The time coverage differs across policy measures. The countries include Australia, Austria, Belgium, Brazil, Canada, Chile, the People's Republic of China, Colombia, Costa Rica, the Czech Republic, Denmark, Estonia, Finland, France, Germany, Greece, Hungary, Iceland, India, Indonesia, Ireland, Israel, Italy, Japan, Kazakhstan, Korea, Latvia, Lithuania, Luxembourg, Malaysia, Mexico, the Netherlands, New Zealand, Norway, Peru, Poland, Portugal, Russian Federation, the Slovak Republic, Slovenia, South Africa, Spain, Sweden, Switzerland, Thailand, Turkey, the United Kingdom, the United States.

[3] Throughout this chapter, a number of concrete policy reform examples are used to illustrate the types of regulatory changes that could correspond to the simulated policy reform scenarios (based on the STRI framework) used in the empirical estimations. The examples should not be interpreted as being directly associated with the estimated impacts. For methodological reasons, the various measures within a policy domain in a sector are treated equivalently within the STRI framework. In practice, however, their "real" degree of restrictiveness might differ. Hence, two different reforms having the same impact on the STRI score should not necessarily be expected to impact FDI in a similar manner. Potential social, political and economic costs associated with the implementation of reforms leading to a reduction in restrictiveness may also differ depending on the existing policy landscape and are not incorporated in the analysis.

[4] Although information on the investors' origin was available in the greenfield dataset specific to Portugal and used in Chapter 1, due to contractual limitations, the OECD could not retrieve data of similar granularity for a larger set of countries required for the econometric analysis.

[5] The results are reported in Tables 2-3 in Annex 3.B.

[6] Potential policy reforms and their impact on Portugal's STRI scores at the sectoral level can be simulated via the STRI Simulator web tool. https://sim.oecd.org/. Throughout this chapter, examples of possible reforms identified via the STRI simulator are used to simulate the potential impact of reforms on investment based on the estimations obtained in the regression analysis. The examples are only illustrative of a possible reform based on existing regulatory practice in peer economies. It might not necessarily be adequate in the Portuguese context.

[7] Furthermore, as explained in Section 3.2, the discrepancies in the estimates might be driven by the differences in the estimation models. In addition, properties of the underlying data might play a role. More specifically, both M&A and greenfield databases cover completed FDI projects, but the greenfield dataset also includes projects that were announced (i.e. projects that might have not been realised or that have been realised later) and the two types of projects cannot be distinguished in the greenfield data.

[8] The results are reported in Tables 2-3 in Annex 3.B.

[9] See Law No. 145/2015 approving the Statute of the Portuguese Bar Association (Art. 213).

[10] See Law No. 119/92 on the Statute for Portuguese Engineers (Art. 13), Law No. 2/2013 on the Statute for Portuguese Technical Engineers (Art. 12), and Regulation 350/2016 on the Registration with the Portuguese Order of Architects and Traineeship (Article 4 and Annex II).

[11] Several other existing regulatory requirements also affect the movement of foreign professionals to Portugal for the provision of such services, affecting "Mode 4" of international supply of such services. While Portugal does not impose quotas nor labour market tests for foreign contractual services suppliers and independent service suppliers to provide accounting and auditing services in Portugal, it imposes several other residency, stay and qualifications requirements for foreign professionals to be able to supply such services in Portugal. See Chapter 2 for more information.

[12] Reducing the number of documents needed to obtain a business (visitor) visa and the required processing time to below eight documents and ten working days, for instance, could help approach the compared restrictiveness level (see the OECD STRI Regulatory Database for more information). The referred visa requirement applies in the case of standard business visitors entering Portugal for short-term business assignments. Other schemes, with varying requirements and eligibility criteria, apply to foreign entrepreneurs and employees aiming at establishing and permanently working in Portugal, respectively (see Chapter 2, Section 2.2.2. for more information on relevant visa and residence programmes).

[13] See Decree-Law No. 262/1986 on the Companies Code (Article 4).

[14] The results for this section are reported in Tables 4-5 in Annex 3.B.

[15] A wide range of measures are classified as operational regulatory hurdles (e.g. nationality requirements for directors and managers, quotas and labour market test for intra-corporate transferees, restrictions on the participation of foreign suppliers in public procurement, among others). See the OECD STRI methodology for further information (Geloso Grosso et al., 2015[18]).

[16] Speeding up visa processing times is an example of a measure that could reduce regulatory restrictiveness to ongoing operations (see the OECD STRI Regulatory Database for more information).

[17] Services can be supplied internationally in four different ways known as "modes of supply" following the definition adopted in the General Agreement on Trade in Services: 1) cross-border trade, where a service is provided from one territory to another; 2) consumption abroad, where a service is provided in the territory of the supplier to a consumer who has moved abroad to consume the service; 3) commercial presence abroad, where a service is supplied by a provider from one territory established in another one; 4) movement of natural persons, where a provider from one territory provides a service in another territory.

[18] See *supra* note 9.

[19] The results for M&As are reported in Table 6 in Annex 3.B. The analysis cannot be performed on greenfield data, as they do not provide the information on the country where projects originate. As the results table shows, the negative correlation between the number of FDI flows and regulatory heterogeneity is present after controlling for the level of regulatory restrictiveness, as measured by the STRI score.

[20] The gains from improved regulatory coherence are found to be larger in countries with less restrictive regulatory environments (Nordås, 2016[17]).

[21] More information on the EU's Single Market Scoreboard can be found at the dedicated website: https://single-market-scoreboard.ec.europa.eu/home_en.

[22] The results are reported in Table 7 in Annex 3.B.

[23] See Decree-Law No. 398/1998 on the General Tax Law (Art. 19.6) and Decree-Law 262/1986 of the Companies Code (Annex, Article 4).

[24] Discriminatory access to payment settlement methods, in the case of Portugal, reflects the restriction preventing non-EU headquartered financial institutions from providing payment services in Portugal unless through the establishment of a branch in the country. In turn, credit institutions authorised in other EU countries are allowed to provide such services in the Portuguese territory either through the establishment of a branch or the free provision of services. See the OECD Digital STRI Regulatory Database for more information on the underlying measures and regulation covered by the index.

[25] Portugal's strategic priorities for the next decade are enshrined in the *Acordo de Parceria Portugal 2030* and, particularly, in the *Internacionalizar 2030* programme. See Chapter 1 for more information.

[26] The results are reported in Table 8 in Annex 3.B.

[27] Although firms in the telecommunications sector tend to rely heavily on fixed assets, they represent less than a fifth of the sample. Most greenfield projects in ICT take place in less capital-intensive activities, such as computer programming, consultancy and software publishing.

[28] The estimation results are not statistically significant with respect to greenfield projects.

[29] The effect of the EPL indicator could not be adequately estimated with regard to cross-border M&As, partly because little or no variation is observed in the EPL indicator over time for too many countries included in the analysis.

[30] While the gravity model has been developed in the context of trade, it has been shown to be a good fit also for foreign investment (Hijzen, Görg and Manchin, 2008[7]; Blonigen and Piger, 2014[9]).

4 The perspective of foreign investors in Portugal

This chapter complements the assessment of Portugal's regulatory framework for investment and broader business environment by conveying the findings of consultations held with foreign-owned businesses and foreign and domestic chambers of commerce in Portugal. It briefly discusses the motivations of foreign investors for choosing Portugal as an investment location. The chapter then reports businesses' perceptions on various aspects of Portugal's regulatory framework and business environment identified as potential obstacles in Chapter 2. This chapter also maps out consulted businesses' use of government funding and incentives, describes the impact of the COVID-19 pandemic and Russia's war of aggression against Ukraine on their business activity and relays investors' thoughts on how the government could better support companies in Portugal in their digital transformation and green transition.

Key findings

- Portugal's skilled labour force was the leading driver of consulted investors' decision to invest or expand in Portugal. Other highly important drivers included lowering production costs (for greenfield investors) and diversifying risk (for M&A investors).
- Reflecting Portugal's regulatory openness to foreign investment, the business consultation did not reveal specific obstacles related to foreign ownership or direct discrimination against foreign-owned companies. Yet, several regulatory areas, affecting all firms operating in Portugal regardless of ownership structure, were viewed as relatively burdensome by investors of different size and origin, across economic sectors and regions.
- Interactions with public administration were often described as complicated and time-consuming, with little predictability regarding process stage and timeline. The most emblematic cases were in licensing and permits and exchanges with tax authorities.
- In terms of regulatory policy, many investors cited frequent changes in legislation as an obstacle, particularly in taxation. Tax regulation was also perceived by many as unnecessarily intricated.
- Highly skilled labour and the quality of higher education institutions were viewed as Portugal's advantages in attracting FDI. However, many investors experienced challenges in attracting and retaining talent and bottlenecks in the entry process of third-country professionals.
- Businesses perceived rules on hiring and firing as a significant obstacle, likely reflecting the relatively high level of employment protection in Portugal, particularly in terms of dismissals of individual employees.
- Long delays in the judicial system, as well as the prevalence of late payments and difficulties in collecting them, were seen as some of the main challenges of Portugal's business environment.
- Portugal's R&D tax incentive was viewed by many investors as effective. However, there might be room to better target other funding opportunities and incentives and increase investors' awareness of initiatives to train employees and support the digital and green transitions.

4.1. Introduction

A country's regulatory environment is but one of several factors determining its attractiveness as a foreign directi investment (FDI) location. Yet, this is one of the few such aspects that governments can influence in the short-to-medium term. In addition to any explicit limitations to foreign ownership and directly discriminatory rules against foreign investors, addressing a broader range of measures that affect the cost of doing business can improve the investment climate and indirectly tilt FDI decisions.

By factoring in the views and experiences of local foreign investors, this chapter complements the rules-based and comparative regulatory assessments in the previous chapters. It does so by summarising the outcomes of a consultation with foreign-owned companies of different sizes and origin, operating in Portugal across selected sectors and regions.

The business consultation served to refine the understanding of which aspects of Portugal's regulatory framework discussed in previous chapters matter the most for investors and which aspects identified as comparatively stringent are, in practice, less problematic than expected. As foreign investors in Portugal benefit from a comparatively open regulatory framework with few statutory barriers to FDI (see Chapter 2), discussions with the consulted firms centreed around regulatory aspects shaping the country's broader business climate and applicable to all firms, irrespective of their ownership structure. The consultation also highlighted deficiencies in the implementation of government policies and other non-regulatory challenges in the business environment. Moreover, these exchanges revealed certain sector-specific challenges in Portugal's priority sectors for investment, complementing thereby the regulatory assessment of Chapter 2.

This chapter is structured as follows: a first section provides a brief description of the profile of the investors that participated in the business consultation. A second section presents the main drivers behind respondents' decisions to invest in Portugal, while a third section provides insights from investors and business associations on regulatory challenges identified in previous chapters. A fourth section discusses investors' use of available funding and incentive mechanisms. The last section presents a brief overview of the impact of the pandemic on consulted firms' operations and their perceptions of short-term threats in Portugal. Companies' digital transformation and green transition efforts, as well as how the government could further support businesses in both areas, are also covered in this last section. The methodology behind the company selection and the structure of the business consultation are described in Annex 4.A.

4.2. Respondent profile

Foreign-owned companies with different profiles across key characteristics, such as sector and activities, size and location in Portugal, investor origin and type of investment, were selected for the business consultation. The process consisted of an online questionnaire, completed by 32 senior executives of foreign-owned firms based in Portugal, and a series of semi-structured interviews covering 25 companies and ten chambers of commerce and industry federations. Although the consultation was not meant to be exhaustive and representative of all foreign investors in Portugal, the insights shared by respondents echo the findings of other recent business surveys with larger respondent pools, as further discussed below.[1] Comments from individual respondents are reported when they help provide further details or illustrate practical examples on issues identified in the online questionnaire or the analysis of previous chapters as (potentially) important for investors.

Particular attention was accorded to Portugal's FDI priority sectors and activities, namely: life sciences, automotive/mobility, aerospace, smart materials, food industry, software and information technology (IT) services, business services, renewable energy. Companies operating in key upstream and auxiliary sectors (e.g. health, telecommunication, financial services, construction and real estate, power generation and distribution, water services, logistics, road transportation and auxiliary mobility services) were also consulted.

The sample includes companies of different sizes across all seven regions of Portugal. Although most respondents have their head offices in the Lisbon area or in Northern Portugal, half of the firms also have industrial, production or research facilities, or other kind of physical presence, in one or several other regions (Table 4.1). Close to 60% of the consulted firms are large companies with a headcount of 250 or more, a quarter are medium-sized companies, and the remaining 16% are small companies (less than 50 employees).

The sample of respondents is nearly equally split between ultimate investors from within and outside of the European Economic Area (EEA), the latter including countries as Brazil, the People's Republic of China (hereafter 'China'), Japan, Peru, Singapore, South Korea, the United Kingdom and the United States. Fifty-three percent of respondents come from companies having entered Portugal via greenfield investment projects, while Portuguese firms acquired by or merged with a foreign company or private equity fund make up the remaining part. All respondents have invested (at firm or group level) also outside Portugal, 44% of them in countries outside the European Union (EU). Several firms have invested in one or more selected peer countries,[2] most commonly in Spain (28% of respondents), the Czech Republic (25%) or Poland (25%).

Almost all the consulted businesses engaged in trade. Seventy-eight percent of the respondents sold products or services in other EU countries, most commonly in France, Spain and Germany, and 59% sold to countries outside the Single Market. Twenty-two percent had exclusively foreign sales, with no products or services sold in Portugal. A large majority of respondents sourced some inputs locally from Portugal, but most of them also from foreign markets. Close to half of them sourced at least a quarter of their inputs from abroad, most commonly from Spain, France, China and Germany.

Table 4.1. Selected respondent characteristics

	Share of online questionnaire respondents
Sector of activity	Industry (47%), services (53%)
Region of headquarters in Portugal	Lisbon (59%), Northern Portugal (19%), Central Portugal (13%), Alentejo (9%)
Region(s) with other physical presence in Portugal	Lisbon (19%), Northern Portugal (21%), Central Portugal (21%), Algarve (12%), Alentejo (14%), Madeira (7%), Azores (7%)
Size (as per headcount in Portugal)	Small (16%), medium (25%), large (59%)
Ultimate investor origin	EEA country (47%), non-EEA country (53%)
Entry mode	Greenfield investment (53%), cross-border M&A (47%)
Trade profile: Source(s) of inputs	Portugal (84%), other EU countries (63%), non-EU countries (53%)
Trade profile: Destination(s) of sales	Portugal (78%), other EU countries (78%), non-EU countries (59%)

Source: Own calculations based on the online questionnaire.

4.3. Drivers of FDI to Portugal

Accessing a pool of local skilled labour was the leading driver of consulted firms' investment in Portugal, regardless of investment type (Figure 4.1). The skilled labour force was a particularly strong driver for firms entering via mergers and acquisitions (M&A), all of whom ranked it as important for their decision to invest or expand in Portugal, compared to 89% of greenfield investors.

Figure 4.1. Access to Portugal's skilled labour is the leading motivator of FDI decisions

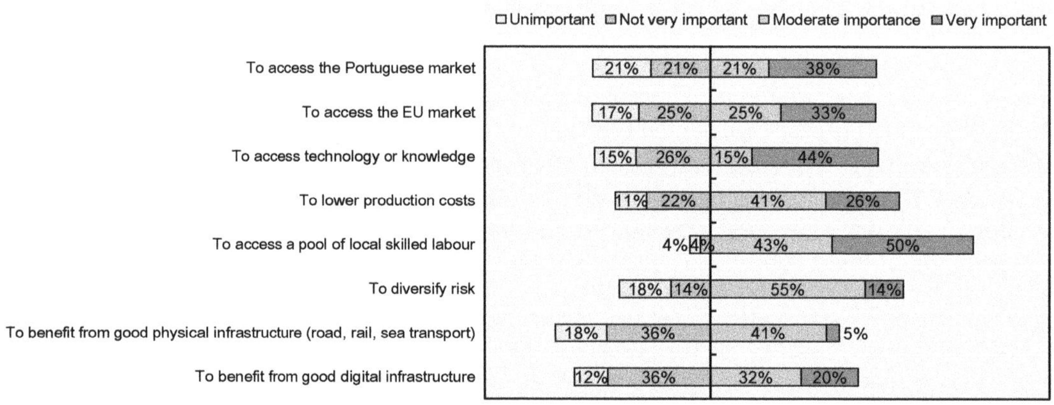

Note: Respondents were asked how important the listed reasons were for their company's decision to invest/expand in Portugal (greenfield investors) or for the foreign company's interest in the Portuguese target company (M&A investors). The figure reports a selection of the answer options. "Not applicable" answer option is not displayed.
Source: Own calculations based on the online questionnaire.

For greenfield investors, lowering production costs was the second most important reason for choosing Portugal (88% identifying it as important), whereas this aspect was less relevant for M&A investors (30%). Many greenfield investors also reported access to the Portuguese and EU markets, and access to technology and knowledge as important drivers. For M&A investors, the most significant drivers of investment after access to skilled labour were diversifying risk (88%) and access to the Portuguese market (64%), while access to the EU market was a less important driver (40%). Additionally, Portugal's strategic geographical location, e.g. for transatlantic trade, was raised as an important consideration in the investment decision of some companies.

Although access to a local talent pool was identified as the top driver for investment, and Portugal's skilled labour and the quality of its higher education institutions received positive comments from several investors, many consulted businesses reported experiencing skill shortages (see Section 4.4.3). In fact, difficulties recruiting skilled workers was one of the two main reasons cited by those investors who were uncertain of making further investment in Portugal in the next three years, with a non-conducive regulatory environment being the other most indicated reason for uncertainty.[3]

4.4. Regulatory challenges affecting the business environment in Portugal

This section describes foreign investors' views on several regulatory aspects, many of them identified in Chapter 2 as potentially affecting foreign investors in Portugal. The section explores the main topics of concern for consulted investors and business associations, namely: lengthy and burdensome administrative processes, including in licensing and permitting; complicated and frequently changing legislation, particularly in taxation; difficulties attracting and retaining talent; excessively rigid labour regulation; long delays in the judicial system; and late payments. It also addresses other aspects of Portugal's business environment, perceived as burdensome by some investors, but to a lesser extent.

The challenges identified in some of the above-mentioned areas seem to have persisted over some time. Since 2014, the judicial system, licensing and taxation have consistently arisen in Portugal's business surveys as the areas where companies, and particularly small and medium-sized firms, identify the most important negative effects on their operations due to rules, procedures, actions and omissions not attributable to the firm or investor themselves (INE, 2022[1]).[4] While generally perceived as a lesser obstacle to business activity, administrative burden (in terms of, e.g. the frequency and complexity of requests from authorities) was relatively more often considered as penalising by large firms and companies in industry sectors (INE, 2022[1]).

Except for obtaining licenses and permits to start or operate a business, other aspects related to setting up a business, such as registering a branch of a foreign company, were generally not perceived as obstacles by the consulted firms. Similarly, the screening of certain foreign acquisitions did not come up as a specific concern for non-EU foreign investors, none of which had experienced it. This result reflects the understanding that no acquisitions have been opposed under the Portuguese foreign investment screening mechanism so far (see Chapter 2). Nonetheless, it is possible that screening may become a more important consideration for foreign investors in the future, should the legal framework or its implementation in Portugal undergo changes that reflect the increasing attention accorded to the policy area in recent years, including at the EU level. More broadly, the consulted businesses did not report any discriminatory treatment towards companies with foreign ownership.[5]

4.4.1. Administrative processes are seen as lengthy and burdensome across the board

Burdensome interactions with public administration were one of the most critical issues raised by investors about Portugal's business environment. Seventy-seven perfect of respondents considered administrative delays and other red-tape as a very important or moderately important obstacle to their operations in Portugal (Figure 4.2). Most firms also signalled discretion of the bureaucracy (73% of respondents) and lack of transparency and predictability in dealing with public administration (65%) as obstacles. Difficulties understanding regulation and frequent changes in legislation (see Section 4.4.2) were considered to exacerbate the above-mentioned challenges.

Figure 4.2. Regulatory transparency and red-tape

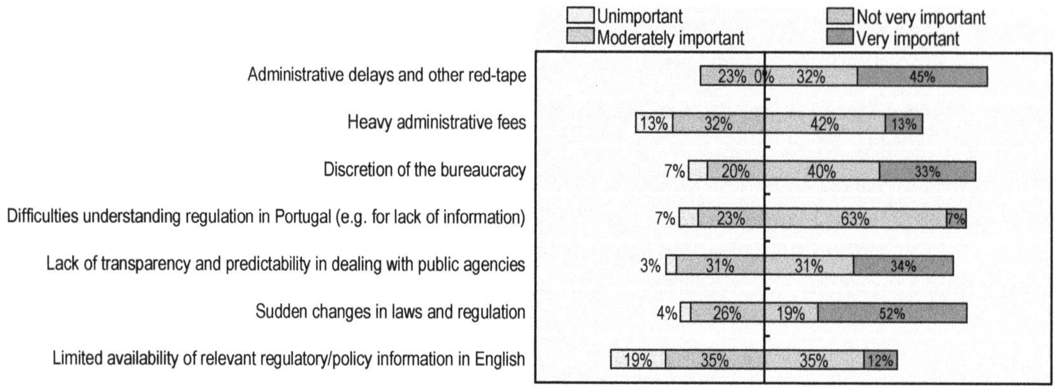

Note: Respondents were asked to what degree the listed factors act as an obstacle to their company's operations in Portugal. The figure reports a selection of the answer options. "Not applicable" answer option is not displayed.
Source: Own calculations based on the online questionnaire.

Based on clarifications obtained in interviews with investors, two-in-three companies had experienced one or several burdensome aspects in licensing and permits. However, long waiting times, difficulty predicting how long processes would take, lack of communication on process timelines, complexity of procedures and requirements and absence of standardised operating procedures were commonly perceived shortcomings also in other processes, such as interactions with the tax authority (see Section 4.4.2). Overall, investors perceived a high level of bureaucracy in Portugal, requiring firms to allocate significant time and resources to interactions with public administration. In a large law firm's experience, companies cannot generally expect most applications and requests to be processed on time. It was also noted that although most applications and requests can be submitted online, the availability of electronic applications is no guarantee for a quick processing time, once submitted.

A few investors in different sectors (e.g. automotive, food, health) considered that dealing with public administration is unnecessarily difficult in Portugal, sometimes more so than in other countries where they operated, and to the point that external legal and consulting services are needed to navigate the processes. Nine interviewed firms and chambers of commerce, however, thought that delays and other challenges with public administration stem not from difficult procedures, but from a general lack of efficiency in their execution. Insufficient human resources, poor internal organisation and inter-agency co-ordination and lack of accountability were mentioned as examples of factors contributing to public administration's difficulties in delivering services to the standard expected by investors.

Slow and unpredictable licensing and permitting represent obstacles for operations

As discussed in Chapter 2, Portugal has made efforts to simplify business licensing in recent years. Reforms undertaken as part of the Simplex+ programme, such as the introduction of the Single Environmental Title and expanding the scope of the digital point of single contact for licensing, are estimated to have reduced administrative burden for companies and resulted in time saving in public administration (EY, 2019[2]). Yet, there remains room to further develop online public services for businesses and increase their uptake compared to best-perfoming EU countries (see Section 2.2.1).

Despite simplification measures, more than half of the respondents considered complicated licensing procedures and delays in obtaining the necessary permits and approvals as important obstacles to starting or expanding operations in Portugal, citing as main issues delays, lack of predictability on the process timeline and communication of the stage of the process, and burdensome requirements or procedures across different sectors of the economy and in different licensing and permit processes. To a great extent, these findings corroborate and exemplify in a more concrete manner some of the findings of other large-scale enterprise surveys (Box 4.1).

Box 4.1. Operating license procedures are more burdensome in Portugal than in peer countries

Overall, firms in Portugal report that it takes close to 90 days on average to obtain the necessary licenses and permits to operate a business; more than twice the time it takes in peer economies (Figure 4.3). About 12% of firms in Portugal report this as a major constraint for their operations, compared to around 9% in the EU. If considering only the responses of medium-sized firms, the average number of days required to obtain such licenses and permits is much higher (114 days). Unfortunately, data are not reported for small-sized firms. As for construction permits, although the time required to obtain a permit may at times be considered high for business, it is roughly aligned with peer countries. The opportunity cost associated with such delays may, however, be quite important for individual investors, particularly for small and medium-sized enterprises, which generally have fewer resources to cope with long delays.

Figure 4.3. Portugal has the longest delays in operating licensing among peers

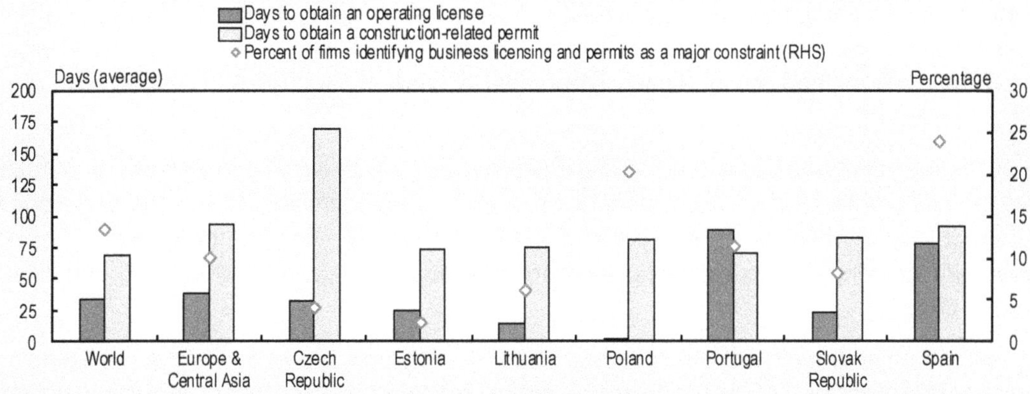

Note: Data are for the latest year available: 2019 data for all countries, except Spain for which 2021 data were available.
Source: World Bank (2019[3]; 2021[4]), *Enterprise Surveys*, https://www.enterprisesurveys.org/en/enterprisesurveys.

Some investors partly attributed delays in licensing to insufficient levels of human resources in public administration, but non-enforcement of procedural deadlines set for authorities was also perceived as affecting investors in specific sectors (e.g. health, life sciences, pharmaceuticals) and more broadly businesses operating in Portugal (according to a Portuguese and a foreign chamber of commerce).[6] The possibility of tacit approval is foreseen in the Code of Administrative Procedure,[7] and silence from the part of the administration can, in principle, result in tacit approval in cases expressly provided for by law or regulation (e.g. industrial licensing,[8] certain environmental licensing processes[9] and certain acts in urbanisation and construction[10]). However, investors raised that it can be hard to benefit from existing rules foreseeing tacit approval due to difficulties presenting proof that tacit approval has been justified.[11]

Additionally, according to respondents, public entities sometimes use the possibility of sending multiple requests for additional information to extend the time limits imposed on their decision-making. Insufficient administrative co-ordination (where a process is being put on hold while a response from one of the public entities involved is still pending), lack of standard operating procedures and insufficient technical expertise were also cited as potential sources of delays across different licensing and permit processes.

A scoped sectoral reform of environmental licensing, which is expected to serve as a basis for other licensing and permit reform processes, is set to address some of the above-mentioned challenges faced by businesses (see Box 4.2). Environmental licensing, as well as construction and occupancy permit processes, were commonly cited as examples of burdensome and lengthy processes affecting a wide range of investment projects. While extensive documentation is often required in environmental licensing to ensure the protection of environmental standards, investors perceived the documentation requirements in Portugal as excessive and requiring specialist help to fulfil.[12] Some level of simplification may likely be welcome, but only if achieved without jeopardising the authority's capacity to ensure business compliance with environmental standards.[13]

Box 4.2. Scoped reform of environmental licensing intends to address process bottlenecks

After extensive stakeholder consultation, a legislative package to amend environmental licensing was approved by the Government of Portugal in December 2022, but the final text had not yet been published as of early January 2023.[1] The reform is a first step of a wider effort to reduce administrative burden and costs for businesses in licensing, as foreseen in Portugal's Recovery and Resilience Plan (Portugal Government, 2021[5]).[2] It is intended to remove some administrative requirements that are considered to create unnecessary costs for businesses without environmental value added. Some civil society organisations have, however, expressed concerns with certain proposed amendments during a public consultation, arguing that they could impair effective compliance with environmental protection standards; they call instead for increased resources to allow the public administration to expedite licensing procedures.[3]

Among the reform measures proposed in the draft law are: a reduction in the scope of situations in which an environmental impact assessment is required, the elimination of the need to renew the environmental license after 10 years and the creation of "Single Environmental Reporting" to reduce time spent on reporting by consolidating existing reporting obligations and offering simplified and automatised filling.

Some proposed amendments are also directed at addressing procedural bottlenecks in licensing and permit processes more widely, beyond environmental licensing. For instance, to minimise delays in licensing, the draft law proposes stricter time limits for the issuance of opinions. The responsible authority would request all opinions simultaneously and proceed with decision-making as soon as the deadline for opinions has lapsed, with opinions issued after the deadline being null and void.[4] Administrative entities would be able to request additional elements (i.e. documents or clarifications) from the applicant only once and the request would not suspend the time limit accorded for the licensing decision if the applicant responds within a ten-day period.

A new certification mechanism is also proposed to enforce the policy of tacit approval. A designated administrative entity would be obliged to issue to an applicant, within three working days from the receipt of the applicant's online request, a document acting as proof of a tacit approval of the applicant's license or authorisation application in the an absence of response from the administration.

1. Ministerial Council communication, 7 December 2022; DL 169/XXIII/2022, 2 August 2022.
2. Simplification reforms are also foreseen (component 18) in urban and spatial planning, industry, commerce, services and agriculture.
3. Liga para a Protecção da Natureza, 16 September 2022; Observador, 16September 2022 and 17September 2022; ZERO, 18 September 2022.
4. Currently, the responsible authority must request opinions simultaneously "whenever possible". Silence of an entity issuing a mandatory, binding opinion can slow down the process, as a final decision can be made without the issuance of such opinion only after an additional request from the responsible authority and an additional time limit of 20 days from such request. See Article 92 of Decree-Law No. 4/2015.

In construction and real estate, three businesses (including a law firm) and a chamber of commerce reported significant disparities in construction permit and occupancy permit process timelines depending on the location in Portugal, with particularly long delays in Lisbon compared to smaller municipalities. Additionally, a few businesses cited a margin of (political) discretion in municipalities' decision-making in permit processes;[14] at the same time, appeal against licensing decisions was not considered an option due to long processing times in Portugal's courts (see Section 4.4.5).

Investors in health and life sciences also lamented long delays in sector-specific licensing. Two investors in the health sector considered that licensing is time-consuming and more complicated in Portugal than in certain other European economies (Denmark, Germany, Poland or the United Kingdom) where they are present. A company in life sciences reported that obtaining the necessary product certification to participate in public procurement took considerable time and required specialist help. An investor in pharmaceuticals considered that Portugal's competitiveness for clinical trials is negatively affected by the relatively long delays in the processing of applications.[15]

Portugal's special regulatory regimes for investment, intended to streamline the licensing process of eligible projects (see Box 2.2 in Chapter 2), received mixed feedback. While a couple of businesses viewed the regimes as effective, a few others considered that obtaining a *Potencial Interesse Nacional* (PIN; for large-scale projects) or *Projeto de Investimento para o Interior* (PII; for projects in interior regions) status for a project does not speed up the licensing process or increase its predictability. Several perceived drawbacks in the special regimes were also raised, such as the need to hire specialised help to obtain PIN or PII status for a project and lack of periodical follow-up with the investor on, for instance, the status of the licensing process.

However, several investors and foreign chambers of commerce reported positive experiences with Portugal's investment promotion agency AICEP's support, such as connecting the investor with regional licensing authorities, albeit some complained that AICEP's support sometimes stops short as licenses and permits processes remain bound by local authorities' capacity and efficiency. Small cities' dynamic approach to licensing, in terms of quicker processes but also additional support, such as help finding suitable land at lower cost, was also appreciated by several businesses.

Being subject to fewer licensing requirements, investors in information and communication technology (ICT) and digital marketing services had no specific complaints in this regard.[16] Likewise, some companies had not undergone licensing or permit processes due to their strategy of expansion via acquisitions of Portuguese firms with existing facilities.

4.4.2. Complex, unstable rules and regulatory divergence pose challenges to businesses

Most investors struggle to understand regulation and cope with frequently changing rules

Over 70% of the firms consulted identified difficulties understanding regulation and sudden changes in the legal framework as important obstacles to their operations in Portugal (Figure 4.2). Investors across different sectors, e.g. automotive, port services, food and manufacturing, as well as a foreign chamber of commerce, commented that due to the complexity of regulation, external help (lawyers and consultants) is vital to do business in Portugal.[17]

Particularly intricate regulatory frameworks were not limited to taxation (discussed below), but extended also to public procurement (see Section 4.4.6) and certain sector-specific legislation (such as the national transposition of the EU Electronic Communications Code; see below). Similarly, frequent changes in regulation were cited in taxation, as well as in the health, energy and tourism sectors, and with regard to the entry framework of non-EU nationals (see Section 4.4.3). Some firms and business associations considered that investors would benefit from improved availability of regulatory information in English.

Furthermore, as discussed in Chapter 2, there is likely room for Portugal to improve regulatory impact assessment and stakeholder engagement in law-making, compared to better-performing peers. While the private sector involvement in the drafting of regulation may not appear so problematic, a few investors and chambers of commerce argued that business perspectives and realities are not always sufficiently considered in the drafting process.[18]

However, the scoped reform of environmental licensing (see Box 4.2 above) was viewed as a positive development in stakeholder engagement by a Portuguese chamber of commerce having participating in the drafting process. More than 250 entitites contributed to the legislative package in environmental licensing,[19] and extensive stakeholder engagagement is planned also for the preparation of other forthcoming licensing reforms foreseen in the Recovery and Resilience Plan (urban and spatial planning, industry, commerce, services and agriculture). The licensing reform process has been developed with the direct participation of various public entities[20] and private stakeholders, and it involves stakeholder participation in every step of the drafting process, including the identification of potential simplification measures, design of policy alternatives and impact assessments.[21]

Tax regulation is considered as complex and difficult to comply with

Portugal's tax system was perceived by many investors as unnecessarily complicated. Taxation has also arisen as an obstacle or a relatively unattractive factor for investors in past business surveys, not only in terms of a complicated legal framework, but also in terms of tax burden.[22]

A large number of exemptions was viewed by investors as contributing to the complexity of Portugal's tax system. A 2019 evaluation identified more than 500 tax benefits dispersed across more than 60 different legal instruments, concluding that the system of tax benefits in Portugal was very complicated and lacking in transparency (Grupo de Trabalho para o Estudo dos Benefícios Fiscais, 2019[6]). Notwithstanding steps taken in recent years to reduce the use of special tax provisions (OECD, 2021[7]), consulted investors largely considered that tax regulation remains difficult to understand and comply with compared to other countries in which they have invested. One interviewed firm reported that even the Portuguese accountants enlisted by the company "sometimes struggle to understand tax requirements"; two others, as well as a Portuguese chamber of commerce, considered that the level and intricacy of reporting requirements in taxation have increased in recent years.

As alluded to above, six businesses and two foreign chambers of commerce also cited frequent changes in tax regulation, for instance regarding tax breaks. This instability was reported to result in increased tax compliance time and difficulties planning investment in the long term. In some investors' experience, the tax authority has not been able to provide clarification on the interpretation of new rules prior to their entry into force, sometimes resulting in the postponement of their implementation and, hence, additional uncertainty for businesses.

Three investors, including a law firm, and a chamber of commerce also lamented that long delays in obtaining a binding opinion from the tax authority contribute to legal uncertainty in taxation. Such binding rulings on the correct interpretation and application of tax regulation can be particularly important for businesses in the case of highly complex transactions. Portuguese legislation imposes a general 150-day time limit for the tax authority to respond to requests for binding information. Following a taxpayer's "justified request" and payment of a fee, the tax authority may recognise the request for binding information as "urgent", in which case a response must be provided within 75 days.[23] However, based on the business consultation, it is unclear whether these time limits are complied with in practice. Tacit confirmation of the taxpayer's interpretation of tax rules, following the silence of the tax authority after the prescribed time limit has lapsed, is only foreseen in the case of requests considered as urgent.[24]

Dealing with the tax authority was mentioned by consulted businesses as an example of particularly burdensome interactions with public entities, despite the fact that Portugal has put in place simplifying measures for tax compliance, such as prefilled tax declarations and online services.[25] In INE (2022[1]), Portuguese firms overall indicated burdensome interactions with tax administration in terms of the frequency, complexity and time limits for responding to information requests; but particularly large firms, nearly half of which reported administrative burden as a high or very high obstacle in this regard. Tax administration was also perceived as an obstacle to a larger extent than in any of the peer countries in international surveys, with 47% of surveyed firms in Portugal identifying tax administration as a major constraint, compared to figures ranging from 3% in the Slovak Republic to 35% in Poland among the benchmark group (World Bank, 2019[3]; 2021[4]).[26] According to World Bank (2020[8]), companies also spent more time preparing and paying taxes in Portugal (243 hours per year) than in any of the benchmarked countries (excluding Poland), with Estonia being the best performer in the group at 50 hours per year.

Due to extensive intra-EEA harmonisation, regulatory divergence is limited to specific areas

Overall, the divergence of Portuguese regulation from that of other countries of interest came out as a relatively small obstacle for consulted businesses. As discussed in Chapter 2, Portuguese regulation is, in many services sectors, mostly harmonised with Single Market rules.

Nevertheless, a few specific examples of regulatory divergence affecting foreign multinationals' operations were raised in the consultation. In transport, consulted businesses mentioned the broad Iberian track gauge (used by railways in Portugal and Spain) compared to the standard gauge as a constraint. In taxation, differences in invoicing requirements between Portugal and other countries were reported to cause difficulties in compliance in the case of foreign suppliers with no presence in Portugal.

An ICT investor raised a few concrete examples of cases where Portuguese regulation might benefit from further harmonisation with the EU's Digital Single Market rules. According to this investor, certain obligations imposed in a 2021 domestic act regulating financial services advertising are difficult to comply with and go beyond requirements observed in other EU countries.[27] Moreover, the investor considered Portugal's approach to the protection of copyright content in the digital environment to be an outlier among EU countries.[28] Finally, the scope of obligations imposed on private network operators in the Portuguese domestic transposition of the EU's Electronic Communications Code was perceived by the investor as unclear and diverging from transposition efforts in other EU countries, for instance regarding notification requirements.[29]

4.4.3. Difficulties attracting and retaining talent thwart efforts to mitigate skill shortages

Overall, foreign investors perceived Portugal's highly skilled talent and the good quality of its higher education institutions as advantages. Access to a local pool of skilled labour was also the most important driver for respondents at the time of their decision to invest in Portugal (see Section 4.3). However, some consulted firms expect skill shortages to hinder their capacity to expand operations in the near future. Bottlenecks in the entry process of third-country talent and difficulties in talent attraction and retention experienced by some firms complicate companies' efforts to mitigate skill shortages in specific sectors or for certain categories of workers. Improving conditions for talent attraction and retention is an increasingly important and distinguishing factor for FDI attractiveness, as skill shortages in certain high-demand fields (e.g. ICT) become more widespread and acute worldwide.

Investors experience skill shortages in certain sectors and professions

Overall, investors reported a good availability of talent for their operations in Portugal and considered Portuguese top managers very qualified. However, nearly half of the interviewed investors raised increasing skill shortages as a challenge, particularly in terms of IT and engineering professionals, but also with regard to technical professions (e.g. electricians, mechanics) in the automotive and aerospace industries.[30] In the experience of a foreign chamber of commerce, firms across different sectors of the economy also struggle with finding qualified middle management and talent with high-demand language skills, such as French. An investor having sought talent with specific language skills for a service centre reported challenges identifying potential candidates within and outside Portugal, partly due to lack of data regarding the number of foreign students in Portuguese universities. In the case of French-speakers, it was considered "impossible" to attract talent from France due to wage differences between France and Portugal, leading some French groups to source French-speaking talent from Northern African countries.

The companies consulted had various ways of mitigating skill shortages, from providing employee training to establishing linkages with educational institutions or recruiting trainees and PhD students. An investor in Northern Portugal reported offering above-average wages and other advantages, such as a relocation premium or compensating commuting costs. For many investors, sourcing talent from outside Portugal was reported as a way to deal with local skill shortages, but not without its own challenges.

Bottlenecks in entry processes slow down efforts to source talent from abroad

Many investors reported recruiting employees from outside Portugal, including at management level; 59% of respondents had foreigners in managerial positions. In addition to sourcing talent from countries within the Single Market (e.g. Czech Republic, France, Italy, Spain), interviewed firms also expressly mentioned hiring from third countries, in particular from Brazil, but also from Japan, Morocco and Pakistan.

Oftentimes, foreign investors' efforts to mitigate domestic skill shortages by sourcing talent from third countries had been made less efficient by long delays in foreign workers' visa and residence permit processes with the Portuguese Immigration and Border Service (SEF).[31] Over 60% of the respondents considered residence permits for third-country foreign talent as particularly challenging for their operations in Portugal. The investors' principal concern related to the long processing times of visa and/or residence permit applications, rather than to e.g. uncertainty regarding the outcome of the process.[32] An investor in the ICT sector stated that long processing times make it difficult for the Portuguese subsidiary to compete for talent within the group. An investor and a chamber of commerce also reported four cases of non-EEA foreign investors giving up or putting their plans of setting up in Portugal on hold due to long and intricated visa and residence permit processes.

Some businesses mentioned having used the Tech Visa programme to bring highly qualified employees to Portugal. Although intended to streamline the entry of highly skilled and specialised workers (see Chapter 2), the effectiveness of the programme received mixed views from investors, half of those having experience with the Tech Visa considering that it had not (sufficiently) accelerated entry processes.

As discussed in Chapter 2, Portuguese legislation imposes maximum time limits for decisions on residence visa applications; however, it is unclear to what extent actual visa processing times remain within the statutory limits. Waiting time to obtain a visa appointment before submitting an application may add to the total length of the visa process beyond the statutory time limit. Several investors also considered that overstaying visa limits is common due to difficulties obtaining the necessary appointment with SEF to move forward with a residence permit process after arrival in Portugal. A foreign, third-country national is entitled to begin work based on the residence visa while the residence permit application for long-term stay is pending; nevertheless, consulted firms considered that delays in the issuance of the residence permit cause practical difficulties and uncertainty for employees, such as not being able to travel outside the Schengen Zone, including for work purposes, due to not having a valid visa or residence permit upon their return. However, Portuguese authorities note that, in practice, SEF considers the visa to be extended in situations where the residence permit application is pending.[33]

Although three investors perceived entry processes as unnecessarily burdensome or unclear for the applicant, most considered that the bottleneck lies in the processing of applications and internal organisation of SEF, possibly due to a lack of manpower to deal with the case flow. Four investors suspected that poor internal processes could be the source of the backlog and suggested the modernisation of SEF's structure and/or accelerated digitalisation of processes.

Recently adopted simplification measures, such as the introduction of a job-seeker visa and the definite elimination of immigration quotas (see Chapter 2), were welcomed by the consulted firms and business associations. However, as highly qualified workers were already exempted from quotas under previously applicable rules, addressing bottlenecks in the processing of applications might be more beneficial to help businesses navigate domestic skill shortages. Some steps have been taken towards easing the administrative burden faced by foreign talent in the recent amendments to the Foreigners Act; for instance, a "pre-residence authorisation" is to be issued together with the entry visa, containing provisional tax and social security numbers, as well as information on obtaining a residence permit.[34] Moreover, foreign nationals entering Portugal with the new job-seeker visa type will automatically be assigned an appointment with SEF for the issuance of a residence permit.[35]

Many investors struggle with attracting and retaining talent

Nearly half of the interviewed businesses and chambers of commerce reported difficulties attracting or retaining foreign talent, often citing as main reasons Portugal's relatively low wage level compared to other European countries and increasing costs of living, particularly around Lisbon and Porto. Personal income taxation was perceived to contribute to these challenges, although one investor in the ICT sector considered that Portugal's non-habitual resident tax regime works well in attracting high-income individuals (see Chapter 2). Additionally, a foreign chamber of commerce considered that minimum thresholds for pension contributions, such as those in place in Portugal, can discourage the movement of certain foreign talent. As a general rule, employees must work in Portugal for 15 years to be eligible for old-age pension, despite social security contributions being deducted from salaries from day one.[36]

Several companies in different sectors also viewed attracting Portuguese diaspora back to the country as difficult, despite targeted tax benefits for those having resided abroad for three years (see Chapter 2). In their view, young Portuguese workers who left during the financial crisis are not coming back, unless they have a personal reason to return or a high-income position lined up. Perceived high personal income taxes were equally raised as a deterrent factor for attracting the diaspora who does not qualify for this preferential tax treatment. One investor in ICT considered that the scarcity of open top management positions contributes to the difficulty of luring the Portuguese diaspora back.

More advantageous salaries and/or taxation in foreign markets were also considered to draw high-demand workers (e.g. ICT professionals) abroad as part of a global competition for skills, making it challenging for businesses to retain talent in the country. An ICT investor reported that, in areas of high demand, it was equally an issue to retain non-EEA recruits in Portugal.[37] Five investors also explicitly mentioned losing an increasing number of Portuguese IT and engineering talent to foreign multinationals offering remote work opportunities.

4.4.4. Investors call for more flexible labour regulation

Striking the right balance between employment protection and labour market flexibility can be challenging. Employment protection legislation (EPL) is central for productivity growth and social equity. It helps to protect workers against unfair dismissals and makes the company laying off an employee take on some of its social costs. Job security may also encourage firms and workers to invest in long-term training. Overly strict rules, however, may have unwanted consequences by potentially raising firms' labour adjustment costs and by excessively incentivising the use of temporary contracts in relation to permanent ones.[38] Through reduced labour mobility, stringent employment protection legislation may also limit productivity and innovation spillovers from foreign firms to Portuguese small and medium-sized enterprises (SMEs) in sectors and regions with low absorptive capacities (OECD, 2022[9]).

Portugal has high levels of employment protection standards, including regarding individual dismissals of employees with regular contracts (see Box 4.3). Likely reflecting difficulties experienced by the consulted companies in individual dismissals of employees with permanent contracts, the rules on hiring and firing came out as the single most important perceived obstacle by 85% of the respondents. Similarly, in EIB (2022[10]), 70% of firms in Portugal considered labour market regulation as an obstacle to investment, compared to 61% of EU firms. Several foreign investors consulted for the present assessment reported not being able to let go staff who no longer contribute to work, due to difficulties establishing that the legal requirements for a fair dismissal have been met. Dismissing an employee with a permanent contract on the grounds of performance was described by several respondents as effectively impossible unless the firm and the employee come to an agreement. Most benchmarked countries' (except for Spain) regulatory frameworks foresee the possibility of dismissal on the grounds of insufficient performance (OECD, 2020[11]).

Box 4.3. Portugal has relatively high employment protection compared to most peer countries

Overall, Portugal has one of the highest levels of worker protection among OECD countries and the highest level among the peer group (except the Czech Republic) regarding both individual and collective dismissals of regular workers (OECD, 2019[12]). Employment protection regarding temporary contracts is also relatively high in comparison to peer economies and the OECD average (Figure 4.4).

Figure 4.4. Individual dismissals and temporary contracts are relatively strictly regulated

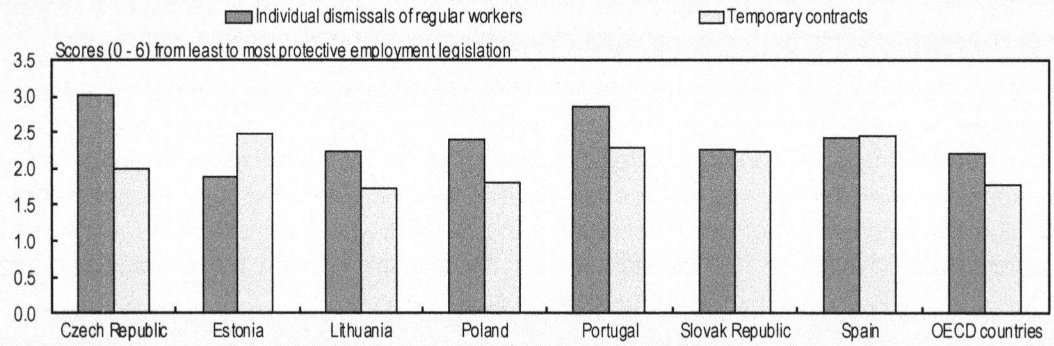

Note: Data are for 2019. The indicator for individual dismissals of regular workers captures dismissal regulation along four dimensions: i) procedural requirements before notice is given; ii) notice period and severance pay; iii) the regulatory framework for unfair dismissals; and iv) enforcement of unfair dismissal regulation. The indicator for temporary contracts captures limitations on the use of fixed-term contracts and temporary work agency contracts and rules on the termination of fixed-term contracts.
Source: OECD (2019[12]), *OECD Indicators of Employment Protection*, http://www.oecd.org/employment/protection.

Strict hiring rules for temporary workers are needed where job protection is high for regular workers to avoid labour market segmentation (OECD, 2020[11]). In Portugal, however, temporary contracts, i.e. fixed-term contracts and temporary work agency contracts, still allow greater flexibility to employers than regular contracts, despite stricter rules introduced recently on contract duration and renewal.[1] Further limitations to the renewal of temporary contracts are currently under discussion.[2]

Relatively low regulation of temporary contracts compared to regular ones helps to partly explain the high incidence of temporary employment in Portugal, where 16.9% of workers (and 59.2% of workers aged 15 to 24) were estimated to be employed under fixed-term contracts in 2021, one of the highest proportions among EU and OECD countries (OECD, 2023[13]). This market segmentation can be an extra obstacle to productivity growth and income equity, as it may curb incentives for investment in knowledge and skill development.

1. Labour Code (Law No. 7/2009), Articles 148 and 149. In 2019, the maximum duration of a fixed term contract was reduced from three to two years and the total duration of renewals was capped to correspond to that of the initial contract period. The maximum duration of an indefinite term contract was also reduced from six to four years.
2. Draft law 15/XV/1 of 6 June 2022.

Several consulted businesses reported negotiation of an agreement and severance pay with the employee as the "only" means for circumventing the difficulty of dismissals. Companies also reported giving particular attention to actions that help to mitigate the risk of hiring an unsuitable candidate, such as making use of referrals in the recruitment process or of the probationary periods foreseen in labour legislation, but also turning to sub-contracting or temporary contracts (see Box 4.3).

4.4.5. Long delays in the judicial system discourage investors from seeking justice

An inefficient justice system was perceived by the consulted firms as one of the most important challenges of Portugal's business environment. Close to 80% of respondents considered the length and complexity of court proceedings as an important obstacle for their operations in Portugal. This perception was shared by investors across different sectors of the economy, and first-hand experiences of long delays were reported in different branches of justice, but particularly in administrative and fiscal courts.[39] These results echo findings of Statistics Portugal's surveys, in which the judicial system has continued to feature as the domain with the highest negative impact on firms' activity (INE, 2022[1]).[40]

As discussed in Chapter 2, court proceedings remain considerably lengthy in Portugal compared to some peer countries, despite some recent improvements. The consulted businesses perceived numerous opportunities for appeals, procedural delays, limited human resources and insufficient specialist knowledge in technical cases as possible reasons behind delays. Some of these aspects were also highlighted as areas of further improvement in OECD (2020[14]), encouraging Portugal to strengthen human resources in court support functions,[41] improve the resolution of insolvency and enforcement cases, consider simplifying procedural legislation and increase the use of out-of-court procedures.

Due to long proceedings, consulted businesses considered litigation as a last resort or abstained from legal recourse altogether. Some investors recounted positive experiences using out-of-court mechanisms for quicker dispute resolution, for instance arbitration in patent, tax and labour disputes.

Investors also reported difficulties collecting late payments, including from public entities, due to a time-consuming and burdensome judicial process for debt collection. An investor active in various sectors cited the need to notarise agreements in order to prove their existence and insufficient electronic signature solutions (not necessarily available for all types of transactions or for foreign nationals) as practical difficulties in debt collection. Moreover, a large law firm mentioned shortcomings in Portugal's legal framework for insolvency; in the firm's experience, restructuring constitutes, in practice, a pre-insolvency process, as "firms apply for restructuring only to delay insolvency".[42]

4.4.6. Other burdensome aspects of the business environment

Beyond the above-mentioned main concerns in Portugal's regulatory environment, some firms reported difficulties accessing public procurement projects, as well as shortcomings in customs, port services and other infrastructure, as burdensome aspects, albeit to a lesser extent.

Challenges in public procurement participation were indicated by 60% of respondents. Based on follow-up interviews, difficulties accessing public tenders seemed to affect particularly ICT sector investors, but also firms active in life sciences, automotive and smart materials. Public procurement processes were described as lengthy and burdensome, sometimes with complicated requirements for participation, such as product certifications. An investor in life sciences reported no longer participating in public tenders in Portugal due to bureaucracy and described participation in large procurement projects as difficult for smaller firms in the sector.[43] Moreover, several ICT firms perceived that some tenders were tailored, by reportedly imposing excessively stringent conditions for participation, which only one supplier would be able to fulfil. The investors' perception was that such strict requirements were often used to secure the continuity of the supplier from one contract period to another. Portugal's online public procurement platform, however, was thought to work well and have improved transparency in public tenders.

Portugal's digital infrastructure received positive comments from investors, but some concerns were raised regarding physical infrastructure and port services. Back in 2018, the World Bank (2018[15]) already reported that the quality of Portugal's trade and transport related infrastructure, e.g. ports, railroads, roads and information technology, was perceived to fall below the OECD average and the level observed in some benchmark countries, namely Spain and the Czech Republic. These challenges seem to have persisted over time. Interviewed firms in e.g. automotive, agro-food and port sectors called for more investment in the country's railroads, roads, airports and ports. While Portugal's Sines is identified as relatively well-performing compared to many other European ports in World Bank (2022[16]), some consulted investors pointed out a need to improve road access to Portuguese ports and expand their operating hours.[44] Moreover, although outside of Portugal's domestic policy making sphere, the prohibition of cross-border use of so-called gigaliners or mega-trucks in the EU was raised as hampering efforts to reduce transport costs and emissions in cross-border traffic in the Iberian peninsula.[45]

65% of respondents also considered lengthy and complicated customs procedures as an obstacle in Portugal, citing limited opening hours of customs in ports, excessive documentation requirements, insufficient degree of digitalisation and a lack of user-centric approach as the main practical problems. As discussed in Chapter 2, international surveys indicate that although Portugal's customs regime is efficient compared to some peer countries, it is not on par with European best performers.

4.5. Funding and incentives

In addition to fiscal incentives (see Box 4.4), domestic and foreign-owned companies in Portugal may also qualify for various funds and grants and benefit from special investment regimes, such as PIN or PII status (see Chapter 2).

When inquired about their experience with some of such incentives and funding opportunities,[46] two-in five respondents reported to have benefitted from Portugal's research and development (R&D) tax credit (SIFIDE II, see Box 4.4), making it the most used incentive among the consulted firms. While a majority of users of SIFIDE II found it effective, the application process received mixed feedback, with some investors finding SIFIDE II easy to implement and others commenting that the process is unnecessarily complicated and time-consuming. Unexpectedly, negative feedback was mostly received from large firms, reporting issues such as burdensome documentation requirements, lack of competence in the public administration to evaluate applications and time-consuming application process (even with the help of external consultants). Nonetheless, SIFIDE II was considered by many firms as the best existing incentive in Portugal. Direct government funding for R&D in the form of grants and loans is also available, but accounts for a relatively small share of public support for business R&D in Portugal in comparison to the benchmark group (OECD, 2021[17]).[47]

The results of the business consultation suggest that there may be room for Portugal to further refine other incentives and funding opportunities and raise companies' awareness of existing support mechanisms. Recent OECD analysis also suggests that Portugal could benefit from ensuring better communication of the support available for investors, as well as from avoiding potential redundancies to improve coherence among the various regulatory incentives currently in place across different parts of the government, such as PIN or PII status or special residence permits for investors and start-ups (OECD, 2022[9]). Incentives offered by the central government were also perceived as a relatively less attractive factor of Portugal's investment climate in EY (2022[18]).[48]

Compared to SIFIDE II, investors reported having difficulties applying for support from various EU funds. Application processes under the Portugal 2020 and Portugal 2030 programmes were perceived as complicated, requiring external specialists. Long waiting times for grant decisions were seen as particularly problematic for this type of support as it imposes long delays on critical investment decisions.[49] Other incentives mentioned by the consulted businesses, but used by much fewer of them, include the tax regime for investment support (used by two investors in manufacturing industries) and the Patent Box regime (see Box 4.4; used by one ICT investor).[50] Several firms reported good experiences with AICEP's support: AICEP had, for instance, helped investors to set up collaborations with local universities, made introductions to key persons in Portuguese firms and acted as an intermediary in discussions with regulators.[51] Some firms had also benefitted from local support by cities, particularly in licensing and permitting (see Section 4.4.1).

Box 4.4. Fiscal incentives for investment

Portugal maintains various tax incentives for investment. The Investment Tax Code of 2014[1] seeks to promote the competitiveness of the Portuguese economy, job creation and maintenance, investment in less favoured regions, innovation and investment by SMEs, via the following incentives:

- An R&D tax credit (*Sistema de Incentivos Fiscais em Investigação e Desenvolvimento Empresarial*, SIFIDE II) allows firms to recover a part of their R&D costs. Beneficiaries are resident corporate taxpayers with their principal activity in agriculture, industry, trade or services, and non-resident companies with a permanent establishment in Portugal.
- The regime of contractual tax benefits for productive investment (*benefícios fiscais contratuais ao investimento produtivo*) applies to investment projects in specified economic activities, contributing to key development objectives defined in the legislation, job creation or maintenance and amounting to EUR 3 million or more. The benefits include: a tax credit of up to 25% of relevant investment, depending on the region where the project is located and the number of jobs created or maintained; exemption or reduction of stamp duty and municipal taxes on real estate transactions and ownership; and simplified customs procedures.
- Under the tax regime for investment support (*regime fiscal de apoio ao investimento,* RFAI), investment projects in specified economic activities but which do not fulfil the eligibility conditions for the contractual regime above, may nonetheless be eligible for a tax deduction and stamp duty exemption or reduction on real estate transactions and ownership.

From 1 January 2023, the previously applicable regimes for the deduction of profits retained and reinvested (*regime de dedução por lucros retidos e reinvestidos*) and the conventional remuneration of share capital (*remuneração convencional do capital social*) are merged to create a new incentive for the capitalisation of companies (*incentivo à capitalização das empresas,* ICE) in an effort to simplify tax incentives.[2] ICE consists of a tax deduction based on eligible capital increases.

Other fiscal incentives include the Patent Box regime (tax benefit for income derived from intellectual property) in the Corporate Income Tax Code[3] and a reduced corporate income tax rate for companies in inland areas under the Tax Benefits Statute.[4] The medium-term agreement on the improvement of income, wages and competitiveness also sets up a selective corporate income tax reduction for firms investing in R&D.[5.]

1. Decree-Law No. 162/2014;
2. New Article 43-D of Decree-Law No. 215/89;
3. Law No. 2/2014, Article 50-A;
4. Decree-Law No. 215/89, Article 41-B;
5. Acordo de médio prazo para a melhoria dos rendimentos, dos salários e da competitividade, 9 October 2022.

When asked about government support to firms for the reskilling of their employees, investors generally responded that they had either not used any training incentives or were not aware of any existing support mechanisms in this area. Only two interviewed companies indicated having benefitted from training initiatives, both reporting good results.[52] For selected examples of Portugal's training incentives, see Box 4.5. Training incentives, particularly in IT and digital, were perceived as necessary to encourage firms to continue qualifying their staff, due to a risk of trained employees subsequently leaving the firm or going abroad (see Section 4.4.3 on talent retention).

Box 4.5. Training incentives to reskill workers

Portugal has implemented several initiatives to reskill its workforce. Some of the incentives support companies in training their employees, while others focus on requalification of unemployed persons. Several training initiatives are co-ordinated by the Institute for Employment and Professional Training (*Instituto do Emprego e Formação Profissional*; IEFP). Some examples of training support include:

- A voucher (*Cheque-Formação*) for professional training, including of employed persons. Employers can apply for financial support for training which their employees undergo with certified training entities.
- Requalification trainings for unemployed and "at-risk" workers in industry, digital, green economy, trade and health, as part of PRO_MOV, led by private companies and IEFP and constituting a pilot project under the European-wide Reskilling 4 Employment initiative.
- To support digital transformation, ICT training is provided to unemployed people under the UPskill programme in collaboration with higher education institutions and private companies.
- A recent measure called *Formação Emprego + Digital 2025* supports employers in their digital transformation efforts by providing training for employees in specific areas of digital skills, as foreseen in Portugal's Recovery and Resilience Plan.

Source: Ordinance No. 229/2015; IEFP, PRO_MOV, consulted on 15 November 2022; Upskill.pt, consulted on 15 November 2022; Ordinance No. 246/2022.

Considering the skill shortages experienced by many investors (see Section 4.4.3), there may be room for Portugal to reassess the offer of employee training incentives, increase companies' awareness of these initiatives and ensure that the content of trainings aligns with business needs. According to a large business confederation, member companies consider that the offer of training centres should be adapted to better match business needs. In aeronautics, for instance, an industry representative considered that it is difficult to accommodate for all sector-specific needs and requirements in the training curriculum at higher skill levels, making the training ineffective in practice. At the level of vocational training (e.g. technicians), the curriculum of reskilling programmes was considered to be well aligned with the needs of the aerospace industry; but attracting participants to this type of training was seen as a challenge, with reportedly less than half of training places being filled.[53] Similarly, an investor in the ICT sector reported challenges in finding participants for IT re-skilling programmes.

4.6. Investment outlook: COVID-19 pandemic, digital and green transitions

This section briefly describes how the consulted businesses have responded to the effects of the COVID-19 pandemic and Russia's war against Ukraine. It also discusses investors' perceptions on government support for companies' digital transformation and green transition, identifying several aspects that may affect the shift towards the digital economy and net-zero emissions.

4.6.1. Impact of the pandemic and the war in Ukraine

The COVID-19 pandemic affected businesses' operations in Portugal in various ways. Most investors (63% of respondents) experienced increased revenues since the onset of the pandemic, but also increased costs

(66%). Only 13%, however, reported a decline in total employment. Over 40% of respondents increased exports, while nearly a quarter saw their exports decline. Thirty-eight percent reported no change in foreign sales. Eighty-one percent of firms indicated having revisited their supply chains in some way in response to the pandemic and/or the war in Ukraine. Diversifying suppliers across multiple countries was the most important strategic consideration for coping with possible supply chain disruptions. Other strategic solutions mentioned were the adoption of automation, 3D printing or similar technologies to cut costs and nearshoring (switching to suppliers closer to or in Portugal).

Volatile energy and commodity prices, economic consequences of the war in Ukraine and rising inflation and interest rates were perceived as relatively significant (potential) threats, with more than a half of respondents expecting these aspects to affect their operations in Portugal severely or in a substantial manner in the next 12 months. Less than one-in-three investors considered health risks, cyber risks or climate change as important challenges in the short-term perspective.[54] Despite the impacts of the COVID-19 pandemic and the war on the economy as a whole, a majority (63%) of respondents were planning further investment in Portugal in the next three years.[55]

4.6.2. Cost of investment and lack of know-how slow down firms' digital transformation

As highlighted in other recent corporate surveys, business in Portugal attach strong importance to digital transformation.[56] Half of the consulted firms have have already gone through one or several kinds of digital transformations. Respondents in manufacturing industries mentioned automation, paperless solutions and advertising technology, among others, as examples of their digital transformation. Remote working tools and practices were mentioned by firms in pharmaceuticals, ICT and business services. Other digitalisation efforts included, for instance, moving to cloud services and the uptake of sales automation tools. Nearly half of the respondents considered that further digital transformations were needed for the company's business model to remain competitive or economically viable in the medium term. Examples of such technologies included digitalisation and automation of processes (where possible), cloud computing, Internet of Things, artificial intelligence, big data and 5G.

Among the respondents, the cost of investment was the most commonly cited factor having prevented and/or inhibited firms' digital transformation or technology uptake, followed by insufficient know-how, for instance in terms of availability of talent or partners with technical knowledge. As also observed in OECD (2021[7]), the prevalence of micro enterprises, which typically struggle more with digitalisation, in Portugal's business fabric was seen as slowing down digital transformation. Some investors perceived the small domestic market and SME customer base as preventing factors, with a large business services firm observing difficulties by (smaller) Portuguese firms to grow online business internationally.

Portugal's various policy instruments in digital transformation (see Box 2.5 in Chapter 2) and the investment and reforms foreseen in its Recovery and Resilience Plan set out expectations for the strengthening of digital skills and increased adoption of digital technologies, including within companies. In fact, Portugal offers government support mechanisms for companies' digital transformation, but these measures received mixed feedback from investors. Some businesses were aware of training support in digital skills and technologies (see Box 4.5 above), R&D and innovation incentives and other financing, including support under the Recovery and Resilience Plan.[57] Several firms, particularly those in manufacturing industries, considered that more support for companies' digital transformation, as well as simpler and faster application processes, are needed. While firms in the automotive industry mentioned already investing in partnerships with universities and technical schools, it was considered that the government could further encourage such partnerships and incorporate more training on new technologies in the curricula of education institutes.

4.6.3. Companies ask for more government support for green transition

Portugal's Recovery and Resilience Plan and the government's carbon neutrality, renewables use and energy efficiency objectives more generally (see Chapter 1) set high expectations for the country's green transition. A recent business survey indicates that many Portuguese firms already have or are planning investment to deal with climate change, and a higher share of Portuguese than EU firms perceive the transition to stricter climate standards and regulation as an opportunity rather than a risk (EIB, 2022[10]).[58]

Government support is available for companies' green transition projects; for instance, under the Industry Decarbonisation system, introduced in 2021, businesses can apply for direct financial support for various low-carbon industry projects, including research and innovation.[59] Two-in-three consulted firms, however, indicated that Portugal's current policies and instruments are either insufficient or largely ineffective in influencing the firm or its stakeholders' green transition, while only 13% of respondents viewed them as providing significant support. Some consulted businesses were aware of support for green energy transition, such as for installing solar panels, considered effective by an industry federation. However, firms in the automotive industry and a Portuguese chamber of commerce viewed existing support instruments as too difficult to apply for, while an investor in the ICT sector considered that incentives should extend to energy storage in addition to energy generation. Three investors in ICT and manufacturing, as well as a foreign chamber of commerce, considered that other (European) countries offer more support for companies' green transition than Portugal does. Some businesses reported having already invested or planning to invest in, for instance, renewable energies, despite a perceived lack of government support or pressure from the government to advance towards carbon neutrality.

Respondents also reported some regulatory hurdles preventing or slowing down their green transition, particularly in renewable energies. A large firm reported that it could not sell back to the grid the energy surplus that could be generated during weekends or other times, e.g. when factories are closed. A respondent in crop and animal production also indicated obstacles in the sale of surplus energy obtained from solar panels, reporting that the concessionary in charge of managing the national grid (REN) "only appreciates the process from time to time and has no deadline for response". A chamber of commerce considered that lack of control regarding whether buyers of grid capacity produce electricity and inject it into the grid contributes to Portugal's relatively high energy prices; this because companies need to obtain a grid capacity reserve title prior to applying for a power production license and, according to the chamber, some companies were holding on to such rights to later resell them at a margin, impeding somewhat the entry of others into the market. However, as Portugal has recently amended its regulatory framework for licensing of electricity production and storage, it is possible that some of the concerns raised by investors reflect past legal situations.[60]

4.7. Conclusions

This chapter has mapped out foreign investors' views on several aspects of Portugal's regulatory framework and broader business environment, describing the results of a consultation held with foreign-owned companies and chambers of commerce in Portugal. The findings of the business consultation indicate that although some aspects of Portugal's investment climate, such as company incorporation processes, skilled workforce and digital infrastructure, are viewed in a positive light by foreign investors, important challenges for business operations remain in several regulatory areas.

While the reported views may reflect only some experiences and the perspectives of consulted investors, their wide-spread prevalence across the sectors of the economy and investors of different origin, size and location provide significant indication that aspects such as bureaucracy in administrative processes, lengthy and unpredictable licensing and permitting, long delays in the judicial system, relatively strict labour regulation and complicated tax regulation, may indeed be burdensome for businesses and make Portugal a less attractive FDI destination. Nonetheless, these findings are backed by other large-scale surveys and should be kept in mind when considering ways to improve the local investment climate.

In addition to outlining investors' perceptions of regulatory aspects, this chapter has mapped consulted businesses' use of government funding and incentives. While Portugal's R&D tax credit was used by several investors and considered by many as effective, there might be room to improve certain aspects of the incentive offering for the reskilling of employees, companies' digital transformation and green transition and increase the business community's awareness of existing incentives. This chapter has also provided some business perspectives on drivers of FDI into Portugal, concluding that access to a skilled labour force is still a leading factor for consulted M&A and greenfield investors' location choices.

Building on the above findings and those from previous chapters, Chapter 5 offers a number of policy considerations to further improve Portugal's regulatory set-up for investment and the broader business environment and to support the country's efforts to attract and retain foreign investment.

References

British Irish Chamber of Commerce and Fragomen (2019), *Brexit Guide: Employers' Handbook to EU Citizen Status and Rights Post-Brexit*, https://www.britishirishchamber.com/wp-content/uploads/2019/05/Brexit-guide_British-Irish-Chamber-of-Commerce_8-May-2019.pdf. [23]

CEPEJ (2022), *Study on the functioning of judicial systems in the EU Member States. Facts and figures from the CEPEJ questionnaires 2012 to 2020*, https://ec.europa.eu/info/publications/two-studies-prepared-european-commission-cepej-european-commission-efficiency-justice-functioning-judicial-systems-eu-member-states-2022_en. [21]

EIB (2022), *EIB Investment Survey 2021. Portugal Overview*, European Investment Bank, https://doi.org/10.2867/614689. [10]

EY (2022), *Portugal, the comfort zone to deal with uncertainty? EY Attractiveness Survey Portugal*, Ernst & Young, https://assets.ey.com/content/dam/ey-sites/ey-com/pt_pt/topics/attractiveness/ey-attractiveness-survey-portugal-july-2022.pdf. [18]

EY (2019), *Assessment of Simplex+ Programme. Final report*, Ernst & Young, European Commission Structural Reform Support Service. [2]

Grupo de Trabalho para o Estudo dos Benefícios Fiscais (2019), *Os benefícios fiscais em Portugal: conceitos, metodologia e prática*, Centro de Estudos Fiscais e Aduaneiros, Autoridade Tributária e Aduaneira, Lisboa, https://www.portugal.gov.pt/download-ficheiros/ficheiro.aspx?v=%3D%3DBAAAAB%2BLCAAAAAAABACzMDQwAgCG5%2BMmBAAAAA%3D%3D. [6]

INE (2022), *Inquérito aos Custos de Contexto 2021*, https://www.ine.pt/xportal/xmain?xpid=INE&xpgid=ine_destaques&DESTAQUESdest_boui=540898022&DESTAQUESmodo=2. [1]

OECD (2023), *Temporary employment* (indicator), https://doi.org/10.1787/75589b8a-en (accessed on 6 February 2023). [13]

OECD (2022), *Strengthening FDI and SME Linkages in Portugal*, OECD Publishing, Paris, https://doi.org/10.1787/d718823d-en. [9]

OECD (2022), *Tax Administration 2022: Comparative Information on OECD and other Advanced and Emerging Economies*, OECD Publishing, Paris, https://doi.org/10.1787/1e797131-en. [19]

OECD (2021), *OECD Corproate Tax Database*, OECD Publishing, https://oe.cd/tax-database. [22]

OECD (2021), *OECD Economic Surveys: Portugal 2021*, OECD Publishing, Paris, https://doi.org/10.1787/13b842d6-en. [7]

OECD (2021), *OECD R&D tax incentives database*, http://oe.cd/rdtax. [17]

OECD (2020), *Justice Transformation in Portugal: Building on Successes and Challenges*, OECD Publishing, Paris, https://doi.org/10.1787/184acf59-en. [14]

OECD (2020), *OECD Employment Outlook 2020: Worker Security and the COVID-19 Crisis*, OECD Publishing, Paris, https://doi.org/10.1787/1686c758-en. [11]

OECD (2019), *OECD Employment Protection Legislation indicators*, https://www.oecd.org/employment/emp/oecdindicatorsofemploymentprotection.htm. [12]

OECD et al. (2022), *Inventory of Tax Technology Initiatives*, https://www.oecd.org/tax/forum-on-tax-administration/tax-technology-tools-and-digital-solutions/ (accessed on 20 October 2022). [20]

Portugal Government (2021), *PRR – Plano de Recuperação e Resiliência*, República Portuguesa, XXII Governo, https://recuperarportugal.gov.pt/documentacao/. [5]

World Bank (2022), *The Container Port Performance Index 2021: A Comparable Assessment of Container Port Performance*, World Bank, Washington, DC, http://hdl.handle.net/10986/37542. [16]

World Bank (2021), *Enterprise Surveys (Spain)*, http://www.enterprisesurveys.org. [4]

World Bank (2020), *Doing Business*, https://archive.doingbusiness.org/en/doingbusiness. [8]

World Bank (2019), *Enterprise Surveys: Portugal 2019*, The World Bank Group, http://www.enterprisesurveys.org. [3]

World Bank (2018), *International Logistics Performance Index*, https://lpi.worldbank.org/about. [15]

Annex 4.A. Methodology of the business consultation

In the context of this report, foreign investors' perspectives about Portugal's business environment were captured through a series of consultations comprising two main elements: (i) an online survey with selected foreign-owned companies in Portugal and (ii) follow-up, semi-structured consultations with selected foreign investors, as well as with foreign and domestic chambers of commerce present in Portugal.

To secure a broad representation of different investor profiles, foreign-owned companies considered for the consultations were those having invested in Portugal in the last five years and matching certain pre-defined characteristics in terms of firm size, sector of activity, regional location in Portugal, investor country of origin and investment entry mode (greenfield vs. M&A). A set of firms matching these characteristics were identified using commercial databases on greenfield investment projects and M&As, respectively the Financial Times fDi Markets and the Refinitiv M&A databases, and based on AICEP's contacts database. The company selection also aimed at securing the participation of companies operating in Portugal's priority sectors for investment, not only in sectors specifically assessed in the comparative regulatory assessment of Chapter 2.

With AICEP's support, a set of some 100 companies were initially invited to participate in the consultations; about half accepted the invitation. A few additional investor contacts were also sought via foreign chambers of commerce in Portugal. These firms were then invited to respond to an online questionnaire from June to August 2022. Full responses were received from 32 senior executives. The online questionnaire consisted of eight groups of questions, collecting information on the following topics: general background information on the respondent company, motives which led the firm to invest in Portugal, regulatory and policy challenges for investment and day-to-day operations in Portugal, the investor's expansion outlook, the company's trade profile, use of incentive schemes, economic outlook in the context of COVID-19 and Russia's war against Ukraine, and the firm's digital transformation and green transition efforts.[61]

Following the online questionnaire, semi-structured interviews were held with 25 companies and ten chambers of commerce and industry federations between 19 September and 10 October 2022. Some of these meetings occurred bilaterally and some in focus groups invited by business associations. Most interviews were conducted in person in Lisbon, others via teleconference. In the interviews, investors were asked targeted questions based on their response to the online questionnaire, where applicable, to obtain additional information and clarifications. Business associations were asked more general questions on the topics covered in the questionnaire. Additionally, written clarification was received from two investors following their response to the online questionnaire.

Notes

[1] EY (2022[18]) measured Portugal's attractiveness in the eyes of 200 investors from various parts of the world from February to April 2022. 15% of the respondents were present in Portugal. EIB (2022[10]) collected information on investment plans, the impact of the COVID-19 pandemic and climate change, drivers and barriers of investment, among other topics, from 481 firms in Portugal from March to July 2021. Statistics Portugal (INE, 2022[1]) assessed "framework regulation costs" incurred by companies in the following areas: starting a business, licensing, network industries, financing, judicial system, tax system, administrative burden, barriers to internationalisation and human resources. Framework regulation costs refer to the negative effects on companies' activity caused by rules, procedures, actions and omissions not attributable to the firm or investor. Answers were collected from 4 672 non-financial firms headquartered in Portugal from February to April 2022. World Bank (2019[3]) surveyed perceptions of business owners and top managers in 1 062 firms from November 2018 to January 2020 regarding e.g. regulation, taxes, finance, infrastructure, trade and workforce.

[2] As in the previous chapters, aspects of Portugal's investment climate are benchmarked against a group of peer economies, namely the Czech Republic, Estonia, Lithuania, Poland, the Slovak Republic and Spain.

[3] Investors' concern with the regulatory environment has also appeared in other more comprehensive business surveys. After uncertainty about the future, business regulation was the second most cited long-term barrier to investment by firms in Portugal in EIB (2022[10]), in which business regulation was perceived as an investment barrier by 80% of surveyed Portuguese firms, compared to 65% of EU firms.

[4] Small and medium-sized enterprises reported more important obstacles than large and micro firms in taxation and licensing, whereas large firms were the most affected by the judicial system (INE, 2022[1]).

[5] A sector-specific concern raised in interviews was that, in the future, Portugal might introduce additional requirements in electronic communications regulation or exclude firms from certain parts of the network based on the investor's country of origin.

[6] According to the general rule of the Code of Administrative Procedure (Article 128 of Decree-Law No. 4/2015), administrative procedures of private initiative must be decided within a period of 60 days, unless another period arises from the law. This period may be extended by the person responsible for directing the procedure, in duly justified exceptional circumstances, up to a maximum limit of 90 days.

[7] Article 130 of Decree-Law No. 4/2015.

[8] Article 16 of Decree-Law No. 169/2012 creating the Responsible Industry System.

[9] See, for instance, Article 19 of Decree-Law No. 151-B/2013 establishing the Environmental Impact Assessment regime; Article 23 of Decree-Law No. 127/2013 establishing the industrial emissions regime; and Article 17 of Decree-Law No. 226-A/2007 regarding authorisation for the use of water resources.

[10] Article 111 of Decree-Law No. 555/99 provides for the possibility of tacit approval only in certain processes in urbanisation and construction, such as applications for occupancy permits (*autorização de utilisação*), excluding municipal licensing processes from the scope of the "silence is consent" rule.

[11] Additionally, in some cases, a license is considered to have been granted tacitly only if there are no grounds for rejection. This is the case under Article 23 of Decree-Law No. 127/2013 (industrial emissions) and Article 17 of Decree-Law No. 226-A/2007 (use of water resources).

[12] Requirements to obtain additional authorisations for installations or expansions already covered by an industrial site's environmental impact assessment were mentioned as an example of excessive bureaucracy in environmental licensing.

[13] In fact, while some degree of simplification of environmental licensing procedures may be welcome by investors, it is important to ensure that the envisaged reform does not compromise environmental protection standards and, more broadly, the capacity of institutions to protect public interests by making informed decisions in licensing and permit matters. An assessment of the extent to which the proposal would indeed reduce bureaucracy without negative consequences to environmental protection is, however, not possible within the scope of this report.

[14] For instance, an investor in real estate considered that technicians in public administration act as gatekeepers in the approval of real estate projects, imposing requirements that do not always have a sound legal basis. In turn, obtaining the involvement of high-level public authorities and navigating permit processes was, at times, easier in smaller municipalities.

[15] The investor reported that the application process took around six months in Portugal, compared to as few as two or three weeks in best-performing European countries.

[16] This observation is aligned with the findings of INE (2022[1]), concluding that information and communication and other services (excluding construction and hospitality) were the segments least affected by licensing, whereas firms in industry, agriculture, and energy, water and sanitation reported a particularly high negative impact of licensing.

[17] Two investors explicitly mentioned an excessive need for legal services in Portugal in relation to other countries they have invested in, even though they could not attest that this had translated into significantly higher costs.

[18] Overall, businesses reported that the private sector was not usually consulted in law-making, at least not within an appropriate timeframe, and even if consultations were held, their concerns were not necessarily taken into account.

[19] Government of Portugal press release, 7 December 2022.

[20] Such as the Cabinet from the Secretary of State for Digitalisation and Administrative Modernisation, other cabinets and the Competence Centre for Planning, Policy and Foresight in Public Administration.

[21] Information obtained in consultations with Portuguese stakeholders in December 2022.

[22] In business surveys conducted by Statistics Portugal in 2014, 2017 and 2021, the tax system has consistently come out as the area representing the highest "framework regulation costs" for businesses, with tax burden being the most cited obstacle in the area of taxation in 2021 (INE, 2022[1]). Similar results are reported by EY (2022[18]) and the World Bank (2019[3]). Businesses consulted for this report also perceive Portugal's statutory corporate income tax rate (CIT; set at 31.5%, national and sub-national CIT combined) to be comparatively high. The second highest statutory CIT rate in the benchmark group (Spain) is about 6.5 percentage points lower (OECD, 2021[22]). Statutory CIT rates incorporate a strong signalling effect, but they do not reflect existing allowances and special tax incentives which some firms can benefit

from. When some tax base provisions are taken into account (e.g. capital allowances), Portugal's effective corporate tax rate is significantly reduced and lower than in some peer economies (see the OECD's (2021[22]) data on forward-looking effective average tax rates). A more comprehensive assessment of the tax burden for business would be necessary to determine possible shortcomings of the current structure, reforms and implications. This is, however, not possible in the context of this report.

23 Article 68 of Decree-Law No. 398/98.

24 Article 68(8) of Decree-Law No. 398/98.

25 Pre-filling is available for expense information in corporate income tax returns, and both sales and purchase transactions in value added tax (VAT) returns (OECD et al., 2022[20]). One-hundred percent of corporate income tax returns and VAT returns are filed via electronic systems (OECD, 2022[19]). Further investment in the digitalisation of public administration, including tax administration, are planned under Portugal's Recovery and Resilience Plan (Portugal Government, 2021[5]).

26 Tax administration data from the World Bank Enterprise surveys, which are administered across countries to a representative sample of firms in the non-agricultural, formal, private economy, are for the latest year available: 2019 for all countries, except Spain (2021).

27 Media entities and websites disseminating financial services advertisements in Portugal must verify the veracity of the information in such ads and insert in them the financial services provider's registration number with the regulatory authority. Article 3 of Law No. 78/2021.

28 In Portugal, an administrative entity has the power to request the removal of or prevention of access to content that has been unlawfully made available online, whereas in the investor's experience, such interventions are subject to judicial control in other EU countries. Law No. 82/2021.

29 Law No. 16/2022 transposing Directive (EU) 2018/1972.

30 In Statistics Portugal's business surveys, the area of human resources has consistently represented more bureaucracy for firms, with increasing negative effects for companies from 2014 to 2021, with the 2021 result reflecting difficulties in accessing qualified technicians (INE, 2022[1]).

31 The recognition of non-EU foreign professional qualifications, although ranked as an obstacle by close to half of the respondents to the questionnaire, was not confirmed as a major concern during the interviews. The consultation showed that recognition of qualifications might be an issue for foreign candidates in the public sector and in some specific activities in the private sector, e.g. health care and professional services.

32 Figures from 2019 indicate that processing times are considerably longer in Portugal than in best-performing European countries and longer than in some peer countries, such as the Czech Republic (British Irish Chamber of Commerce and Fragomen, 2019[23]).

33 Information obtained in consultations with Portuguese stakeholders in December 2022. The possibility to extend the validity of the visa as long as the residence permit application is pending is foreseen in Article 72 of the Foreigners Act (Law No. 23/2007).

34 Law No. 18/2022 (25 August 2022) amending Article 58 of Law No. 23/2007.

35 Law No. 18/2022 (25 August 2022) introducing a new Article 57-A to Law No. 23/2007.

[36] Decree-Law No. 187/2007, Article 19. The minimum period of 15 years applies to all workers, including Portuguese ones; however, time worked in other countries may count towards the 15-year limit based on bilateral or multilateral agreements to which Portugal is a party, with the EU being a notable example.

[37] One investor reported being hesitant of recruiting from non-EEA countries, considering it somewhat risky to go through the burdensome process of recruiting from abroad for then possibly seeing the non-EEA employee follow the route of Portuguese talents moving abroad for more competitive job offers.

[38] See OECD (2022[9]) for a literature review on the economic impacts of EPL.

[39] Some firms reported that contesting the tax authority's decisions is, in practice, made ineffective by the long duration of proceedings in administrative and fiscal courts. Two investors considered that the tax authority tends to litigate, relying more on auditing than creating guidelines or procedures for tax subjects regarding the correct application of (new) rules.

[40] In INE (2022[1]), over half of the firms considered the duration of proceedings as a high or very high obstacle. Large firms reported a slightly more important negative impact of the judicial system than small and medium sized enterprises, while micro firms were affected to a lesser extent. Fiscal disputes were perceived as presenting more obstacles than commercial or labour related disputes.

[41] At 2.9 non-judge staff per judge in 2020, the ratio between non-judge staff and professional judges in Portugal is slightly below the EU median (3.3) and below the level observed in any of the peer countries (CEPEJ, 2022[21]). There has been no significant change in Portugal in these figures since 2012.

[42] The underlying reasons supporting the interviewed firm's opinion could not be further explored during the consultation.

[43] There may be more widespread barriers on SME participation in public tenders in Portugal, with relatively small proportions of bids from SMEs (44% of all bids) and of SME contractors (42%) compared to most other EU countries. European Commission, Single Market Scoreboard, consulted on 10 November 2022.

[44] World Bank (2022[16]) ranks Sines as the sixth best performing container port in Europe and North Africa, and second-best performing small port globally, in terms of total port hours per ship call.

[45] Directive 96/53/EC does not currently allow Member States to authorise cross-border use of gigaliners, even if both Member States have authorised their use at the domestic level, as in Portugal and Spain.

[46] For instance, the R&D tax credit (SIFIDE II), funding under the *Agendas para a Inovação Empresarial* programme, support for low-carbon industry projects under the Industry Decarbonisation programme, technology transfer between companies and universities via *Programa Interface*, Digital Innovation Hubs, Start-up Visa programme and local support from cities. Additional feedback, not limited to the above-mentioned initiatives, was collected in interviews.

[47] Recently, the offering of direct support mechanisms has been strengthened by the implementation of new measures. The *Agendas para a Inovação Empresarial* programme (Ordinance No. 43-A/2022) promotes innovative projects that can support Portugal's economic recovery from the COVID-19 pandemic. Eligible investment include collaborative R&D projects carried out by companies and research entities. The programme, however, received mixed reviews from consulted investors: one respondent said it was "very effective" for supporting R&D activities, another reported that the application process was "very bureaucratic" and time-consuming. Under the Industry Decarbonisation programme (Ordinance No. 325-A/2021), firms in extractive industries and manufacturing industries can apply for direct support for low-carbon industry projects, including research and innovation processes.

[48] Central Government's incentives were seen as "very attractive" by 5% of surveyed firms, whereas regional and municipal authorities' support and incentives were considered slightly more attractive (11% of firms) in EY (2022[18]).

[49] According to respondents, Portugal 2020 and Portugal 2030 programmes' rules prevent applicants from going ahead with their investment projects while waiting for a positive decision because any investment made before receiving a decision cannot be contemplated in the support scheme.

[50] Two-in-five respondents indicated that they had not used any incentives or funding opportunities; perhaps partly due to challenges regarding e.g. eligibility, bureaucracy or long waiting times, as 55% of respondents reported difficulties accessing local funding, grants or subsidies as an obstacle to their operations in Portugal. Some investors also considered that support for large firms had overall become scarcer over the years.

[51] Portugal's investment promotion agency AICEP provides various support services, information and contacts to foreign investors seeking to establish or expand a business in Portugal. Support can include, for instance, organisation of site visits, provision of site proposals and establishing contacts with local entities. AICEP Portugal Global, AICEP support, consulted on 14 November 2022.

[52] For instance, a firm in the automotive industry had used grants for employee training. An investor in the ICT sector had participated in a requalification programme, committing to hiring talent who undergo a six-month training in a university, to mitigate skill shortage in the sector.

[53] It is to be noted, however, that the aeronautics sector is a relatively newly developed one in Portugal and competence-building work is ongoing.

[54] In EIB (2022[10]), 72% of firms in Portugal considered that climate change and related changes in weather events already affected their business, albeit most reported the impact of climate change as minor.

[55] As of 23 August 2022. This finding is aligned with the results of EY (2022[18]), in which 62% of surveyed investors had plans to establish or expand operations in Portugal over the next year, up from 37% in 2021.

[56] In EY (2022[18]), 52% of surveyed investors identified the digital economy as the leading sector to drive Portugal's growth in the coming years, up from 45% in 2021. Forty-two percent of firms surveyed in EIB (2022[10]) had already taken action to become more digital as a response to the pandemic, and 58% expected COVID-19 to have a long-term impact on their business, in terms of increased use of digital technologies.

[57] The Recovery and Resilience Plan foresees EUR 650 million worth of investment in companies' digital transition, through training programmes in digital skills (see Box 4.5), a national network of test beds, coaching and support for the digitalisation of SMEs, among others (Portugal Government, 2021[5]).

[58] EIB (2022[10]) found that 36% of firms in Portugal had already invested to deal with climate change and 50% were planning do so in the next three years. Thirty-seven percent of Portuguese firms perceived the transition to stricter climate standards and regulation as an opportunity, compared to 28% of EU firms. The survey, however, does not provide an explanation for such difference with the EU average.

[59] Ordinance No. 325-A/2021.

[60] In 2022, the regulatory framework for the electricity sector was renewed by the adoption of Decree-Law No. 15/2022, in effect from 15 January 2022, establishing the organisation and functioning of the National Electric System. The law consolidates the legal framework in the sector, aligns the National Electric System

with Portugal's energy and climate objectives and transposes EU energy directives into national law. The previously established requirement to obtain a grid capacity reserve title before the investor can apply for a production license has been retained in the new law. Under the new regime, the reserve titles are transferable until the issuance of a production license.

[61] The content of the online questionnaire can be consulted in detail at: https://www.oecd.org/daf/inv/OECD-EU-Portugal-Questionnaire-Impact-Regulation-Foreign-Direct-Investment.pdf.

5 Policy conclusions

This chapter summarises the key findings of the report and outlines policy considerations that can support Portugal in its efforts to attract and retain more FDI and improve the country's general business environment. It proposes policy measures that can help to improve the investment climate economy-wide – such as in relation to operating licenses and permits, tax compliance, access to skilled domestic and foreign talent, regulatory governance, investment incentives and judicial system – as well as in selected sectors (professional services, transports, logistics and digitally enabled services) providing strategic support to Portugal's priority sectors for investment. The suggested policy actions focus on facilitating market entry and promoting competition in such strategic sectors.

Key policy considerations

- Continue to facilitate the entry of foreign firms by keeping up investment in online solutions for company incorporation and lowering the minimum capital requirement for public limited liability companies. Promote transparency, accountability and flexibility in the implementation of the foreign investment screening mechanism.
- Further strengthen regulatory impact assessment and stakeholder engagement in law-making to ensure that business regulation meets its intended objectives, further minimise unnecessary administrative burden for businesses and help firms anticipate forthcoming changes.
- Implement planned reforms to streamline business licensing while preserving the institutions' capacity to make informed decisions and protect public interests. Standardised operating procedures, increased resources, digitalisation and enforcing tacit approval can contribute towards speedier decisions and legal certainty for investors.
- Continue simplifying corporate taxation and ensure timely communication and guidance on forthcoming changes to reduce tax compliance costs for companies. Further developing tax (assistance) services can also contribute to this goal while increasing predictability and legal certainty for taxpayers.
- Take further steps to increase the efficiency of the judicial system to tackle the case backlog in courts and improve investor confidence in Portugal's business environment.
- Help businesses mitigate skill shortages by speeding up entry processes for third-country talent. Recent amendments to the Foreigners Act are a step to the right direction. Increase firms' awareness of employee training incentives and continue investing in digital skills training to maintain the attractiveness of Portugal's talent pool for investors.
- Continue efforts to reduce labour market segmentation between workers with permanent and temporary contracts to promote productivity growth.
- Assess existing investment incentives with a view to revising and possibly streamlining them to ensure effectiveness and reduce unnecessary complexity for applicants. Promote greater take-up of incentives also by increasing transparency and raising investors' awareness of support mechanisms. Better differentiate the available support to target specific types of FDI.
- Implement targeted reforms in professional services, transports, logistics and digitally enabled services to lift remaining regulatory hurdles for foreign providers and promote the competitiveness of these key supporting sectors. Improved foreign investment entry and competition conditions can result in an increase of investment projects in these sectors and be beneficial to firms, including domestic ones, in downstream industries economy-wide.

5.1. Introduction

Alongside an impressive economic rebound, foreign direct investment (FDI) in Portugal has grown rapidly over the last decade, resulting in one of the highest levels of inward FDI stocks among OECD countries. Yet, with overall investment levels remaining relatively low, Portugal would benefit from mobilising further FDI to respond to long-term structural challenges weighing on productivity growth and to accelerate the country's digital and green transitions. Ensuring that Portugal continues to be an attractive destination for foreign investors is therefore essential.

Although foreign investors benefit from Portugal's relatively open regulatory framework, previous chapters of this report have highlighted areas where further regulatory reforms could help Portugal build a more enabling and competitive environment for investment. This chapter outlines the key findings of the report in this regard and suggests policy actions to support Portugal's efforts to attract and retain FDI. The first section of this chapter provides policy considerations regarding broader aspects that affect businesses across different sectors of the economy, while the second section outlines sector-specific considerations. The third section concludes by suggesting next steps for the implementation of investment climate reforms.

As discussed in Chapter 3, regulatory liberalisation is not an end in and of itself. Strict policy approaches to investment or business more broadly can sometimes be needed to serve important public interests. Nonetheless, regulation that is overly strict in proportion to its intended objectives may have the unintended consequence of increasing business costs. Drawing from best practice regulation and relatively less burdensome rules adopted in peer countries, as identified in previous chapters, this chapter proposes measures that could help Portugal achieve its policy objectives while improving operating conditions for foreign investors and domestic firms alike. The timing could not be more apt to consider alternative policy approaches, as structural reforms envisaged in Portugal's Recovery and Resilience Plan are currently being scoped and in some instances implemented across many areas addressed in the present chapter.

5.2. General policy implications

Overall, Portugal has a relatively open regulatory environment for FDI, with only a few statutory limitations on foreign investment and more competition-friendly regulation than OECD countries on average. Yet, there is potential to further improve Portugal's investment climate by undertaking reforms in several areas affecting a wide range of companies across different sectors of the economy. In addition to regulatory reforms, the policy considerations outlined in this section call more broadly for an increasingly service-oriented approach in the implementation of business regulation.

5.2.1. Facilitate market entry

Foreign investors in Portugal, including investors from outside the European Economic Area (EEA), benefit from relatively open market entry. New domestic and foreign-owned firms also face a relatively light administrative burden in Portugal, compared to most benchmarked countries. Although policies related to starting a business and investment screening did not arise as a priority in the business consultation undertaken in the context of this report (see Chapter 4), a few targeted measures to further facilitate foreign investors' establishment of new firms in Portugal and acquisitions of existing ones would be welcome.

Since 2005, Portugal has implemented simplified company incorporation procedures and electronic registration services to start a business, such as the *Empresa na Hora* and *Empresa Online* initiatives. However, despite Portugal's impressive track record in improving digital government services, there is still room to improve the online availability and use of public services for entrepreneurs to start a business and conduct daily operations. Furthermore, even if Portugal has eliminated minimum capital requirements for private limited companies in 2011, it still maintains a stricter minimum capital requirement for public limited liability companies (EUR 50 000) than some peer countries and the minimum level required by European Union (EU) legislation (EUR 25 000).

- Continue expanding the offer of online solutions for company incorporation, including for foreign nationals, as has been done in e.g. Estonia. Implement the planned "e-Residency" platform, which would allow foreign companies to incorporate in Portugal fully remotely. Invest in simplifying other online procedures adopted during the company lifecycle (such as licensing and permits, management and closure), as foreseen in the Recovery and Resilience Plan, and further encourage the use of online services by businesses and citizens.
- Reduce the cost of incorporation by aligning the minimum capital requirement for public limited companies with peer countries, such as Estonia and the Slovak Republic, which maintain the

minimum level required by EU law. As discussed in Chapter 2, minimum capital requirements have generally not had the intended effect of protecting creditors.

Certain non-EEA foreign acquisitions of strategic assets in Portugal are potentially subject to government review and may be blocked if they are deemed to jeopardise national defense and security or security of supply of essential services. Amendments to ensure transparency in the implementation of the foreign investment screening mechanism and to allow for tailored responses could be considered, should Portugal decide to modernise the current mechanism in the near future in line with reforms in other EU countries.

- Promote transparency and accountability in the implementation of the screening mechanism by requiring the executive to periodically report to the parliament and/or the public (aggregated) information on screened transactions and outcomes, while ensuring confidentiality.
- Increase predictability for investors and flexibility in the implementation of the screening mechanism by introducing a possibility of negotiating or imposing obligations or conditions for the transaction to address security concerns, as an alternative to blocking the acquisition. In the peer group, the Czech Republic and the Slovak Republic's screening legislation already foresees the use of such mitigation measures.

5.2.2. Strengthen good regulatory governance

Public consultations on draft regulation proposed by the executive are open to all interested persons, including businesses, and an online consultation portal ConsultaLEX was launched in 2019 to facilitate stakeholder engagement in the drafting of secondary legislation proposed by the executive branch. Competition impact assessment has recently been introduced as a mandatory element of the executive's proposals for new regulation. Yet, OECD indicators show that there remains room for Portugal to strengthen good regulatory practices in comparison with peer countries and the OECD average, particularly in terms of regulatory impact assessment (RIA) and stakeholder engagement in law-making (see Section 2.2.3).

Some of the foreign investors and chambers of commerce interviewed for this report also felt that the private sector was not consulted enough in the drafting of regulation, or was not consulted within an appropriate time frame, and business perspectives and realities were not sufficiently considered in law-making. The recent consultation process in preparation of an environmental licensing reform, however, was welcomed by a consulted chamber of commerce as a positive development in involving the private sector in law-making. Additionally, many investors identified difficulties understanding regulation and frequent changes in the legal framework as obstacles to their operations in Portugal.

- Continue promoting RIA and stakeholder engagement practices in both domestic law-making and transposition of EU directives to ensure better understanding of the effects of new regulation on companies and further reduce unnecessary administrative burden. The process developed for the preparation of licensing reforms (see Section 4.4.2 in Chapter 4) is a step towards more active stakeholder involvement and the good practices implemented therein could be generalised to the drafting of other business regulation.
- Broaden the use of ConsultaLEX to cover all levels of regulation and also non-legislative initiatives (e.g. strategy documents and action plans of relevant agencies), use RIA to support discussions with stakeholders, strengthen timely communication of regulation under preparation and engage with stakeholders in earlier stages of the drafting process to identify alternative policy options, and make more extensive use of *ex post* reviews of regulation to ensure that it fulfils its intended objectives (OECD, 2021[1]; 2022[2]). Follow the example of e.g. Estonia, Poland, the Slovak Republic and Spain and make RIA documents publicly available online.

- Ensure sufficiently long transitional periods in new regulation to allow time for businesses to adapt to changing obligations. Improved transparency and more active stakeholder engagement in law-making, as described above, can also help firms anticipate forthcoming changes in regulation.

5.2.3. Increase the speed and predictability of business licensing

Large-scale business surveys indicate that firms in Portugal perceive obtaining operating licenses and permits as more time-consuming and to some extent more burdensome than in peer countries (see Box 4.1 in Chapter 4). Despite simplification measures implemented as part of systematic efforts to reduce administrative burden for companies, the foreign investors consulted in the context of this report also cited burdensome interactions with public administration in the context of obtaining the necessary operational licenses and permits to start or expand a business in Portugal, such as environmental licenses or construction permits. Sector-specific challenges were observed, for instance, in the authorisation of clinical trials in the pharmaceutical industry. Commonly perceived shortcomings in licensing and permitting included long delays, lack of transparency and predictability on process timelines, complex procedures and requirements, the discretion of the bureaucracy and uncertainty stemming from lack of standardised operating procedures.

- Continue to simplify licensing procedures, following the example of recently streamlined environmental licensing and as foreseen in the Recovery and Resilience Plan, while preserving the capacity of institutions to make informed decisions and protect public interests more broadly. Consider introducing a single license to simplify the start and expansion of operations; for instance, in the Netherlands, building, planning and zoning, and environmental permissions are generally covered by an "all-in-one" permit.[1]
- Ensure the capacity of institutions to issue licenses and permits within statutory deadlines, e.g. by strengthening human and/or financial resources and accelerating the digitalisation of both internal processes and interactions with businesses to further help expedite decisions. For instance, speeding up the approval of clinical trials could contribute to increasing Portugal's competitiveness and attractiveness for investment in the pharmaceuticals sector.
- Enforce tacit approval to increase legal certainty for investors when there is no timely response from authorities, without jeopardising monitoring and compliance standards, as contemplated in the scoped reform in relation to streamlining environmental licensing but also administrative processes more broadly.
- Consider standardising licensing and permit procedures (e.g. applications and required documents), as well as other processes involving interaction with the authorities, across the relevant institutions in different parts of the country to improve the efficiency of processing requests and compliance monitoring by relevant authorities and increase predictability for investors.
- Leverage foreign investors' positive experiences with smaller municipalities' dynamic approach to licensing and broader support to attract foreign investors outside the Lisbon and Porto areas. Sub-national offices of AICEP and IAPMEI could be leveraged to strengthen the investment promotion and support capabilities of municipalities and inter-municipal councils, for instance by encouraging the sharing of good practices (OECD, 2022[2]).

5.2.4. Reduce tax compliance time and costs

Although steps have been taken in recent years to simplify the tax system by eliminating several special provisions and Portugal has made available tax simplification measures, such as prefilled declarations and online services, taxation has consistently come out as an obstacle or relatively unattractive factor in surveys of Portuguese firms, with businesses spending more time on tax compliance in Portugal than in most of the peer countries (see Section 4.4.2 in Chapter 4). Investors consulted for this report also largely considered that Portuguese tax regulation is still relatively difficult to understand and burdensome to comply with. Investors also cited frequent changes in tax regulation and difficulties obtaining clarification on the interpretation of new rules as aspects contributing to uncertainty, difficulties planning long-term investment and increased time spent on tax compliance.

- Continue efforts to implement a simpler and streamlined corporate tax regime to bring down tax compliance costs for foreign investors and domestic-owned firms alike (OECD, 2021[3]).
- Ensure timely communication of changes to taxpayers and appropriate transitional periods for them to adjust to new obligations (IMF/OECD, 2017[4]). More extensive regulatory impact assessment and more actively involving business stakeholders in the drafting of new tax rules could help policy makers to pinpoint possible ambiguities at an earlier stage of drafting and companies to anticipate forthcoming changes and get accustomed to them ahead of their implementation.
- Strengthen Portugal's offering of tax information and assistance services to increase predictability and legal certainty for taxpayers and facilitate tax compliance. For instance, ensure timely issuance of guidance notes and rulings, adopt further digital assistance services (e.g. chatbots) and promote the use of software integrating tax services in the systems that corporate taxpayers use to run their business, such as payroll systems (OECD et al., 2022[5]; OECD, 2021[6]).[2] Strengthening the tax authority's capacity to issue guidance and binding rulings could also help prevent excessive tax litigation (IMF/OECD, 2017[4]).

5.2.5. Continue increasing the efficiency of the judicial system

Portugal has undertaken reforms in its justice system and improved the efficiency of its courts in recent years. Yet, the duration of court proceedings remains long compared to peer countries, particularly in administrative cases, which take more than eight times as long to resolve in first instance courts in Portugal than in the benchmark group's best performer Lithuania (see Section 2.2.4 in Chapter 2). Long judicial proceedings may undermine Portugal's FDI attractiveness while also affecting domestic investors.

The prevalence of late payments and difficulties in collecting them are also viewed by investors as a particular challenge in Portugal. Even with a declining number of cases, enforcement cases (including contract enforcement and insolvency) still account for much of the backlog in courts.

- Continue efforts to further reduce the length of court proceedings in all branches of justice to tackle the backlog in courts and improve investors' confidence in Portugal's business environment. Speed up insolvency processes, increase digitalisation in courts and reform administrative and tax courts, as foreseen in Portugal's Recovery and Resilience Plan. Strengthen human resources in court support functions to help address backlogs and improve efficiency (OECD, 2020[7]).
- Make more extensive use of existing out-of-court mechanisms and create new ones, for instance for firm liquidation (OECD, 2020[7]). An assessment of businesses' use and awareness of the current out-of-court mechanisms, including those for firm recovery, could be a first step towards improving the dissemination of information on such mechanisms and increasing their take-up.

5.2.6. Ensure that the talent pool remains attractive for investors

Portugal's highly skilled labour force is one of the leading drivers of foreign firms' decision to invest or expand in the country, and the quality of Portugal's higher education institutes is seen as an advantage in attracting FDI. At the same time, skill shortages (e.g. in information technology and engineering professionals, technicians and middle management) is one of the most important concerns for investors in some sectors.

Portugal's Recovery and Resilience Plan and the Digital Transition Action Plan foresee reforms to increase the population's educational and professional qualifications, as well as investment to increase the number of graduates in science, technology, engineering and mathematics, namely through the implementation of the *Impulso Jovens STEAM* and *Impulso Adultos* programmes. Boosting the domestic supply of skilled labour via the educational system is important to ensure that Portugal's talent pool remains attractive for investors in the long term.

However, fully leveraging existing and planned skills development initiatives and facilitating the entry of foreign talent can be an additional and prompter way to address skill shortages in the short term. Some firms use employee training with good results to address talent shortage, but many investors are either not aware of existing government support for training or do not find it effective. Businesses also see bottlenecks in the entry processes of third-country professionals, mainly from the Immigration and Border Service (SEF)'s long processing times and difficulties obtaining an appointment for the issuance of a residence permit. Recent amendments to the Foreigners Act, easing the entry conditions of foreign talent, are thus welcomed by foreign investors. The issuance of a "pre-residence authorisation" together with the residence visa, with provisional tax and social security numbers and information on obtaining a residence permit, can ease some of the administrative burden faced by foreign talent. However, taking further steps to cut waiting times for visas and residence permit appointments may still be needed to help businesses bring talent from third countries.

- Continue investing in skill upgrading programmes and increase businesses' awareness of government support for employee training, including in digital skills and technologies, for instance via ensuring clear and up-to-date incentive guidelines and targeted information campaigns. Strengthen the alignment of training programmes, as well as PhD degrees, with business needs and the objectives of Portugal's smart specialisation, innovation and entrepreneurship strategies and ensure greater co-ordination between existing and planned initiatives (OECD, 2022[2]).
- Evaluate the possibility of redesigning internal processes as part of the planned restructuring of SEF,[3] better leveraging digital tools and/or allocating more resources to the processing of applications to speed up the entry of foreign talent from third countries.
- Foreign nationals entering the country with the newly introduced job-seeker visa are automatically assigned an appointment with SEF for the issuance of a residence permit. Portugal could consider expanding this new approach of automatic residence permit appointment to other visa types, including residence visa on the grounds of employment (i.e. for those already having an employment contract or job offer when entering Portugal), to reduce the number of steps to obtaining a residence permit.

5.2.7. Promote fair and flexible labour market policies

Workers in Portugal enjoy relatively high employment protection standards compared to peer countries. Labour market regulation came up as a relatively more important obstacle to investment in Portugal than in the EU on average in a recent large-scale business survey, and likely due to experiences with strict regulation of dismissals of employees with regular (permanent) contracts, the rules on hiring and firing are perceived by investors as one of the main challenges of Portugal's business environment (see Section 4.4.4 in Chapter 4). Firms tend to mitigate the difficulty of dismissals of unperforming regular workers through, for instance, probationary periods, sub-contracting or temporary contracts.

Even if Portugal has highly guarded regular contracts, it continues to have relatively low protection of temporary contracts, i.e. fixed-term contracts and temporary work agency contracts, and the incidence of temporary employment is particularly high. Taking further steps to reduce labour market segmentation along the type of contracts is important to address Portugal's productivity challenge and improve labour market conditions of more vulnerable workers (e.g. youth, women and low-skilled).

- Continue efforts to address labour market segmentation by reducing the gap in the protection of workers with temporary contracts compared to relatively highly protected permanent contracts, in line with the recommendations of OECD (2021[3]; 2019[8]). Consider strengthening the framework to make performance-based dismissals of employees with permanent contracts an effective possibility, as in most benchmark economies, while continuing to ensure strong protection against unfair dismissals (OECD, 2022[2]). Implement the scoped reform, which would, among other proposals, further limit the renewal of fixed-term contracts, to improve the employment protection of workers under temporary contracts.

5.2.8. Strengthen targeted funding and incentive offering

Portugal has put in place various funding opportunities, (fiscal) incentives and special regulatory regimes to promote investment. While two-in-five foreign investors consulted for this report had benefitted from Portugal's research and development (R&D) tax incentive and many of them viewed it as effective, the business consultation, previous OECD analysis and a large-scale business survey suggest that there may be room to further refine other funding opportunities and incentives and raise investors' awareness of some of these mechanisms to increase their take-up.

For instance, while some investors found Portugal's special regulatory regimes for investment (such as *Potencial Interesse Nacional* status for large-scale projects) as effective in streamlining the licensing of eligible projects, others considered that the initiatives did not speed up licensing or offer sufficient follow-up and support in project implementation. As discussed elsewhere in this chapter, many investors are also not aware of existing government support for employee training (see Section 5.2.6 above) and firms' digital and green transitions (see Section 5.2.9 below).

- Assess existing funding opportunities and incentives, including tax benefits, regularly with a view to revising and possibly streamlining the available incentives and ensuring that they reach their intended objectives while keeping added complexity to e.g. the tax system at a minimum (OECD, 2022[2]; Grupo de Trabalho para o Estudo dos Benefícios Fiscais, 2019[9]). For instance, ensure through systematic reviews that incentives remain effective, in terms of their benefits outweighing administration costs and the scope of R&D and innovation incentives following the development of new technologies (OECD, 2022[10]). Clarity on how the different schemes meet the needs of investors can help Portugal to ensure policy coherence (i.e. to avoid potential inconsistencies and redundancies arising from operating too many incentives at too small a scale in different parts of the government) and develop more targeted and differentiated financial and technical support for specific types of investors (e.g. for firms of different sizes) (OECD, 2022[2]; 2022[10]).
- Promote a greater take-up of existing incentives among investors by increasing transparency and investors' awareness of incentives, for instance by ensuring clear and up-to-date information on the eligibility criteria and awarding process and promoting support mechanisms via incentives guides (including in English), consolidated information on incentives dispersed across different pieces of legislation and information campaigns (Dayan, 2021[11]). Consider simplifying application procedures for funding, grants and subsidies to the extent possible. The R&D tax incentive scheme (SIFIDE II) was viewed by investors as relatively easy to apply for and could thus serve as a benchmark for the design or reformulation of other tax incentives.

5.2.9. Boost support for companies' green and digital transition efforts

Foreign investors are already contributing to accelerate Portugal's green and digital transitions, with considerable FDI interest in Portugal's renewable energies, digital technologies and infrastructure in recent years. However, many consulted investors were either not aware of Portugal's various existing support mechanisms for companies' digital and green transitions, or perceived shortcomings in, for instance, the application procedures, scope of support and effectiveness of different mechanisms. Ensuring that support mechanisms match business needs and that they are effectively promoted to firms already present in Portugal and prospective foreign investors can help to further leverage FDI in Portugal's transition towards a carbon-neutral and digital economy. Further strengthening climate policies may also be beneficial for attracting more FDI in renewable energies (Knutsson and Ibarlucea Flores, 2022[12]).

- Raise awareness and evaluate, in particular, the effectiveness of current incentives in supporting companies' digital transition and promoting investment in renewable energy development and the adoption of more energy-efficient technologies and practices in companies' business operations and infrastructure management.
- Where possible, simplify application procedures to encourage firms' use of existing mechanisms and adjust the scope of support to better respond to business needs, for instance by strengthening the support for energy efficiency measures.

5.3. Sector-specific policy considerations

Portugal has a relatively open market compared to the benchmark group in several services sectors, but foreign investors and domestic firms alike could benefit from further aligning the regulatory framework with the more liberal rules in place in peer economies in certain sectors. This section offers policy considerations to address key regulatory obstacles to investment in selected sectors – professional services, transports, logistics and digitally enabled services. Portugal would benefit from facilitating market entry and lowering barriers to competition in these sectors, as they provide strategic support to the country's priority sectors for investment, as well as inputs into other sectors of the economy.

5.3.1. Open professional services markets to foreign providers

Among professional services, there is room to lower regulatory barriers compared to peer economies with more open regulatory set-ups in accounting and auditing, legal, and engineering services. While regulation of these activities serves the legitimate public interests of ensuring consumer protection, proper qualification of professionals and quality of services, such objectives can be balanced with relatively less stringent rules, for instance on non-licensed professionals' equity participation in professional services firms, as it is the case in most peer countries (see Section 2.3.1 in Chapter 2). Ownership restrictions for non-licensed professionals, combined with rules restricting access to the profession for foreign practitioners, currently limit possibilities for foreign investment in Portugal's professional services sectors, particularly in auditing and accounting.

However, as envisaged in Portugal's Recovery and Resilience Plan and in line with the recommendations of OECD (2018[13]), the parliament recently approved a bill amending access conditions to regulated professions (see Section 2.3.1).[4] The approved amendments will open the ownership and management of professional firms to non-licensed professionals once the amending Act takes effect and the statutes of the relevant professional associations are amended accordingly.[5] This is a welcome development, as the expected positive impact of lifting regulatory barriers, in terms of increase in FDI projects, is particularly significant in professional services (see Chapter 3).

- Proceed with a swift implementation of the reform of regulated professions' legislation to open investment in these firms by non-licensed professionals, including foreign investors. The revision of the statutes of the relevant professional associations as part of the implementation process provides an opportunity to address also other barriers to competition and entry of foreign professionals not covered by the reform.

5.3.2. Reinforce the competitiveness of transport and logistics services

Portugal's regulatory framework for transport and logistics services is relatively liberal compared to some peer countries. Yet, addressing remaining domestic regulatory barriers to competition and investment in these sectors and improving the efficiency of customs procedures could benefit a wide range of foreign and domestic-owned firms.

In road freight transport, domestic legislation imposes limitations on the activity of transport manager and additional minimum capital requirements to transport undertakings compared to EU-level requirements. In maritime freight transport, foreign-flagged vessels have limited possibilities of providing cabotage services, which in principle are reserved for EU-flagged ships. Rules for the award of port service concession contracts (such as cargo-handling, pilotage and towage) restrict competition in Portugal's ports, and consulted investors called for improved port services in terms of operating hours. Finally, although outside of Portugal's domestic policy making space, the EU-level prohibition on the cross-border use of so-called gigaliners or mega-trucks may hamper firms' efforts to reduce transport costs and emissions.

- Eliminate additional domestic limitations and requirements for transport managers and undertakings in the road freight transport sector to align the regulatory framework with other, more open EU countries (OECD, 2018[14]).
- Open the maritime cabotage market to foreign-flagged vessels, as is the case in several EU countries (e.g. Denmark, Ireland, Latvia, the Netherlands and Norway), to promote competition in the sector.
- Adopt more competition-friendly rules for the award of contracts for the provision of port services, whereby objective and transparent criteria determine the length of the concession based on the level of investment by the concessionaire and new tenders must be held for the renewal of concessions (OECD, 2018[14]).
- Expand port operating hours to better correspond with business needs to support the day-to-day operations of firms engaging in trade.
- Portugal may also have an interest in co-ordinating with Spain to address at the EU level the cross-border use of gigaliners with a view to possibly authorise cross-border traffic in the Iberian peninsula.

In logistics, foreign investors' ability to own shares in customs brokerage firms is limited due to restrictions on equity participation by non-licensed professionals, combined with a reciprocity requirement for third-country nationals to access the customs broker profession. Individual licensing requirements on warehousing and freight forwarding limit the ability of logistic services providers to integrate their activities. International surveys and the business consultation for this report indicate that there is still room to improve Portugal's customs regime for the benefit of firms in transport, logistics, courier and distribution services.

- As in professional services (see Section 5.3.1 above), implement amendments to eliminate barriers to the ownership and management of customs brokerage firms to open investment in these firms by non-licensed professionals, including foreign investors.
- Consider lifting licensing requirements in warehousing and freight forwarding and replacing them by a lighter notification procedure and risk-based inspections, if necessary. In the peer group, the Czech Republic and Estonia do not require a license for either activity. Alternatively, introduce a single operating license covering the provision of both types of services to make it easier for providers to integrate their activities.[6]
- Promote the efficiency of customs procedures: improve information availability by making a minimal set of information available online in English, extend opening hours of customs in ports to better correspond with user needs and adapt digital solutions to improve the customer experience, such as to allow for electronic payment of all duties, taxes, fees and charges.

5.3.3. Strengthen the regulatory framework for digitally enabled services

Portugal has a comprehensive regulatory environment for trade in digitally enabled services, but regulatory barriers to digital trade are slightly higher than in most peer economies. Addressing the few remaining barriers in this area can help Portugal strengthen its regulatory framework for digital trade and complement efforts to support the development and access to technology-based innovations, promoting the country's digital transformation. As discussed in Chapter 3, liberalising Portugal's regulatory set-up for digital trade to align with the level of openness observed in the Single Market's best performer Estonia could result in 7% more cross-border M&A deals and 2% more greenfield projects. The regulatory set-up for digital trade is particularly relevant for sectors such as distribution, audio-visual, telecommunications and financial services, among others.

- Lift the requirement for foreign companies, exercising activities for more than one year in the country, to designate a permanent representative in Portugal to ease cross-border digital sales for firms established abroad, in cases not covered by the EU-wide requirement for e.g., online marketplaces to designate a representative in the Union.
- Consider also to what extent divergence from approaches taken in other EU countries in the national transposition of certain Digital Single Market directives, such as the Electronic Communications Code, is necessary in Portugal's domestic context. As indicated in Chapter 3, further reducing regulatory hurdles for EEA investors and strengthening regulatory coherence with EEA countries could stimulate FDI from these countries.

5.4. Next steps towards a more attractive investment destination

This report has highlighted areas where further regulatory and policy reforms could contribute towards a more attractive environment for foreign investment in Portugal. The policy considerations outlined in this chapter are intended to inform domestic reform efforts and strategic discussions.

To fully capitalise on the potential of such reform efforts, Portugal could consider adopting a whole-of-government approach to ensure their effective planning and implementation, involving also foreign investors and the country's broader business community in the process. For instance, Portugal could create a working group bringing together key actors from the public and private sectors to develop an action plan for the implementation of the regulatory and policy reforms outlined in the present report. A recent example of such co-ordinated industry-government policy action can be found in the development of Australia's Services Exports Action Plan.[7]

References

Commonwealth of Australia, Department of Foreign Affairs and Trade (2021), *Australia's Services Exports Action Plan: A Government and Industry Strategy to Boost Services Exports*, https://www.services-exports.gov.au/sites/default/files/2021-03/australias_services_exports_action_plan.pdf. [16]

Dayan, S. (2021), *Improving transparency of investment incentives: Draft discussion note*. [11]

Grupo de Trabalho para o Estudo dos Benefícios Fiscais (2019), *Os benefícios fiscais em Portugal : conceitos, metodologia e prática*, Centro de Estudos Fiscais e Aduaneiros, Autoridade Tributária e Aduaneira, Lisboa, https://www.portugal.gov.pt/download-ficheiros/ficheiro.aspx?v=%3D%3DBAAAAB%2BLCAAAAAAABACzMDQwAgCG5%2BMmBAAAAA%3D%3D. [9]

IMF/OECD (2017), *Tax Certainty. IMF/OECD Report for the G20 Finance Ministers*, https://www.oecd.org/tax/tax-policy/tax-certainty-report-oecd-imf-report-g20-finance-ministers-march-2017.pdf. [4]

Knutsson, P. and P. Ibarlucea Flores (2022), "Trends, investor types and drivers of renewable energy FDI", *OECD Working Papers on International Investment*, No. 2022/02, OECD Publishing, Paris, https://doi.org/10.1787/4390289d-en. [12]

OECD (2022), *FDI Qualities Policy Toolkit*, OECD Publishing, Paris, https://doi.org/10.1787/7ba74100-en. [10]

OECD (2022), *Strengthening FDI and SME Linkages in Portugal*, OECD Publishing, Paris, https://doi.org/10.1787/d718823d-en. [2]

OECD (2021), *Building Tax Culture, Compliance and Citizenship: A Global Source Book on Taxpayer Education, Second Edition*, OECD Publishing, Paris, https://doi.org/10.1787/18585eb1-en. [6]

OECD (2021), *OECD Economic Surveys: Portugal 2021*, OECD Publishing, Paris, https://doi.org/10.1787/13b842d6-en. [3]

OECD (2021), *OECD Regulatory Policy Outlook 2021*, OECD Publishing, Paris, https://doi.org/10.1787/38b0fdb1-en. [1]

OECD (2020), *Justice Transformation in Portugal: Building on Successes and Challenges*, OECD Publishing, Paris, https://doi.org/10.1787/184acf59-en. [7]

OECD (2019), *OECD Economic Surveys: Portugal 2019*, OECD Publishing, Paris, https://doi.org/10.1787/eco_surveys-prt-2019-en. [8]

OECD (2018), *Australian Services Trade in the Global Economy*, OECD Publishing, Paris, https://doi.org/10.1787/9789264303911-en. [15]

OECD (2018), *OECD Competition Assessment Reviews: Portugal: Volume I - Inland and Maritime Transports and Ports*, OECD Competition Assessment Reviews, OECD Publishing, Paris, https://doi.org/10.1787/9789264300026-en. [14]

OECD (2018), *OECD Competition Assessment Reviews: Portugal: Volume II - Self-Regulated Professions*, OECD Competition Assessment Reviews, OECD Publishing, Paris, https://doi.org/10.1787/9789264300606-en. [13]

OECD et al. (2022), *Inventory of Tax Technology Initiatives ("Corporate income tax"; "Tax rule management and application")*, https://www.oecd.org/tax/forum-on-tax-administration/tax-technology-tools-and-digital-solutions/corporate-income-tax.htm (accessed on 12 December 2022). [5]

Notes

[1] Certain notifications and permits, such as water permit, continue to fall outside the scope of the all-in-one permit. Business.gov.nl, consulted on 10 January 2023.

[2] For example, among the peer group, the Slovak Republic and Spain have made tax regulation available in a machine-readable format, allowing rules to be incorporated in taxpayers' software (OECD et al., 2022[5]). The Spanish tax administration has made available a series of virtual tax and customs assistance tools, including a VAT chatbot (Agencia Tributaria, consulted on 12 December 2022). In Estonia, solutions are in place for companies to submit data from their accounting software to the tax administration's server, facilitating tax declarations (Invest in Estonia, consulted on 10 January 2023).

[3] A restructuring of SEF, as part of which administrative migration processes would be taken over by a new agency, is expected to take place in the first quarter of 2023. Observador, 20 December 2022.

[4] Draft law No. 108/XV/1 of 1 June 2022, approved on 22 December 2022.

[5] At the time of writing, the amending Act had not yet been promulgated and hence not yet entered into force. The Government of Portugal will have 120 days from the entry into force of the amending Act to present bills to amend the statutes of professional associations and other relevant legislation.

[6] For instance, in Spain, holders of cargo transport operator licenses are entitled to provide freight forwarding and storage services.

[7] After the publication of an OECD report on the competitiveness of the Australian services sector (OECD, 2018[15]), the Australian Government initiated a partnership among the Department of Foreign Affairs and Trade, Austrade and the business community to identify barriers on services exports (Australian Government, Department of Foreign Affairs and Trade, Australia's Services Exports Action Plan, consulted on 15 February 2022). A number of industry working groups were created to provide recommendations feeding into an action plan. Launched in 2021, Australia's Services Exports Action Plan (Commonwealth of Australia, Department of Foreign Affairs and Trade, 2021[16]) defines key outcomes and actions needed to achieve these outcomes. Progress on the Action Plan is monitored and updated on a regular basis.

www.ingramcontent.com/pod-product-compliance
Ingram Content Group UK Ltd.
Pitfield, Milton Keynes, MK11 3LW, UK
UKHW051503290926
15471UKWH00008B/1381

9 789264 843745